Building
Bioinformatics Solutions

Building Bioinformatics Solutions

with Perl, R and MySQL

Conrad Bessant
Ian Shadforth
Darren Oakley

OXFORD

UNIVERSITY PRESS

OXFORD
UNIVERSITY PRESS

Great Clarendon Street, Oxford OX2 6DP

Oxford University Press is a department of the University of Oxford.
It furthers the University's objective of excellence in research, scholarship,
and education by publishing worldwide in

Oxford New York

Auckland Cape Town Dar es Salaam Hong Kong Karachi
Kuala Lumpur Madrid Melbourne Mexico City Nairobi
New Delhi Shanghai Taipei Toronto

With offices in

Argentina Austria Brazil Chile Czech Republic France Greece
Guatemala Hungary Italy Japan Poland Portugal Singapore
South Korea Switzerland Thailand Turkey Ukraine Vietnam

Oxford is a registered trade mark of Oxford University Press
in the UK and in certain other countries

Published in the United States
by Oxford University Press Inc., New York

British Library Cataloguing in Publication Data

Data available

Library of Congress Cataloging in Publication Data

Data available

Typeset by Newgen Imaging Systems (P) Ltd., Chennai, India
Printed in Great Britain
on acid-free paper by
CPI Antony Rowe

ISBN 978–0–19–923019–8 (Hbk.)
ISBN 978–0–19–923023–5 (Pbk.)

10 9 8 7 6 5 4 3

Acknowledgements

We would like to take this opportunity to acknowledge the many hundreds of people who have contributed to the open source software and publicly available databases used herein. Without these tools, bioinformatics would be infinitely more difficult and we could never have written this book.

Thanks are also due to Cranfield University, for providing the opportunity for the three of us to get together, develop our abilities, and ultimately share our skills and experiences through this book. We'd also like to thank all the students who have passed through Cranfield's MSc in Applied Bioinformatics—teaching this course has given us insight into the concepts that are most important to beginners and helped us understand how best we can get these concepts across. Similarly, our laboratory-based research collaborators have been invaluable in helping us to identify real world bioinformatics challenges.

Finally, we would like to thank those who have supported us throughout the creation of this book: the friends and family who have turned a blind eye to the time spent with the keyboard, rather than with them, the colleagues who have generously given of their time to check sections of the book, and the staff of Oxford University Press for trusting in us to deliver and for bringing it all together. Particular thanks to Helen Eaton, Carol Bestley, Fady Mohareb, and Will Stott.

Preface

Modern bioinformatics encompasses a broad and ever changing range of activities related to the management, analysis, and visualization of data from molecular biology experiments. From its origins in the study of DNA sequences, bioinformatics has grown to include microarray data analysis, proteomics, metabolomics, and systems biology. As a result there is now a plethora of bioinformatics software, from both the academic and commercial sectors, available for dealing with the data from these techniques. However, what happens if you're involved in novel research for which an off-the-shelf tool does not exist and you need to develop a new software solution to tackle the problem?

To the uninitiated, this is a daunting prospect, with a seemingly infinite range of design choices and complex concepts to learn, but our experience in many different areas of bioinformatics has taught us that we can start from a generic approach for most applications, using a common set of tools. This book introduces this approach, which is based primarily on three open source, platform independent, tools used throughout the bioinformatics community: Perl, R, and MySQL. We explain how these tools can be used to build software for storing, organizing, analysing, and visualizing data. We then go on to show how solutions developed using these tools can be deployed via the web, allowing you to share data and tools with others.

Our aim in producing this book has been to impart the information and confidence required to start using the tools we cover, to allow more people to get into bioinformatics and enjoy the rewards that it brings. We certainly enjoyed the challenge of putting the book together—we hope you find it useful.

Conrad, Darren & Ian
March 2008

Table of Contents

CHAPTER 1

Introduction

1.1 From data to knowledge: the aim of bioinformatics

The term bioinformatics can mean different things to different people, but for the purpose of this book we define bioinformatics as the process of extracting novel biological knowledge from bioanalytical data. Bioinformatics is therefore a key element of bioscience, because knowledge is what we need to understand biology, to combat disease, and to mitigate environmental catastrophes, but what we actually have is lots of data—genome sequences, protein structures, metabolomic profiles, and more. In this sense, bioinformatics is neither tied to a particular type of experimental data nor to a particular application. Indeed, the data may come from any of today's many bioanalytical methods, such as high throughput sequencing, gene expression microarrays, nuclear magnetic resonance, or proteomic mass spectrometry, and the knowledge sought can be as varied as the identity of a new disease biomarker, a phylogenetic tree, or a system-wide understanding of a particular biological process. Similarly, the tasks involved in bioinformatics range from simply organizing data for future use, through to sophisticated analysis, visualization, and sharing of that data and the results derived from it. Bioinformatics is therefore a truly interdisciplinary subject, requiring an understanding of at least some biology, analytical science, information technology, and mathematics.

There are, of course, many generally available bioinformatics tools that can be used to analyse data with a view to extracting new knowledge and many of these tools are free of charge. However, due to the typically large size of biological data sets and the speed with which the field is developing, it is often necessary to produce your own software to organize, analyse, and visualize data. In this book, we introduce the tools and general approaches employed to produce such software.

The book is primarily aimed at readers with a background in the life sciences who have some bioinformatics knowledge, but little or no experience in the development of software and databases. A typical reader might have dabbled with online databases such as GenBank or Ensembl (if not, these are introduced briefly later in this chapter), and experienced the power of tools such as BLAST (Basic Local Alignment Search Tool) or GeneSpring, and now want to take the next step and develop their own bioinformatics tools, either for their own use or for sharing with their collaborators or with the life science community at large. Our aim in writing this book was to fill the gap between texts that introduce the field of bioinformatics, such as *Introduction to Bioinformatics* (Lesk, 2005), and software development books, such as those published by O'Reilly (e.g. Laurie & Laurie, 2000; Wall *et al.*, 2000; Tahaghoghi & Williams, 2006). We therefore cover computing material from a fairly basic level (for example, Appendix A explains how to use a command line interface), while the biological background necessary to understand the examples is assumed.

1.2   Using this book

The book has been written with the intention of being read linearly from beginning to end, with a structure that mirrors a typical bioinformatics project. First, it is necessary to assemble the data, be it from a laboratory or from online resources, into a structured database using a relational database management system (RDBMS), such as MySQL. Then, due to the size of bioinformatics databases, some programming is usually required to automate some of the data manipulation—Perl is the tool of choice for this among bioinformaticians. Some advanced numerical data analysis is often then required to extract useful information from the data gathered, which is where R comes in. Finally, in Chapter 5, we bring everything together and the real power of integrating Perl, R, and MySQL becomes apparent, as we show how to combine these ingredients with HTML, CGI, and the Apache web server to make complex bioinformatics tools available via the web. Having said all that, Chapters 2, 3, and 4 have been written to be reasonably standalone, so if you have an urgent need to go straight to a particular chapter, then that is possible. Where necessary, cross-references are provided to help locate explanations of concepts that appeared earlier in the book. Similarly, if you are already experienced in one of the three main tools covered, you should be able to skip that chapter without any problems.

One thing that this book is definitely not is a reference manual. The index should help you find a relevant passage in the book when you need it, but don't expect to see every single Perl function, R package, or Apache configuration option listed here. A simple reason for this is that there just isn't enough space, but more importantly these tools have excellent on-line documentation and we find such documentation to be a much more convenient format for reference materials because it is easy to search and frequently updated. This book is a companion to those reference materials, and a starting point in terms of knowing where the reference materials are and how to use them efficiently.

1.2.1   About the coverage of this book

Deciding what to include and what not to include in this book wasn't easy. Whole books have been written about MySQL, Perl, and R, not to mention all the various types of bioinformatics applications to which they can be applied. It is, therefore, impossible to claim that this book provides exhaustive coverage of all the subjects covered. Selecting the topics to cover was very much like writing a tourist guide to a particular country—it is impossible to cover everything of interest, so information needs to be carefully selected, so that it helps newcomers orientate themselves, outlines the practicalities of survival, covers a few highlights that give a flavour of what is possible, and tells you where you can go to find out more. This is the approach we have taken in this book.

1.2.2 Choice of tools

The toolkit for building bioinformatics solutions that we put forward in this book is loosely based on the LAMP toolkit, which is widely used by developers in all sorts of domains, not just bioinformatics. LAMP is an acronym for four popular open source software packages: Linux (the operating system), Apache (web server), MySQL (database), and Perl[1] (for programming). Together, these packages make a powerful combination for gathering, storing and serving up data over the internet. To this mix we add R, which brings with it the sophisticated data analysis and visualization capabilities frequently needed in bioinformatics applications. A key factor in the appeal of this suite of tools is that they are open source and freely available. To be frank, the technical benefit of these tools being open source is minimal for the typical user. Although we are able to view and edit the source code of the tools we are using, the chances are that we will never need to do so and, if we did, the complexity of these packages is such that making worthwhile modifications would be very time-consuming. Even the fact that the packages can be obtained free of charge is of little direct relevance if you have a software budget. What really makes the use of open source tools appealing is that they are ubiquitous and this widespread uptake has two very important consequences. First, there are a lot of people around who know how to use them, so getting help should not be a problem. Secondly, if someone wants to produce a piece of software or an add-on, they are most likely to do it with these tools to allow maximum exposure. This latter benefit is really the most important, as it means that there is, for example, a constant stream of add-on modules for Perl and packages for R that perform common bioinformatics tasks. Having these tools out there in the community saves us a huge amount of development effort and allows us to concentrate on the science, which is, after all, the main priority in bioinformatics.

1.2.3 Choice of operating system

Throughout this book we have worked to ensure that everything is operating system independent as far as possible. All examples have been tested on Windows XP with service pack 2 (see section 1.6.4 later for information about Windows Vista), Mac OS 10.5 (Leopard), and Ubuntu Linux 7.10 (Gutsy Gibbon). This is not just a ploy to maximize sales of the book, but a reflection of the fact that, in real world bioinformatics, all three operating systems are commonly used. In general, Linux is the operating system of choice in bioinformatics, because it is well suited to running servers and is very scalable, allowing solutions to be developed for

---

1 Depending on who you ask, the P might actually stand for a similar language called PHP, or even just programming in general. It doesn't really matter.

anything from individual desktop PCs through to multi-processor supercomputers. However, the familiarity, usability, and large-scale availability of Windows and Mac OS ensure they are widely used, particularly by those starting out in bioinformatics, and among the biologists using the software that we produce.

Where there are differences between operating systems, typically when installing software, we have provided instructions for all three major operating systems. Obviously, we have not been able to test the material in this book on every available Linux distribution, or on versions of Windows or Mac OS that were released after the book went to press. If you have any problems getting the examples in the book to work, we recommend that you head over to the book's website (www.bixsolutions.net) in search of a solution.

1.2.4   www.bixsolutions.net

To help you as you work through this book, we maintain a companion web site, www.bixsolutions.net, where you can find the main example programs and data from the book, as well as up to date lists of recommended reading. The site also has a discussion forum, which is monitored by the authors, who are happy to help if you have any difficulties while working through the examples. Obviously, we have checked the examples very carefully and believed them to work correctly when the book went to press, but they may not work forever. This is because the tools and, indeed, the operating systems, used in this book are constantly evolving—new versions are released frequently, so functions can get depreciated, database schemas change, and new features become available. As we become aware of any changes that affect material in the book we will post updates or workarounds on the web site. For more general bioinformatics assistance, we provide links from www.bixsolutions.net to other helpful websites.

1.2.5   Software engineering in bioinformatics

With this book, a computer, and an internet connection, you have everything you need to produce powerful bioinformatics software. This is mainly thanks to the open source software movement making incredibly powerful software tools freely available via the web, complete with detailed reference documentation and support forums where you can get answers to even the most specialized questions. However, this turns out to be both a blessing and a curse.

It is a blessing in that people with very little software development experience are able to pull various pieces of software together, pasting in program code from here and there, adding in a couple of powerful Perl modules and R packages, and release the result back into the community. The curse is that this approach (often called *hacking*) has some very real limitations in terms of the size and maintainability of the system you can build, and it is not always obvious where these limits lie. Consequently, it is easy to spend a few days knocking together a perfectly respectable little program and then fritter away years struggling unsuccessfully to build it into something more substantial.

The problem is that hacking allows you to make very rapid progress at the start of the project, but if that project starts to grow you may unwittingly cross some boundary that starts to makes your approach unproductive. The more boundaries you cross, the worse your problems become until eventually you stop making any form of real progress. You may be working very hard and writing lots of code, but your effort is entirely spent fixing problems and every problem you solve creates several more to take its place. Over the past 30 or so years, the discipline of software engineering has been developed specifically to ease the development of large and maintainable systems.

Many of today's bioinformaticians have no reason to become experts in software engineering. They simply want to spend a few hours writing a self-contained program for their own use, and may discard it in a matter of days or weeks. However, some people in the field are constructing larger and more complex systems for widespread use, which will need to be maintained over decades. For these bioinformaticians expertise in software engineering becomes essential as they build the teams needed to undertake such ambitious work.

If you want to learn about software engineering, then there are many books on the subject, ranging from those that introduce the field as a whole (e.g. Sommerville, 2006) to those that espouse specific approaches in detail (Martin, 2002; Krutchen, 2003). However, you can also make a start by incorporating a few good engineering practices into your projects like those suggested in the books *Pragmatic Version Control* (Thomas & Hunt, 2004) and *Test-Driven Development: By Example* (Beck, 2003). This will not only help you gain some of the knowledge, skills, and experience you need for working on bigger projects, but it also opens the door for you to make effective contributions to open-source projects, where you can improve your software engineering expertise in the company of like-minded people.

1.3   Principal applications of bioinformatics

Since its origins in genomic sequence analysis, bioinformatics has spread across the whole of molecular biology, in its broadest sense. There are already many fine texts explaining the various applications of bioinformatics (e.g. Lesk, 2005), so we don't replicate such material here. However, we include below a brief outline of the main areas of contemporary bioinformatics with particular emphasis on the application to these areas of the tools introduced in this book.

1.3.1   Sequence analysis

Sequence analysis is a massive field, covering all manner of analysis of textual sequences representing genomes (DNA) and proteins (sequences of amino acids). Applications within genomics are wide ranging and include sequence assembly, prediction of coding regions (i.e. genes), determination of genomic structure, research into the purpose of non-coding DNA, translation of DNA into protein sequences, comparison of sequences to infer evolutionary relationships, rates of evolution, and prediction of gene function and regulation. DNA sequence analysis is also used in the design of experiments that employ techniques such as PCR and microarray technology.

Protein sequence analysis has a similarly wide range of applications, including protein structure prediction (which naturally leads on to structural biology), inference of protein function based on sequence similarity, determination of protein similarity for building protein families and understanding protein evolution, and identification of structural or functional subsequences (*motifs*). Protein sequences are also used when designing and interpreting the results from protein expression experiments.

From a technical point of view, a distinguishing feature of sequence analysis applications is the frequent use of relatively large data sets such as whole genome sequences (for example, the human genome, which consists of about 3,000,000,000 bp). As well as having to deal with the sequences themselves, it is also necessary to handle the *annotations*, without which the sequence data is meaningless. Such annotations include things like the species from which a selected sequence originated, its location in the genome, and any functions or gene products that have been associated with it. A RDBMS, such as MySQL is essential to store such data in a useable way. Another distinguishing feature of sequence analysis is the need to efficiently process textual data, essentially long strings of As, Cs, Gs, and Ts, or the 20-letter alphabet used to represent amino acids. Typical tasks include looking for motifs within much larger sequences and looking for similarities between sequences. Handling large amounts of textual data is something at which Perl excels, as we will see in Chapter 3.

1.3.2   Microarray data analysis

DNA microarrays or *gene chips* allow the expression level of multiple genes to be measured in a single experiment and such is the capacity of these devices that they can now be used to measure the expression level of all known genes in an organism (e.g. about 25,000 genes for humans) with a single array. This obviously has the potential to yield massive data sets, as studies tend to involve multiple samples and these may be monitored at multiple time points. Just storing the expression data and associated information about that data (the so-called *metadata*, which describes the sample and experimental conditions) can be an issue, but the major challenge lies in the processing and statistical analysis of gene expression data. Typically, the raw data is in the form of an image that needs to be processed and cross-referenced with metadata describing the array design (i.e. which spot relates to which gene) to yield numerical expression values. Once these expression values have been extracted and tabulated, we can begin statistical analysis to identify biologically important features, such as differentially expressed genes in a comparative study or co-regulated genes in a temporal study. Due to the large data sets and sometimes sub-optimal experimental designs (the number of genes monitored usually exceeds the number of samples analysed) the statistical methods required can be complex. This is where R is extremely valuable as the common processing algorithms and even some of the more exotic methods have already been implemented for us in R packages, such as Bioconductor. Chapter 4 will get you started with R and, having worked through it, you should be in a position to start working in earnest with packages like Bioconductor.

1.3.3   Proteomics

Gene expression studies are essential in understanding gene regulation and related phenomena, but to gain a real insight into how a biological system functions it is arguably more useful to look at the expression of the functional molecules themselves—the proteins. Proteomics is the science of identifying and, where possible, quantifying proteins in a sample. At the time of writing the majority of proteomics methods are based on mass-spectrometry (MS), coupled with prior protein separation and digestion steps to help ensure that peptides are delivered to the mass spectrometer individually. Due to the complexity and variety of proteomic protocols, handling the data from these experiments can be a major challenge. Some laboratories separate proteins using two-dimensional gel electrophoresis, after which image analysis is employed to identify and define gel spots, prior to excision and MS analysis. Other laboratories use liquid chromatography (LC) instead of gels to achieve a much higher throughput, resulting in large data sets comprising several thousand spectra per sample.

Whichever separation technique is used, data analysis is required to identify the peptide represented by each mass spectrum. The most common techniques are peptide mass fingerprinting (PMF) or, if peptides have been subjected to secondary fragmentation in a subsequent MS stage, a search against simulated spectra derived from a database of known protein sequences for the species being studied. Identified peptides then need to be assigned to proteins, which is not easy due to the small size of the peptides and the many proteins that could potentially be present in a sample—in human tissue this could be several hundred thousand if splice variants and post translational modifications are taken into account. Due to the large datasets and the experimental metadata needed to make use of this, a well designed relational database (perhaps in MySQL) is essential to organize the information, and the increasingly high throughput nature of proteomics necessitates analysis pipelines to be built (often in Perl) if data analysis is to keep pace with data acquisition.

Having identified proteins from all the samples in a given study, statistical analysis then needs to be performed across samples to extract the biologically significant information from the acquired experimental data. At the time of writing, most proteomics protocols are only qualitative—they aim to determine which proteins are present in a sample, but not how much of each protein is present. However, a raft of quantitative protocols has been proposed, which can reveal not just the identities of proteins, but also their abundance. Statistical techniques similar to those used for gene expression analysis are clearly applicable to this data, so as these protocols are adopted more widely it is likely that relevant R packages will emerge.

1.3.4   Metabolomics

Metabolomics deals with the identification and quantification of small molecules in biological samples. Analysis of metabolites is really the oldest of the bioanalytical techniques that we come across in bioinformatics. The primary technologies used—nuclear magnetic resonance (NMR) and gas chromatography mass spectrometry (GC-MS)—have been around considerably longer than microarrays or proteomic MS. Indeed, it is even possible to buy pocket-sized devices for personal monitoring of medically important metabolites, such as glucose and cholesterol. However, metabolomics brings a new emphasis on high throughput analysis and the desire to quantify as many analytes as possible in each sample. The desire for such a global view of the metabolome is being driven mainly by the search for diagnostic biomarkers and the growth of systems biology. As in proteomics, increasing data volumes are encouraging people to put together relational databases and software pipelines for metabolomic data analysis. As metabolite analysis is well established, so are the core algorithms for dealing with the data from such analysis—such methods often come under the banner of *chemometrics*, about which some very good introductory texts have been written (e.g. Brereton, 2007; Otto, 2007). R is a perfect environment for such analysis, as demonstrated by some of the examples in Chapter 4.

1.3.5   Systems biology

Traditionally, bioanalytical science, and even the bioinformatics that supports it, is broken down into the areas outlined previously—genomics, proteomics, and metabolomics. In terms of how organisms function, these delineations are artificial because, in reality, the genes, proteins, and metabolites are free to interact. Systems biology recognizes this and, in practical terms, comprises integration of both data storage and analysis to permit system-wide analysis and modelling of living organisms without being constrained to a particular class of molecule. This is likely to be a theme of bioinformatics for some time to come, because the potential outcome of such work—cell and tissue models with application in areas such as toxicology—is so valuable, but the challenge of achieving this is immense. The core elements of database design, programming, and numerical data analysis covered in this book are all important in systems biology, and much of the effort in systems biology is focused on the design of databases for meaningful storage of heterogeneous data and novel methods for data analysis and visualization.

1.3.6   Literature mining

PubMed, which contains bibliographic information about journals primarily associated with biomedicine (see section 1.5.1), is growing by around 2000 references every day. Keeping up with the work described in all these papers by reading them is impossible, and that is before we consider the backlog of several million papers already out there. There is, therefore, a lot of interest in literature mining methods that may be able to facilitate the high throughput machine reading of papers to extract salient information, and advanced ways of searching through and annotating papers to assist human reading. Perl's text handling capabilities make it ideal for this type of work, as does its ability to automate querying of bibliographic databases and retrieve papers from web sites. There can also be a need to visualize the results of literature mining, which can be handled by Perl or R. For example, if we wrote a Perl program to extract protein–protein interactions from text, it would be convenient to display the resulting network of interactions graphically, as this is a representation with which biologists are familiar.

1.3.7 Structural biology

Structural biology is the study of the physical architecture of biological molecules—particularly proteins. Research typically focuses on topics such as the relationship between structure and function, structural similarity between proteins,
simulation of interaction between proteins and other molecules, and the relationship between protein sequences and their structure (particularly the process
of protein folding). Some of these topics can be tackled using the tools introduced
in this book, but due to the mathematical complexity of molecular simulations,
it is common for researchers to use commercial modelling tools or to produce
bespoke software in lower level languages, such as C. Such tools are sometimes
pipelined using Perl, with a program being written to retrieve a structure from a
repository of protein structures, such as PDB (see section 1.5.1), pass it to a modelling program and deposit the final result of the modelled experiment into a local
database.

1.4   Building bioinformatics solutions

The premise of this book is that, regardless of the particular type of data being
analysed, or the scientific purpose behind the analysis, the tools, and general
approaches used to solve a bioinformatics problem are often the same. This is
because most bioinformatics projects share a similar aim—to bring together data
(be it public or proprietary) with analysis tools (be they existing or novel) to generate new biological knowledge. We refer to this as building a bioinformatics
solution because it best describes what we are doing—putting things together to
solve a problem.

  A schematic representation of this idea is shown in Figure 1.1. Regardless of
the particular type of data being analysed or the scientific purpose behind the
analysis, the general structure of a bioinformatics solution tends to follow this pattern, although not all components are required in all applications. For example,
it may be possible to analyse novel data collected locally without recourse to any
public databases. Similarly, we might be able to rely entirely on our own in-house
analysis software, instead of sourcing tools from the public domain. Conversely,
we may not have access to any novel data or novel analysis routines, and instead
focus entirely on the analysis of public data using publicly available tools. The way
in which results are output from our system may also vary. The figure shows two
potential routes, which may be used together. These are deposition of the results
in a local database, and presentation of the results to one or more users via a web
browser. Unless the software is truly single user—intended only for use by the
developer—some kind of user interface is required, and a web-based interface is
convenient because web interfaces are both familiar to users and relatively easy
to implement. The web obviously allows you to make your software available to
remote users around the world, but even if you are developing a solution for local
use in a single group or organization, a web interface is often the best way to go.

  So, the key components of a system like the one shown in the figure are the analysis pipeline, the local database, and the web interface. The process of building a

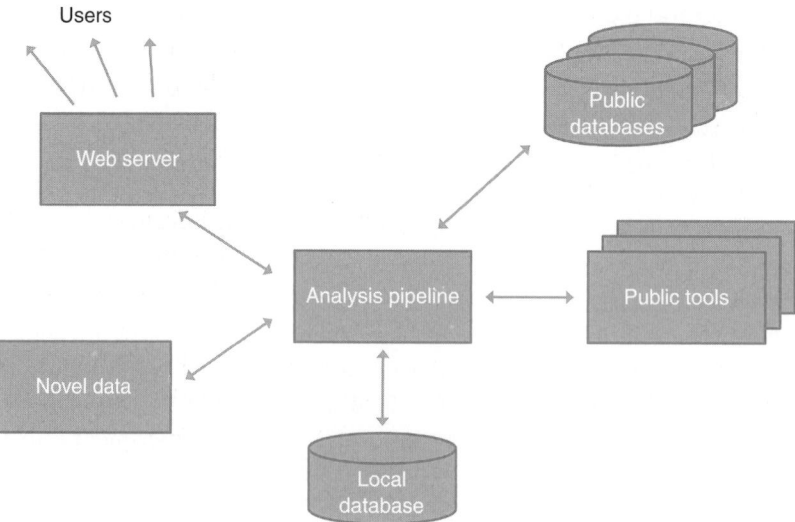

Fig. 1.1 A generic bioinformatics solution showing typical components that may be used.

bioinformatics solution starts with capturing the project requirements, typically by manually carrying out analysis on a small subset of the data being collected. This should reveal which components are needed and what functionality they should have. These components can then be produced using the tools described in the following chapters, specifically the pipeline (with Perl and R), the local database (with MySQL), and the interface (with HTML, Perl-CGI and Apache). For completeness, a brief overview of the other potential components—the public tools and databases—is provided in the next section.

1.5   Publicly available bioinformatics resources

We are very fortunate to have a substantial body of high quality, freely available bioinformatics resources accessible via the internet. These resources can be broken down into databases and analysis tools. Most of the core resources are hosted by two major organizations—the American National Centre for Biotechnology Information (NCBI) and the European Bioinformatics Institute (EBI), which is based in the UK. Resources provided by these organizations are easily accessed via their web sites (www.ncbi.nlm.nih.gov and www.ebi.ac.uk, respectively). What follows is a brief overview of the key resources at these sites and on the wider internet.

1.5.1   Publicly available data

There exists a substantial global collection of data covering a wide range of biological areas, from gene sequences to protein structures and medical information. Furthermore, this collection is growing all the time, both in terms of the number of databases and the amount of data in each database. Indeed, many of the databases are growing exponentially.

This impressive collection of data forms the basis for much bioinformatics work, especially among the many researchers who don't have laboratories or laboratory-based collaborators. Even when we are working with novel proprietary data, we often need to analyse this in the context of publicly available data. For example, if we are looking at SNP data, we may want to map this to existing genomic annotations to identify potential consequences of that SNP. In gene expression studies, it is common to use publicly available information about gene function to provide context for the analysis. In tandem MS proteomics, it is common practice to identify peptides by searching acquired spectra against protein sequence databases.

Due to the extent and rapidly changing nature of the database landscape, we don't provide a thorough review of all available resources here. Instead, we would refer you to the annual *Database Collection* published in the journal *Nucleic Acids Research* (www.oxfordjournals.org/nar/database/c), which has summaries of many hundreds of databases. However, it is worth taking a little space here to introduce what we consider to be the key core databases at the current time, as these are referred to in later chapters.

Genome sequences

The core repositories for nucleotide sequence data are Genbank (at NCBI), EMBL (at EBI) and DDBJ (at the Japanese National Institute of Genetics). These three databases comprise the International Nucleotide Sequence Database Collaboration (INSDC), which collectively capture all the public genome sequence data ever collected. There is even some putative dinosaur DNA in there if you look hard enough (accession number[2] U41319). As part of the collaboration, the contents of these three databases are automatically synchronized daily, so a sequence submitted to one will appear in the other two. All three databases therefore contain the same data. This may seem wasteful, but having the databases in different geographical locations increases data security and ensures that most researchers have the data reasonably close to them, which improves speed of access. Also, the three databases are distinct in that they have different user interfaces.

Although the three INSDC databases are exhaustive in terms of cataloguing all available nucleotide data, the organization of the data is fairly rudimentary and, as a result, they are not the easiest databases to browse around. Consequently, many *secondary databases* have appeared, in which the primary data from repositories such as those in the INSDC has been compiled and indexed into a form that is highly structured, easy to browse, and well integrated with other resources. An excellent example of this is Ensembl (www.ensembl.org), which provides information about a number of completed eukaryotic genomes. As well as the original sequence data, assembled into whole chromosomes, Ensembl also provides annotations for this data, such as known genes, gene predictions, gene structure, gene products, orthologues, and SNPs. As well as being accessed via the web interface,

---

2 An accession number is a unique identifier to a particular record in a database. The record can be found simply by searching for this number.

Ensembl can also be accessed by programs directly via an application programming interface (API), or can even be downloaded in its entirety for working with locally, which will clearly be faster and more secure than connecting to the database via the internet.

Protein sequences

The most comprehensive central resource for protein sequences and functional annotation is UniProt (www.uniprot.org). UniProt comprises two main components: a large database called TrEMBL, which contains protein sequences produced by automatic translation of EMBL nucleotide sequences and a much smaller database of manually curated protein sequences called Swiss-Prot. Thanks to the manual curation, which includes the addition of cross-references to many other databases, the quality of data in Swiss-Prot is recognized as being very high and it is generally considered to be the gold standard protein sequence database. Many other protein databases exist, providing information related to or derived from UniProt sequences. A notable example is InterPro (www.ebi.ac.uk/interpro), which provides information about protein families, domains, and functional sites.

Gene expression data

There are two main databases of gene expression data (primarily from microarrays): Array Express (www.ebi.ac.uk/arrayexpress) and the Gene Expression Omnibus—GEO (www.ncbi.nlm.nih.gov/geo). A key element in getting these databases off the ground was finding agreement within the community for a common format in which to report all the relevant details of a microarray experiment. This was finally achieved by the definition of the MIAME (Minimum Information from A Microarray Experiment) reporting standard, and databases such as GEO and ArrayExpress are fully MIAME compliant. Having this consistent method of representing data is excellent because it means that we can automatically download microarray data complete with all the metadata required to interpret it. Also, having a common data standard means that people are willing to spend time developing the software that supports it. Indeed, we will see in Chapter 4 that there are R packages to deal directly with this type of data.

Protein expression data

Proteomics is following microarrays both in terms of uptake in the laboratory and in terms of data repositories. Like microarray data, proteomic data is only useful if metadata is available to provide context to that data and this issue is gradually being addressed through the Proteomics Standards Initiative (PSI). One of the first databases to be committed to these standards is PRIDE (www.ebi.ac.uk/pride), which is a database of published peptide and protein identifications. PRIDE, like several other proteomics databases, also contains the mass spectra from which peptides have been identified.

Molecular structures

The pre-eminent protein structure database is the Protein Data Bank—PDB (www.pdb.org). This contains protein structures determined primarily using X-ray diffraction or NMR. The information about each structure is quite exhaustive, including information about who determined the structure and how they did it, biochemical information about the protein and, of course, the structure itself, both in formats that can be viewed within the PDB's web interface, and formats that allow the structure to be downloaded and analysed locally. Other protein structure databases, many derived from the PDB, are available, as well as databases of smaller molecules.

Interactions and pathways

The databases mentioned thus far are primarily collections of experimental data from laboratory instruments, albeit augmented with manually generated annotations. Pathway databases are slightly different in that they contain interaction data *derived* from experiments, rather than the experimental data itself. Such databases are becoming increasingly important as systems biology studies become more common. One of the most well established pathway databases is KEGG (the Kyoto Encyclopaedia of Genes and Genomes) Pathway (www.genome. ad.jp/kegg/pathway.html). KEGG comprises several databases, with the Pathway database dedicated to data pertaining to molecular interaction networks. Much of this information has been available for some time in books and papers, but having it online in electronic form obviously facilitates easier access, new applications, and better integration with other resources.

Literature

When we think of scientific literature, journals come to mind and, indeed, it is here that most scientific literature can be found. Despite the existence of the repositories of experimental data described above, journal articles still serve an essential role in acting as the glue that links a lot of this data together and gives it context. It is also where the biological knowledge extracted from this data is reported. Today, the vast majority of journal articles are available online, although not all are available free of charge. However, a large body of bibliographic information about such papers, including abstracts, is available in the PubMed database (www.pubmed.gov).

Journal articles are not the only source of textual information. One notable repository is OMIM (www.ncbi.nlm.nih.gov/omim), which contains textual descriptions of all known genetic disorders. These descriptions include links to supporting data in many of the repositories described above. Similarly, there are links to OMIM from many of these repositories.

Ontologies

In bioinformatics terms, ontologies are essentially lists of terms with strictly defined meanings that have been agreed upon by the scientific community. Where more than one word can be used to describe the same thing, synonyms are listed along with the definition. To avoid any confusion or duplication, each term has a specific accession number associated with it. The most commonly used ontology in bioinformatics is the Gene Ontology—GO (www.geneontology. org). It may sound like an ontology is little more than a dictionary, but an important additional feature is that relationships between terms are also captured. For example, in GO the term 'carbohydrate binding' is defined as a subset of the molecular function 'binding', and many specific types of binding, such as 'glucose binding' are linked to that more general 'carbohydrate binding' term.

Ontologies have many uses in bioinformatics. At their simplest, they can be used as *controlled vocabularies*—lists of terms that users are restricted to using when entering data. A typical way of enforcing a controlled vocabulary on users is to only allow input via a drop-down box, which contains only the permitted terms. Retrieving and analysing data using automated systems is a lot easier if it is annotated in this way, rather than with free text descriptions. For this reason, many of the standard data formats, such as the MIAME microarray standard, make use of ontologies for their metadata. Ontologies can also be used to facilitate advanced querying of data. For example, searching for documents using a normal keyword search for 'carbohydrate binding' would simply return documents containing that term, whereas a search augmented by GO could additionally return documents that do not contain the term 'carbohydrate binding', but do contain terms that GO defines as being related to this, such as 'glucose binding'. Thanks to such utility, ontologies appear in almost every area of bioinformatics.

GO is currently the most ubiquitous of biological ontologies, as it covers three key areas of interest: biological process, cellular component, and molecular function. However, there are many complementary ontologies, most of which can be found at the Open Biomedical Ontologies foundry (www.obofoundry.org). Although there are various ontology formats, the important thing is that these ontologies are freely available, easily machine readable, and can therefore be incorporated into our own programs with relative ease.

1.5.2 Publicly available analysis tools

As well as data, there is also a wealth of data analysis tools freely available via the web. Some of these are add-ons for specific software such as Perl (Perl modules) and R (R packages), which we will deal with in the later chapters. Many other tools are available in stand-alone form, either accessible via web front ends, or as programs that you can download and run locally. The most frequently used tools have been assembled into *toolboxes* by the EBI (www.ebi.ac.uk/Tools) and NCBI (www.ncbi.nlm.nih.gov/Tools). For historical reasons, these toolboxes tend to be biased towards sequence analysis tools, with BLAST and the ClustalW multiple sequence analysis tool arguably being the most famous. However, other tools, such as OMSSA (at NCBI) for proteomic mass spectrometry and DaliLite (at EBI) for pairwise structure comparison clearly cover other data types.

For occasional analyses, as done by the typical laboratory-based biologist, the web-based interfaces to these tools are very convenient. The good news for those of us seeking to build bioinformatics solutions with higher throughput is that most of these tools can also be accessed programmatically, allowing us to incorporate them into our own software and automate analysis. This can be done either by downloading versions of the tools that can be run locally and incorporated into your programs (we see how to do this in Chapter 3), or connecting to a server at the EBI or NCBI, and running the tool there. The latter is achieved using an API that allows data and commands to be sent directly to the tool on the server, and results returned. The details of how to do this vary from tool to tool, but comprehensive instructions and examples are available at both the NCBI and EBI toolbox web sites.

Another suite of tools worth knowing about, especially if you are working with sequence data, is the European Molecular Biology Open Software Suite—EMBOSS (emboss.sourceforge.net). This open source suite mainly comprises tools for sequence analysis, such as sequence alignment, picking primers, and looking for sequence motifs. The programs that make up EMBOSS are well respected and easy to incorporate into your own software, making them a popular choice for bioinformatics developers.

There are many other freely available tools out there, but because these tools tend to be developed by different academic groups, they can be hard to find. In our experience, the best way to discover new tools is by monitoring relevant journals, although even that is a challenge, as tools might be announced in bioinformatics or domain-specific journals, such as those covering genomics, proteomics, and metabolomics.

1.6 Some computing practicalities

Finally, before we get onto the substance of this book, we need to mention a few practical issues that apply to all of the following chapters.

1.6.1 Hardware requirements

A question we are often asked by people looking to develop their bioinformatics skills is 'what kind of computer do I need?' For some people, the expectation is that, with all the talk about large data sets, whole genome analysis, and complex visualizations, substantial computing resources must be required. In practice, however, most bioinformaticians are able to do what they want on a standard desktop computer, and that is definitely the case for this book. Any recently produced PC or Apple Macintosh, in either desktop or laptop format, connected to the internet, should be fine for running the examples in this book.

The alternative is to adopt a client–server approach, as practiced in many organizations. In this scenario, a powerful computer is set up as a server and core software is installed on it. In bioinformatics, the server would typically be running a Linux operating system, with MySQL (or an equivalent such as Oracle), Perl, R, and Apache installed. You would connect to the server from a separate (client) computer to query databases, execute commands, and run software that you have created. This may sound like a lot of unnecessary hassle, but it has several benefits if multiple users or software developers are involved. First, because it is not necessary to physically sit at the server to use it, it can be used simultaneously by a number of people. This makes it possible to share, for example, a single installation of MySQL or even a specific database. This considerably reduces administrative duties, because the software only needs to be installed and configured once, regardless of the number of users. This approach is therefore very popular in larger organizations, such as universities and companies that are big enough to have dedicated system administrators. The client–server approach also provides separation between the server and the personal computer on which you write program code, check your email, surf the web, etc. This has several advantages:

* The server can be in a remote location, such as a data centre with better security and an uninterruptible power supply.

* You can run a different operating system on your personal computer to the operating system that is installed on the server.

* You can switch off, reboot, or otherwise abuse your computer without affecting the server.

All this is particularly useful if you are developing bioinformatics tools that need to be accessible to other people and therefore need a high level of reliability.

Having said that, when starting out we recommend you use a single computer for which you have administrator rights. This is what we assume throughout the book. However, if you are in an organization where you wish to or are forced to use a server, you shouldn't have any major problems with the examples. You will just need to liaise with the server administrator to find out what software is available on your particular server and how to access it.

1.6.2   The command line

In most of the examples throughout this book we interact with the computer via command line interfaces. In a command line interface, we tell the computer what do simply by typing commands and feedback is returned to the screen. This may seem like a step backwards in a world of mice, touch screens, and graphical user interfaces (GUIs), such as Mac OS and Windows Aero, but for some tasks commonly carried out in bioinformatics, such as querying databases or manipulating large data sets, command line interfaces can actually be much more efficient than GUIs. Furthermore, if we can get the computer to do something by typing in a command, there is a good chance that we can incorporate that command into a program as part of an automated process.

For those readers who are unfamiliar with command line interfaces, we provide a basic primer in Appendix A. If you are not confident with working at the command line, you should take a look at that before moving on to the following chapters.

1.6.3   Case sensitivity

When using command line tools or writing software, it is essential to be aware of whether the tool or language you are using distinguishes between capital and lower case letters. For example, would it consider something called 'bioinformatics' to be distinct from 'BIOINFORMATICS' or, more subtly, 'Bioinformatics'? This can lead to all sorts of problems, especially for beginners, because commands that superficially look correct don't work. To make things even more confusing it is not just the tools that differ in their case sensitivity—the behaviour of operating systems differs too. Specifically, Windows ignores case, so a file called 'DNA.TXT' could be referred to on the command line as 'dna.txt'. If you tried to do this on Linux or Mac OS you would receive an error saying that the file could not be found. Indeed, in such case sensitive operating systems two distinct files 'dna. txt' and 'DNA.TXT' could co-exist in the same directory, although this is hardly a desirable situation.

Our recommendation throughout this book is to assume case sensitivity, regardless of the tool, language, or operating system you are using, but make sure that you avoid using names that would be identical if the case was ignored. This is the approach we have followed in the examples in the chapters that follow. Not only does this avoid confusion, it also helps ensure that any programs you write are portable between operating systems.

1.6.4 Security, firewalls, and administration rights

Ever since people started connecting their computers to networks there have been concerns about preventing unauthorized people connecting to your computer and downloading data from it. This is clearly a concern for those in bioinformatics working with sensitive data, such as novel compounds, or clinical data that needs to be guarded for ethical reasons. There is also the danger of criminals taking over networked computers and using them to send out spam email, which can have serious consequences for organizations as they can end up being *blacklisted*—having all their outgoing mail flagged as spam. For these reasons, organizations have become increasingly strict in limiting what users can do with their computers and operating systems, and server software has become loaded with more security features. Basic security features include the use of password protected user accounts to access a computer or particular data, and a firewall to filter network traffic to and from the computer.

We mention this here because the material in this book goes beyond what many organizations expect you to be doing with your computer. In particular, you will need to install software on your computer if you don't already have it and in Chapter 5 we explain how to set up your computer as a web server. Installing software requires you to have administrator rights on the computer and running server software may require you to modify your firewall settings if you want to access the server from another computer. Neither of these things are inherently dangerous, but getting such access can be tough if your computer belongs to your organization, and is set up and administered by them. If you are working or studying in an organization, our advice is to talk to your IT support people and explain what you want to do. Depending on the organization, it is possible that the software you need may already be installed, either locally or on a server.

Even if you are using your own computer, you may need to spend a little time ensuring you have administrator rights and tweaking firewall settings, particularly if you are using a PC running Windows Vista, as Microsoft has incorporated a raft of new security features into their latest operating system. In our experience, the result of this is an increase in the number of security warning messages and more difficulty in persuading your computer to do things that go beyond everyday use, such as installing software and running servers.

The good news, however, is that security issues are only likely to be a problem when installing and setting up the tools used in this book, i.e. at the start of the chapter. Once you have successfully got MySQL, Perl, R, or Apache up and running you should be able to proceed through the chapter without further hindrance. Also, software installation and configuration is a generic issue, not specific to people using this book or even to people working in bioinformatics, so there is likely be help available on the web for almost every eventuality. Indeed, you can always head over to www.bixsolutions.net to report the issue and seek a solution.

References

Beck, K. (2003). *Test-Driven Development: By Example* (Addison-Wesley: Boston, USA).

Brereton, R. G. (2007). *Applied Chemometrics for Scientists* (Chichester: Wiley).

Krutchen, P. (2003). *The Rational Unified Process: An Introduction* (Addison-Wesley: Boston, USA).

Laurie, B. & Laurie, P. (2000). *Apache: The Definitive Guide* (O'Reilly: Sebastapol, California, USA).

Lesk, A. M. (2005). *Introduction to Bioinformatics* (Oxford: Oxford University Press).

Martin, R.C. (2002). *Agile Software Development, Principles, Patterns and Practices* (Prentice Hall: Upper Sadle Riva, NJ, USA).

Otto, M. (2007). *Chemometrics: Statistics and Computer Application in Analytical Chemistry (Chichester:* Wiley).

Sommerville, I. (2006). *Software Engineering* (Addison-Wesley: Boston, USA).

Tahaghoghi, S. M. M. & Williams, H. E. (2006). *Learning MySQL* (O'Reilly: Sebastapol, California, USA).

Thomas, D. & Hunt, A. (2003). *Pragmatic Version Control using CVS* (Pragmatic Bookshelf: Raleigh, North Carolina, USA).

Wall, L., Christiansen, T. & Orwant, J. (2000). *Programming Perl* (O'Reilly: Sebastapol, California, USA).

## CHAPTER 2

Building biological databases with MySQL

A database is, at its simplest, a set of stored information, such as a filing cabinet or a computer's hard disk. Generally, pieces of similar or related information are gathered together in the same place, as common sense would dictate, and as you probably already do when you create folders and subfolders for information held on your computer. Database concepts provide a way of formalizing the gathering together of this data such that the relationships between pieces of information are consistent. They can therefore be more efficiently used, whether through manual or automated processes, and the structure provides a means by which data consistency may be maintained.

This chapter focuses primarily on a type of database called a *relational database*. Relational databases are powerful because they enforce a great deal of security and consistency on the data within them. The software tools that are used to create and manage relational databases are called *relational database management systems* or RDBMSs. These allow the data contained within a database to be queried in immensely powerful ways, often using very simple commands created using a special programming language called the Structured Query Language (SQL).

Also briefly introduced in this chapter are two other types of database commonly encountered in bioinformatics: flat text files, such as FASTA files containing sequence information, and Extensible Markup Language (XML) files, which are a key component of most modern data standards, such as the PSI standards for protein identifications. Understanding these types of database is easier than for relational databases, so they do not form the bulk of this chapter.

At first glance, the ordering of this chapter may seem strange—the installation of a relational database system follows extensive sections on databases and database design, and database access through SQL is covered last. This is deliberate. The hardest aspects of understanding and dealing with databases occur at the design stage, and this is also the most important. Installing a RDBMS is straightforward and also unnecessary for good database design. However, a working system is needed to experiment with accessing databases and, hence, installation and connection issues are discussed after database design, but before database interaction.

2.1　Common database types

2.1.1　Flat text files

As stated above, a database is merely a store of data, one of the simplest forms of which would be to write the data as a set of text files, often termed *flat files*. These flat files could be any text file created in a commonly readable format, such as the `.txt` files created in text editors like Windows Notepad. A collection of text documents on a hard disk is one example of a database of flat files. In order to assist automated access and, indirectly, readability, it helps if some sort of structure is imposed upon the data within a text file. In terms of scientific papers, this order is often along the lines of Introduction, Materials and Methods, Results, Discussion, and References, or variants of this type. The structure helps the reader to quickly locate information of interest by navigating first to the relevant section. Sub-headings further help this cause. For automated reading, or *parsing*, of data within a file, it helps if the structure is highly consistent. The headings within scientific papers may be different due to a number of factors, such as different journal formats. On the other hand, if we consider a basic implementation of the FASTA flat file format for storing sequence files, presented below, the structure is much simpler, but allows for both intuitive human and machine reading.

A simple example of a FASTA format file:

```
>ENSP00000630516 | a protein description
SEQUENCEAPPEARSHERE

>ENSP00000295897 | another protein description
THESEQUENCEOFTHISPROTEIN
```

The FASTA file features four structural elements:

1　Information about each protein is introduced by a greater than (`>`) character.

2　The first piece of data to follow the `>` character is the protein accession number, in this case the Ensembl accession number. This is followed by a bar (`|`) character.

3　Following the bar, we have the protein description. There is then a newline character that is not directly visible, but results in a new line being started. This is the indication that the protein sequence follows. In terms of human readability, this is clearly indicated by the start of a new line on which text that looks like a sequence is presented, but in machine readability terms, it is the invisible newline character that is used to differentiate between protein description and protein sequence.

4　Another newline character is used to terminate the sequence followed immediately by one more return character. Visually, this results in a blank line separating successive proteins.

The pattern of these structural elements is repeated until the end of the file.

The important point to note about the above description is that it separates the data contained in the file from the structure of that data. No information about what a protein naming convention, description, or sequence actually is, or what this data looks like, is required to correctly assign data elements into one of three groups—protein accession numbers, protein descriptions, and protein sequences. Furthermore, each piece of data is explicitly related, by its location in the file, to the other two belonging to the same protein. The data structure is therefore valuable in itself, regardless of any data contained within the file.

Far more complicated forms of structured flat file exist and are used in everyday bioinformatics applications. A good example is the GenBank format used to store sequence data—each individual sequence *record* contains not just the sequence, but many additional *fields* of metadata, such as the species name and genomic location (see www.ncbi.nlm.nih.gov/Sitemap/samplerecord.html). Regardless of the specific format, the principle of flat files remain the same: There is a set of consistently used structural elements that allows data to be sorted into like types and also grouped as appropriate, e.g. by protein, as in the preceding example.

2.1.2 XML

Extensible Markup Language (XML) is a commonly used file format in bioinformatics applications. It adds a *syntax* to the concept of a structured text file. A syntax defines the order of language elements, such that what is written is generally comprehensible. In the case of the English language, sentences are most readily understood if the correct grammar and punctuation is used. These elements therefore form the syntax for English. In other languages, such as Perl, or in this case XML, a strict syntax helps both humans and computers to understand exactly what is meant.

As with FASTA files, XML files may be written and viewed in a simple text editor. However, the structures have been designed to be primarily machine readable, not necessarily human readable, and therefore can appear a lot harder to understand. Having said this, the basic XML syntax is made up of a small number of structural elements that are easily understood.

XML structure

Each XML file can begin with a declaration of certain information, such as the type of XML being used, the way characters in the file are encoded and other information, for example:

```
<?xml version="1.0" encoding="UTF-8"?>
```

You will find this at the top of the XML file before the information-containing body of the file starts.

The generic structural elements in XML are called *names*, *attributes*, and *values*. This structure is used for the declaration too, but note the use of the question marks, indicating that this information is part of the declaration, not the body information. Textual content may also be entered into each element. Generically, these are written in the following way:

```
<name attribute_1="value_1" attribute_2="value_2"
...attribute_n="value_n">Some text about this named
element</name>
```

A named set of information is thus introduced using the syntax `<name`; the attributes and values belonging to this follow until the closing `>` symbol. To close a named group, the syntax `</name>` is used. For example, if we were representing the proteins identified in a proteomics experiment, the following could be used:

```
<protein_identified id_number="1" probability="1.00">Protein
identified using mass spectrometry</protein_identified>
```

Named elements may be nested below one another, such that a subset of information belongs to the named element that surrounds it. So, the various names by which an identified protein may be known follow the opening of the `protein_identified`, but precede its closing statement, as in:

```
<protein_identified id_number="1" probability="1.00">
...
<annotation protein_description="Cerulaplasmin precursor"
ipi_name="IPI00017601" refseq_name="NP_000087"
swissprot_name="P00450" ensembl_name="ENSP00000264613"
trembl_name="Q9UKS4" locus_link_name="1356">
...
</protein_identified>
```

A real world example

The above examples have been formatted with some bold text, so that they are clearer for us to read. However, this formatting is not part of the XML format and the convention may not be used in all situations. For instance, Fig. 2.1 provides a sample of an XML file that was generated by ProteinProphet, a system for identifying proteins from mass spectrometry data. In this file, there is little formatting, rendering it very difficult to read initially.

This is pretty much incomprehensible to the untrained eye and even if the reader understood the XML structure as we do now, this would not be a preferred manner in which to view it. Rather, XML files are often viewed through an interface, such as a web-browser, which itself refers to a second document, a stylesheet (XSL document), for instructions as to how to display data contained within the XML structure. This XML file, when viewed with its style sheet, is shown in Fig. 2.2.

To highlight each element as it appears in the body of the example, this is reproduced as Fig. 2.3 with names appearing in bold, attributes in grey and values in normal text.

```xml
<?xml version="1.0" encoding="UTF-8"?><xml-stylesheet type="text/xsl"
href="regis/sbeams/archive/edeutsch/HUPOPPI2/HUPO12_run31/HsIPI_v2.21/interact-prot.xsl"?>
<protein_summary xmlns=http://regis-web.systemsbiology.net/protXML xmlns:xsi=http://www.w3.org/2001/XMLSchema-
instance"xsi:chemaLocation=http://regis-web.systemsbiology.net/protXML/tools/bin/TPP/tpp/schema/protXML_v3.xsd
summary_xml="regis/sbeams/archive/edeutsch/HUPOPP12/HUPO12_run31/HxIPI_v2.21/interact-prot.xml">...

...<protein_group group_number="1" probability="1.00"><protein protein_name="IPI00017601"
n_indistinguishable_proteins="1" probability="1.00" percent_coverage="9.0"
unique_stripped_peptides="KLVYREYTDASFTNRK+IYHSHIDAPKDIASGLIGPLIICKK+LVYREYTDASFTNR+YKK
VVYR+LVYREYTDASFTNRK+KLISVDTEHSNIYLQNGPDR+HYYIGIIETTWDYASDHGEKK+IGGSYKKLVYREYT
DASFTNRKER+IYHSHIDAPK+IGGSYKKLVYREYTDASFTNRK" group_sibling_id="a" total_number_peptides="15"
pct_spectrum_ids="1.18"><annotation protein_description="ceruloplasmin precursor" ipi_name="IPI00017601"
refseq_name="NP_000087" swissprot_name="P00450" ensembl_name="ENSP00000264613" tremble_name="Q9UKS4"
locus_link_name="1356" /><peptide peptide_sequence="KLISVDTEHSNIYLQNGPDR" charge="2"
initial_probability="1.00" nsp_adjusted_probability="1.00" weight="1.00" is_nondegenerate_evidence="Y"
n_enzymatic_termini="2" n_sibling_peptides="8.00" n_sibling_peptides_bin="6" n_instance="1"
is_contributing_evidence="Y" calc_neutral_pep_mass="2299.4919"></peptide><peptide
peptide_sequence="IYHSHIDAPKDIASGLIGPLIICKK" charge="2" initial_probability="1.00"
nsp_adjusted_probability="1.00" weight="1.00" is_nondegenerate_evidence="Y" n_enzymatic_termini="2"
n_sibling_peptides="8.00" n_sibling_peptides_bin="6" n_instances="1" is_contributing_evidence="Y"
calc_neutral_pep_mass="2761.1919"><modification_info modified_peptide="IYHSHIDAPKDIASGLIGPLIICKK"<
mod_aminoacid_mass position="23" mass="161.138794"/></modification_info></peptide>
```

Fig. 2.1 A sample of an XML file generated by a protein identification system, ProteinProphet.

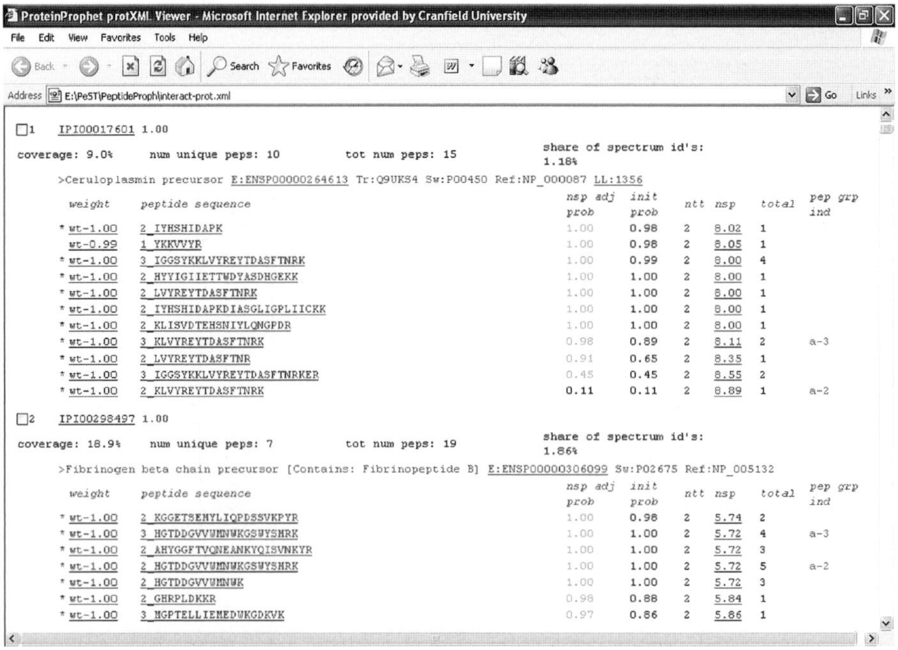

ProteinProphet protXML Viewer - Microsoft Internet Explorer provided by Cranfield University

File Edit View Favorites Tools Help

Address E:\PeST\PeptideProph\interact-prot.xml

1 IPI00017601 1.00

coverage: 9.0% num unique peps: 10 tot num peps: 15 share of spectrum id's: 1.18%

>Ceruloplasmin precursor E:ENSP00000264613 Tr:Q9UKS4 Sw:P00450 Ref:NP_000087 LL:1356

weight	peptide sequence	nsp adj prob	init prob	ntt	nsp	total	pep grp ind
* wt-1.00	2_IYHSHIDAPK	1.00	0.98	2	8.02	1	
wt-0.99	1_YKKVVYR	1.00	0.98	2	8.05	1	
* wt-1.00	3_IGGSYKKLVYREYTDASFTNRK	1.00	0.99	2	8.00	4	
* wt-1.00	2_HYYIGIIETTWDYASDHGEKK	1.00	1.00	2	8.00	1	
* wt-1.00	2_LVYREYTDASFTNRK	1.00	1.00	2	8.00	1	
* wt-1.00	2_IYHSHIDAPKDIASGLIGPLIICKK	1.00	1.00	2	8.00	1	
* wt-1.00	2_KLISVDTEHSNIYLQNGPDR	1.00	1.00	2	8.00	1	
* wt-1.00	3_KLVYREYTDASFTNRK	0.98	0.89	2	8.11	2	a-3
* wt-1.00	2_LVYREYTDASFTNR	0.91	0.65	2	8.35	1	
* wt-1.00	3_IGGSYKKLVYREYTDASFTNRKER	0.45	0.45	2	8.55	2	
* wt-1.00	2_KLVYREYTDASFTNRK	0.11	0.11	2	8.89	1	a-2

2 IPI00298497 1.00

coverage: 18.9% num unique peps: 7 tot num peps: 19 share of spectrum id's: 1.86%

>Fibrinogen beta chain precursor [Contains: Fibrinopeptide B] E:ENSP00000306099 Sw:P02675 Ref:NP_005132

weight	peptide sequence	nsp adj prob	init prob	ntt	nsp	total	pep grp ind
* wt-1.00	2_KGGETSENYLIQPDSSVKPYR	1.00	0.98	2	5.74	2	
* wt-1.00	3_HGTDDGVVWMNWKGSWYSMRK	1.00	1.00	2	5.72	4	a-3
* wt-1.00	2_AHYGGFTVQNEANKYQISVNKYR	1.00	1.00	2	5.72	3	
* wt-1.00	2_HGTDDGVVWMNWKGSWYSMRK	1.00	1.00	2	5.72	5	a-2
* wt-1.00	2_HGTDDGVVWMNWK	1.00	1.00	2	5.72	3	
* wt-1.00	2_GHRPLDKKR	0.98	0.88	2	5.84	1	
* wt-1.00	3_MGPTELLIEMEDWKGDKVK	0.97	0.86	2	5.86	1	

Fig. 2.2 The ProteinProphet XML file, shown in Fig. 2.1, viewed in Internet Explorer with the help of a stylesheet.

All of the information presented in Fig. 2.3 relates to the `protein_group` with a `group_number` of 1, because it falls in between the opening of this group (`<protein...>`) and the closing tag (`</protein_group>`). Later in the file, another `protein_group` may be started with a `group_number` of 2. This would be a different protein and, hence, have a different set of alternative protein names nested within it as annotations. In this way, information that is naturally related is linked together within the XML structure, very much as information is linked within the tables of a relational database, as we shall see in the next section.

2.1.3 Relational databases

Relational databases take the concepts of order and structure of data one step further. This is achieved through compartmentalizing data into boxes of related elements and then linking these boxes such that pieces of data in one box may be accessed alongside related information in another box. The essence of a relational database, and much of their power comes from the design of these boxes and their relationships to one another.

As a physical example of a relational database, we might consider a library indexing system. We can think of a library as a store of information with all of the books in one very big box. The books are often stored in a number of smaller, subject-specific boxes and then indexed alphabetically by author name. To find any book in the library for which you know the author and subject area, you can

```
...<protein_group group_number="1" probability="1.00"><protein protein_name="IPI00017601"
n_indistinguishable_proteins="1" probability="1.00" percent_coverage="9.0"
unique_stripped_peptides="KLVYREYTDASFTNRK+IYHSHIDAPKDIASGLIGPLIICKK+LVYREYTDASFTNR+YKK
VVYR+LVYREYTDASFTNRK+KLISVDTEHSNIYLQNGPDR+HYYIGIETTWDYASDHGEKK+IGGSYKKLVYREYT
DASFTNRKER+IYHSHIDAPK+IGGSYKKLVYREYTDASFTNRK" total_number_peptides="15"
pct_spectrum_ids="1.18"><annotation protein_description="ceruloplasmin precursor" ipi_name="IPI00017601"
refseq_name="NP_000087" swissprot_name="P00450" ensembl_name="ENSP00000264613" trembl_name="Q9UKS4"
locus_link_name="1356"/><peptide peptide_sequence="KLISVDTEHSNIYLQNGPDR" charge="2"
initial_probability="1.00" nsp_adjusted_probability="1.00" weight="1.00" is_nondegenerate_evidence="Y"
n_enzymatic_termini="2" n_sibling_peptides="8.00" n_sibling_peptides_bin="6" n_instances="1"
is_contributing_evidence="Y" calc_neutral_pep_mass="2299.4919"></peptide><peptide
peptide_sequence="IYHSHIDAPKDIASGLIGPLIICKK" charge="2" initial_probability="1.00"
nsp_adjusted_probability="1.00" weight="1.00" is_nondegenerate_evidence="Y" n_enzymatic_termini="2"
n_sibling_peptides="8.00" n_sibling_peptides_bin="6" n_instances="1" is_contributing_evidence="Y"
calc_neutral_pep_mass="2761.1919"><modification_info modified_peptide="IYHSHIDAPKDIASGLIGPLIICKK"<
mod_aminoacid_mass position="23" mass="161.138794"/></modification_info></peptide>
</annotation></protein></protein_group>
```

Fig. 2.3 The same sample of XML as provided in Fig. 2.1 featuring, in the lower portion, highlighted structural elements. Here, name elements appear in bold and attributes appear in grey, with their values remaining in the normal font. For completeness name group terminators have been added at the bottom of this section.

look in the correct subject area and work your way through the books until you hit the correct author, and then work through all of their works until you find the one you want. However, if what you want is to find all of the books in the library written by a specific author, regardless of subject, you may be in for a long search using this method—you would have to search through all the subject areas in the library to be sure of finding all those written by the author of interest. To help in this case we may create another box, such as a filing cabinet, in which to store the author, book title, and key subject information in another way, as a series of cards linking each author to all the books they have written. Now, if you know the name of an author, you can look in this box, work through the list until you find the one of interest, and written next to the name should be the list of books, each one assigned the correct subject area. It would then be possible to fairly quickly locate all the books in the library that had the same author.

To recap, the above example features two boxes of naturally-related data items. The first of these, the library, contains sets of books grouped by subject and then by lead author; the second contains key cards listing below every author's name their complete set of published works and the subject areas in which they could be found. In database terms, these boxes are called *tables*. Each table has a number of pieces of information stored within it: subject, author name, title, and book contents in the case of the library, and author name, book title, and subject in the case of the filing cabinet. Most importantly, each box is also linked to the other by three pieces of information:

• every book in the library contains at least the author's name and the title;

• it may be found in a subject-specific area;

• every record in the filing cabinet contains at least a list of titles, and their subject areas, published by every author.

In this way, the two boxes of information are related. In database terms, the tables are now related by three of their fields. This situation can be rendered pictorially, as shown in Fig. 2.4.

One further important concept highlighted by the above example is that to describe the process of accessing data and to represent the information that is stored, we have not had to refer at all to a specific author, title, or publisher. Compare this with the examples of flat text files and XML formats presented above. In each of these the example contains the stored data. In the case of Fig. 2.4 we have a representation of the data, but no data is shown. The representation

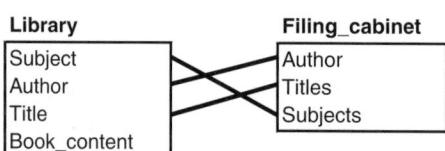

Fig. 2.4 Schematic representation of the contents of a library linked to author information stored in a filing cabinet. The library and filing cabinet are represented as two distinct *tables*.

of the database forms an abstract layer describing the underlying data and, therefore, we can discuss each item of data generically without referring to a specific example.

When dealing with database design and access we are therefore able to talk about access and manipulation generically, a very powerful concept. Why? To go back to the library example, the books in each section are assumed to be ordered alphabetically by author name. This makes a lot of sense, but what if we want to locate a book by title? If we don't know the author, then a rather long search may be required. We can get around this by having a set of index cards that link titles to authors, but this duplicates data, which leaves us prone to errors caused by mismatches between the titles and authors printed on the covers of the books themselves, and those on the index cards. In this case, because the data and the representation of the data are inextricably linked, we have to choose one ordering mechanism and use additional means if we wish to use an alternate order. With a relational database, however, we can order the information contained in a table by any attribute we wish. It is like having a library that will automatically move all the books around to suit the type of search we are doing, whether searching by subject area, author, or title.

As we have seen, the fundamentals of a relational database are not complicated. However, there is a lot of complicated jargon and even mathematics associated with formal database design that can be very off-putting for beginners. In the next section we present a natural approach to database design that, for most applications, allows new databases to be created without the need to wade through this complexity.

2.2   Relational database design—the 'natural' approach

The steps to producing a fairly robust, useable database schema without worrying about the complexities of formal database design are as follows:

1 Gather together a list of pieces of data to be contained within the database.

2 Group these so that they fit naturally together.

3 Assign consistent and descriptive short names to each piece of data.

4 Define the type of each piece of data—number, text, binary, etc.

5 Check for atomicity—can any data item be broken down further?

6 Index your database.

7 Link the tables of your database through relationships.

Each of these steps is described in detail through a worked example in the following sections. As will be seen, the above steps are ordered, but it may be necessary to repeat certain of them as part of an iterative design process. It may be useful for you to attempt to design a database of your own, whilst working through the example given here, or you might prefer to work through the example and then re-read the section with your own database design in mind. Either way, to get the most out of this chapter you should carefully consider each step as it happens—why are you doing it and what has it achieved? In this way, your appreciation of the operations will be enhanced and the easier you will find it to apply these concepts in any situation.

2.2.1 Steps 1–3: gather, group, and name the data

The first important point to keep in mind when designing a database is to think about what you want to get out of the database, not just what you want to put into it. There are a number of reasons for this, the most compelling of which is that you are designing a database for a purpose, and it is that purpose that should define its form and content. It is unlikely that you are designing a database only to store your data—you, and perhaps other people, will want to access it too.

Having said that, we have to start from somewhere and often the easiest point to start from is, indeed, to consider just what is available. For the rest of this chapter we will concentrate on a specific example to illustrate database design and implementation. In this example, we are interested in building a repository of information about PCR experiments that have been carried out in a particular organization. The benefits of such a repository to the organization are to make the results of the PCR more readily available, to avoid duplication of effort, and to facilitate sharing of best practice between experimentalists. The example was inspired by a Cranfield MSc—if you want to find out more we refer you to the relevant thesis (Simecek, 2007), which is available via the web (hdl.handle. net/1826/1773).

Data to be captured from a PCR experiment

Rather than considering the experimental process as a whole, we first break the process down into potential sources of information for the database. Here, we may have five sources of information from an experiment:

1 The PCR kit used.

2 Experimental parameters (annealing temperature, cycle times, etc.).

3 Primers used.

4 The scientist performing the experiment.

5 Results of the experiment.

You may disagree with the above, wish to combine or regroup the sources, or split them down further, but in essence you will achieve the same result—a set of headings under which it is simpler to list the individual pieces of information that are to be stored than would be the case if you were to consider the whole experiment in one go. The result of assigning information under these five headings is shown in Table 2.1.

It is at this point in the design process that you can start asking yourself questions. The first might be 'Is this complete?' This would be a fair question, but tends to lure the unwary database designer down a never-ending quest for completeness that is not necessary to meet the application for which the database is intended.

Table 2.1 Example items of information from a PCR experiment grouped under source headings

PCR kit	Experimental parameters	Primers used	Scientist	Results
Manufacturer	Denature temperature	Primer 1 sequence	Name	Gel image
Kit name	Denature time	Primer 2 sequence	Title	
Order number	Annealing temperature	Primer concentration	Department	
Supplier plus their address	Annealing time	Primer design software used	Telephone number	
Cost	Elongate temperature		Email	
Buffer	Elongate time			
Buffer concentration	Number of cycles			
Enzyme	Completion temperature			
Enzyme concentration	Completion time			
Nucleotide mix				
Nucleotide concentration				

There are some items that are undoubtedly missing from Table 2.1 that you may wish to include. One might be the purpose of the experiment. There may be other experimental parameters that you wish to capture or variations in protocol that could be used. The results column is currently very sparse—would readings summarizing the information content of the gel resulting from the PCR be useful? You might also think that some of the pieces of information are not particularly useful and we might even be misguided to put them in. For instance, if the laboratory follows a set protocol for the majority of PCR experiments—might it not be safer (and more efficient) to point the user to the standard protocol sheet and, hence, eliminate the need to store, and potentially enter incorrectly, most of the pieces of information in the first two columns?

So, to get a better feel for what the database should be able to store, we need to consider how we intend to use the database. For the purposes of this example, it is to provide a record of protocols and kits that have been used in an attempt to amplify sequences that have proven tricky to analyse using standard methods. The benefit of storing the results from these experiments is that the database will provide a reference point across the laboratory for scientists to quickly determine if the sequence they are working with has been considered before and, if so, what the best protocol to use is.

With this in mind, it can be seen that perhaps the only extra pieces of information required would be the sequences that are to be amplified and some sort of judgement as to how successful each protocol was in amplifying each sequence. Perhaps we may also wish to add in some more data, such as the time and date of the experiment, and also an experiment identification number so that we can use this as a quick way of referring to the protocol and its outcome.

Refining Table 2.1 to include these additional pieces of information results in Table 2.2. At this stage, there don't appear to be any pieces of information that should be removed from these lists.

A secondary use of the database might be to research whether there are certain trends in the data that might indicate suitable starting points for amplifying novel sequences. Are there any further pieces of information that would be needed for this?

Once you are satisfied that the pieces of information you have collected are sufficient to fulfil the purpose of the database, the next stage is to turn these lists into a database design.

Schema design and normalization

Database design can be broadly approached in two ways. The officially 'correct' way to design a database is to start with a single database table containing all of the pieces of information that you are seeking to store in the database and then use a process called *normalization* to break this table into a set of tables linked by common pieces of information.

Table 2.2　A refinement of the items of information to be stored from a PCR experiment, once again grouped under source headings. Additional fields are highlighted in *italics*

PCR kit	Experimental parameters	Sequence and primer information	Scientist	Results
Manufacturer	*Experiment identifier*	*Sequence to be amplified*	Name	Gel image
Kit name	*Date*	*Purpose of experiment*	Title	*Assessment of method*
Order number	*Time*	Primer 1 sequence	Department	
Supplier plus their address	Denature temperature	Primer 2 sequence	Telephone number	
Cost	Denature time	Primer concentration	Email	
Buffer	Annealing temperature	Primer design software used		
Buffer concentration	Annealing time	*Primer supplier*		
Enzyme	Elongate temperature	*Cost*		
Enzyme concentration	Elongate time			
Nucleotide mix	Number of cycles			
Nucleotide concentration	Completion temperature			
	Completion time			

A more natural approach to database design can be followed that takes advantage of a lot of the thought that we put into collecting the information above. This is a method that we have evolved and tested many times with feedback indicating that it is more intuitive than the formal method, but also allows a quicker understanding of the steps involved in the normalization process. For these reasons this 'natural design' approach is presented in this chapter. However, if you are going to be doing database work regularly then you should definitely investigate other design approaches as each has its own strengths and weaknesses, and therefore suitability to different tasks. There are many papers and books dedicated to the subject: Codd first introduced the concept of normalization in 1970 (Codd, 1970), followed by numerous other papers. For complete guides to database design you may like to consider the popular *Database Design for Mere Mortals* (Hernandez, 2003) or, by the same publisher, *Database Solutions: A Step-by-Step Approach to Building Databases* (Connolly & Begg, 2003). If you would prefer a MySQL specific guide to both design and the fundamentals of the MySQL system, try *Beginning MySQL Database Design and Optimization* (Stephens & Russell, 2004).

If you talk with database administrators in your organization, they may wish to ascertain the level of normalization of your proposed schema. For most purposes a schema designed to the '3rd Normal' specification will provide a good balance of functionality and robustness. The approach outlined in this chapter tends to result in a schema that is 3rd Normal and, therefore, should suit your needs.

Here, we will cover how to present a schema and some of the more standard terminology used in database design.

Presenting the schema

The information in Table 2.2 is fairly clear for this small example, containing names for tables and the types of information within each table. It does not, however, look very much like a database schema. Before continuing to develop the database it is useful to draw it in a slightly different fashion. Specifically, each table should be presented in its own box with the table name above the box and the types of information contained within each appearing within the box, as shown in Fig. 2.5. At this point it is useful to choose simple, but descriptive names for each of the tables and for each type of information. Such names should be consistent with one another. For instance, there is currently one table named Scientist and another named Results. The first of these is singular and the second plural. Although this seems to be intuitive, it can make using the database harder in the future as not only does one have to remember the name of the table, but also if it is plural or singular. A standard convention is to name all tables in the singular, so Results becomes Result.

The types of data contained in each database are referred to as *fields*. Each field should also be named descriptively and consistently. Field names should generally not be long as they may need to be typed often and so prove frustrating, but they should convey the sort of information contained in the table. For example, naming each field 'a', 'b', 'c', etc., may be consistent and certainly speeds typing the names, but it will be impossible for anyone, including the database designer, to remember what is actually contained in the database.

It was with these guidelines in mind that the schema shown as Fig. 2.5 was created.

The immediate improvement in the clarity of presentation of each table is clear when comparing Fig. 2.5 with Table 2.2. This now looks much closer in form to the simple library schema given in section 2.1.3.

During the process of providing tables and fields with short, but descriptive, names, a number of interesting issues have come to light. For instance, does the information now contained in `Sequence` look right? There are eight fields in this table; six of them are related to primers and primer design, and the other two are related to the experiment. In this case, the renaming operation has helped to guide the formation of the database—we can now see that the fields `sequence` and `purpose` in the table `Sequence` may be better placed in the table `Experiment`, as they represent the sequence that is to be amplified in this experiment and the reason why we are doing the experiment. Once they are removed, all other information in the table relates to primers and so the table might be better named `Primer`. These changes are shown in a revised schema later in the chapter (Fig. 2.6).

Kit

| manufacturer |
| name |
| order_number |
| supplier |
| supplier_address |
| cost |
| buffer |
| buffer_conc |
| enzyme |
| enzyme_conc |
| nucl_mix |
| nucl_conc |

Sequence

| sequence |
| purpose |
| primer_1 |
| primer_2 |
| primer_conc |
| design_software |
| primer_supplier |
| primer_cost |

Experiment

| ID |
| date |
| time |
| denature_temp |
| denature_time |
| anneal_temp |
| anneal_time |
| elongate_temp |
| elongate_time |
| cycles |
| completion_temp |
| completion_time |

Scientist

| name |
| title |
| department |
| tel_number |
| email |

Result

| gel_image |
| assessment |

Fig. 2.5 Schema representation of Table 2.2.

We now have the outline of a schema. It is not yet complete, there are a number of further operations to perform before it is, but much of the conceptual hard work has been done. The following sections describe the processes by which this loose set of disconnected tables may be made more robust, to help ensure data integrity, and also linked together into a truly relational database.

2.2.2   Step 4: data types

The above processes have been fairly intuitive—gathering information, grouping it, and naming each piece. We now need to assign a specific data type to each piece of data. Specifying data types is important because it helps to maintain the integrity of the database, as well as to minimize its size, and maximize the speed with which we can get data in and out.

There is a set of standard data types defined within the ANSI (American National Standards Institute) standards for SQL. Most or all of these are used within RDBMSs, such as MySQL, Oracle, and Access, but are often given different names in each RDBMS. For this reason, there may be some problems when designing a database schema for one particular RDBMS and implementing it on another. For this reason, it is always worth checking that the data types you have used are compatible between the two and, if not, how they should be modified.

As this book assumes that you will be working with open-source software, the data types discussed in this section are for MySQL. Most of these will be the same or there will be equivalents in other systems, but the online help for each RDBMS will identify any differences.

Numeric data types

A number of the most commonly used numeric data types are given in Table 2.3. These can be split into two types—integer (whole number) types and floating point types (which can include numbers with fractional parts after a decimal point). Once you have decided whether your data requires a decimal point or not, the choice of the exact type will depend on how large you expect your stored numbers to be and to what level of precision you require the number to be stored. For instance, if you are only storing integers between 1 and 10 in a field, then the MySQL data type TINYINT would be adequate.

To store monetary data, two decimal places may always be required and, therefore, the data type could be set to DECIMAL(n, d), where n specifies the total precision and d the number of digits that follow the decimal point, in this case $d=2$ and n defines the maximum amount that can be stored in the column. (It is worth noting here that MySQL versions since 4.1 store DECIMAL fields as a text string, not as a numeric type, which can have implications when programming.)

Finally, to store the results of calculations that may result in real numbers, FLOAT may be used. In general it is not necessary to define a precision for FLOAT and, indeed, your schema will be more transferable if you don't, but the option is there in MySQL.

Table 2.3 Standard SQL and MySQL-specific numeric data types. Adapted from the MySQL Reference Manual

SQL type	MySQL type	Minimum value (signed)	Maximum value (signed)	Notes
	TINYINT	−128	127	An unsigned attribute is also available in MySQL. The range of this may be calculated by adding the numeric parts of the signed range (e.g. 0–255 (=128 + 127) for TINYINT)
SMALLINT	SMALLINT	−32768	32767	
	MEDIUMINT	−8388608	8388607	
INTEGER	INT	−2147483648	2147483647	
	BIGINT	−9.22337E + 18	9.22337E + 18	
DECIMAL	DEC or DECIMAL or DECIMAL (n,d)	−1E + 38	1E + 38 − 1	Fixed precision: Decimal numbers are expected to match the precision defined (e.g. currency data)
FLOAT	FLOAT or FLOAT (M,D)	−1.79E + 38	1.79E + 38	Floating point number with optional (non-standard) user definable precision
DOUBLE PRECISION	DOUBLE or REAL	−3.4E + 38	3.4E + 38	15 digits of floating precision

Text data types

Once again, there are a number of choices when deciding how to store textual information. The most commonly used of these are shown in Table 2.4. If the text itself is to be stored in the database in a readable form, then a text type is used. CHAR(n) sets aside storage space for a character string of length n, no more and no less. VARCHAR(n) defines a more flexible data type that allows any length of string to be entered to a maximum length of n, with storage only being used for approximately the length of string entered. Always using a VARCHAR(255) may seem like an attractive option for storing any text information (as long as it is shorter than 256 characters). However, if the data entered is likely to be of uniform length, such as serial numbers or certain accession numbers, then a CHAR of suitable length will generally be more efficient in terms of storage space.

For longer text strings, the variants on the TEXT type may be used. These may seem just like longer VARCHAR strings and do behave rather like them, but care should be taken when grouping and sorting using TEXT values as MySQL defaults to using only the first 1024 characters[1] for such operations. So, if two TEXT strings start the same, but diverge after 1024 characters, they will be treated as being equal for sorting and grouping, which may not yield the desired result.

Binary Large OBjects (BLOBs) are treated as binary strings (as opposed to character strings). Files such as PDFs, Microsoft Word documents, image data, etc., could be stored within the database as BLOBs, ordered and searched by comparing their

---

1 The comparison is actually restricted to the first 1024 bytes, so it will compare fewer than 1024 characters if you are using a character set that requires more than 1 byte to encode each character.

Table 2.4 Standard SQL and MySQL-specific text data types. Adapted from the MySQL Reference Manual

SQL type	MySQL type	Capacity	Notes
CHAR(n)	CHAR	$n = 0\text{–}255$	n sets the stored size of the string
VARCHAR(n)	VARCHAR	$n = 0\text{–}255$	n sets the maximum length of the string
	TINYTEXT	2^8 bytes	Up to 255 characters
TEXT	TEXT	2^{16} bytes	Up to 65,535 characters
	MEDIUMTEXT or LONG or LONG VARCHAR	2^{24} bytes	Up to 16,777,215 characters
	LONGTEXT	2^{32} bytes	Up to 4,294,967,295 characters
	TINYBLOB	2^8 bytes	256 bytes
BLOB	BLOB	2^{16} bytes	~65 KB
	MEDIUMBLOB	2^{24} bytes	~16.7 MB
	LONGBLOB	2^{32} bytes	~4.3 GB

binary strings. As with TEXT, such comparisons are limited by default to the first 1024 bytes of the string.

Choosing and representing the data types for our example

Back in Fig. 2.5 we captured all the fields in our database—each of which needs to be assigned a data type. Fig. 2.6 presents the data types assigned to each field in a tabular format. Consider the field types that have been suggested. Do they make sense? Can you see any problems with any of them or restrictions that they may impose? Some of these will be discussed below. Importantly, it is fine if you disagree with a number of these assignations. They are not perfect for all eventualities, but when you design your own databases you will need to carefully consider the application for which it is to be used and pick data types accordingly.

As mentioned above, VARCHAR(255) has been suggested for most of the text fields in this example. An exception to this is the order_number field in Kit, which assumes that the order numbers assigned by the department are of length 16 and, hence, there is no need to use a variable string length.

All temperatures and times have been assumed to be integer-based, with time in minutes. This assumption may be correct or a finer scale of temperature or time could be required. A FLOAT data type would be considered under these circumstances.

DATE and TIME are special data types that have not been discussed up to now. MySQL has a number of ways of representing these, which can be found in the MySQL Reference Manual (dev.mysql.com/doc/#manual). However, these are the most common, with DATE representing yyyy-mm-dd and TIME hours:mins:secs.

Kit cost and Primer primer_cost are both represented as decimals with two decimal places and a maximum number of six figures, allowing a maximum

Kit

Field	Type
manufacturer	VARCHAR(255)
name	VARCHAR(255)
order_number	CHAR(16)
supplier	VARCHAR(255)
supplier_address	TEXT
cost	DECIMAL(6,2)
buffer	VARCHAR(255)
buffer_conc	FLOAT
enzyme	VARCHAR(255)
enzyme_conc	FLOAT
nucl_mix	VARCHAR(255)
nucl_conc	FLOAT

Primer

Field	Type
primer_1	VARCHAR(255)
primer_2	VARCHAR(255)
primer_conc	FLOAT
design_software	VARCHAR(255)
primer_supplier	VARCHAR(255)
primer_cost	DECIMAL(6,2)

Scientist

Field	Type
name	VARCHAR(255)
title	VARCHAR(255)
department	VARCHAR(255)
tel_number	VARCHAR(255)
email	VARCHAR(255)

Experiment

Field	Type
ID	INT
sequence	VARCHAR(255)
purpose	TEXT
date	DATE
time	TIME
denature_temp	INT
denature_time	INT
anneal_temp	INT
anneal_time	INT
elongate_temp	INT
elongate_time	INT
cycles	INT
completion_temp	INT
completion_time	INT

Result

gel_image	MEDIUMBLOB
assessment	TEXT

Fig. 2.6 Fields and suggested data types by table, for PCR database example.

cost of 9999.99 to be represented in each of these fields. The unit of currency is not specified or stored in these fields.

As gel images can be large, these have been assigned a MEDIUMBLOB type that will allow storage of files just over 16 MB. Alternatively, a link to the location of the image on a hard drive or server could have been placed here (in the form a text string) to save space within the database, whilst still providing easy access to the image. This may often be a better solution than storing the image itself, as few database operations will be usefully employed on an image.

Finally the assessment of the experimental result has been assigned a TEXT type allowing a longer description, of up to around 65,500 characters to be stored here. This may be excessive and perhaps a TINYTEXT type would be more appropriate.

One point of note where the use of VARCHAR(255) might seem a little odd is the tel_number field in Scientist, which intuitively may have been an INT. However, often telephone numbers contain other characters, such as +, spaces and brackets that would not be compatible with a numeric type. This problem arises mainly because the telephone number is not atomic, which brings us neatly on to the next topic.

2.2.3   Step 5: atomicity of data

The term *atomicity* may at first appear overly complex, but all it means is that each piece of information in a field should be as small as it can be—i.e. it should only contain data about one item. If we consider the example of the phone number above, this seems to be just one data item, a phone number. However, it may contain three or more distinct pieces of information, such as country code, area code, and the number itself. As discussed above, the ways of representing such pieces of information generally require that characters other than numbers be entered. This, in itself, can introduce inconsistency and error into the database, and any way of avoiding this would be desirable.

One way of doing this is to split the data up into its smaller parts and thereby create a field for country code, one for area code, and one for the number. All of these will contain only integer values and so the type INT can be used. This may appear to make the database more complicated—we have just replaced one field by three—but these steps serve in the longer term to make the database more robust and, in many cases, more useful. For instance, it is now possible to search within the database for scientists with offices in specific countries using the country code.

Another example of this is in the supplier_address field in Kit. An address generally consists of a number of parts, including: Number/name of building, street name, town/city, county/state, postcode/zip, and country. supplier_ address is therefore not atomic. To correct this, six other fields need to be created and the supplier_address field removed.

The field name in Scientist should be treated similarly. The revised schema is presented as Fig. 2.7.

For each field in your proposed database, ensure that it cannot be split into smaller parts and you will have achieved atomicity. The full advantages of this will be seen in the next section, but for the time being it is worth thinking of this as a useful way of making each piece of data in the system as simple as it can be- simple things are always easier to deal with.

2.2.4   Steps 6 and 7: indexing and linking tables

We now have an atomic database containing all of the information that we think we need to know about the PCR experiments being performed. However, this database is not yet relational—there are no links between tables and, therefore, the information contained within them is not linked. This format works for a paper example, as we think intuitively that if we talked about two different experiments then we could imagine two separate pages containing the data, one for each experiment. This is very much a spreadsheet view of the data. Much of the power of a relational database comes from being able to search through the data contained to spot trends, order by different variables, such as scientist or manufacturer to identify systematic errors, and generally to search the data as

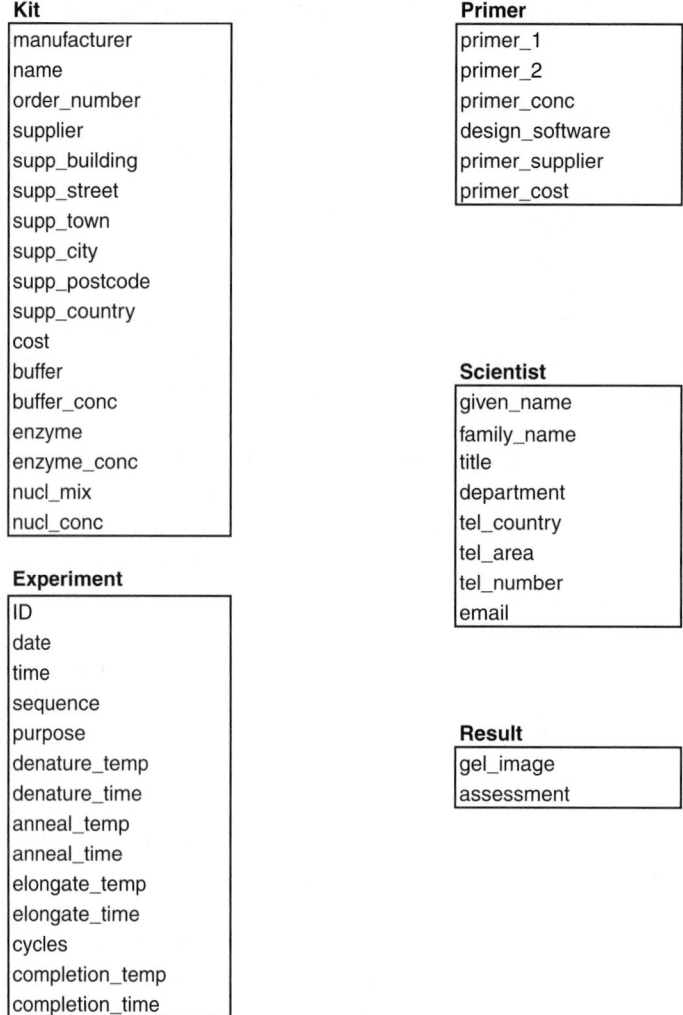

Fig. 2.7 Atomic schema for the PCR database example.

an interlinked whole, not as a series of discrete items. For this reason, we will need to add some fields into the database that allow the tables to be linked to one another.

Before we attempt this we need to first ensure that our tables can be efficiently searched individually. For this they should be indexed. As in a printed dictionary, what indexing does is provide a structure (and order) to the data, such that it can be searched and the correct information retrieved. In a dictionary the sorting is by alphabetical ordering of the first few letters in each word and the correct information for each word is retrieved because each word is generally unique. This is sometimes not true and it is good to think about the difficulties that can be caused when two words are spelt the same, but have different meanings—it would be more convenient if the datum or meaning of the word could be unambiguously accessed by a truly unique key or word. This is what we are attempting to do by indexing our database.

An index therefore allows us to unambiguously select any row of data from any of our tables, with each table having its own index *key*. Such a key can consist of one or more of the pieces of data within the table. A simple example of this is in the table `Experiment`. In this table, each experiment has been given an identification number (`ID`). If this identification number were simply an integer, each one greater than the last identification number, it would be sufficient on its own to uniquely identify any experiment in the table.

A number of database designers will recommend that each table within the database has a unique identifier based on an incremental number. This may result in certain performance increases under some circumstances, but we disagree with this approach on two fronts. The most important of these is that it complicates the database by introducing unnatural fields, with nothing to do with the data, into each table. This makes the database harder to think about, design and query. The second is that it breaks one of the formal rules when designing databases, which is that all information in a table should be directly related to the key of that table—if we introduce an arbitrary running number into the key results we break this relationship.

So, how can keys be created other than by using numeric identifiers? In just the same way as any object is identified everyday, through distinct characteristics. As an example of this, let's consider the table `Scientist`. Here, a candidate for a primary key immediately presents itself: the scientist's name. In this table an index key could be created on just the `family_name`. However, many family names are common and, hence, we might add in the given name of the scientist. In this way we could build a *compound key* to the table, consisting of both the given name and the surname. If we could guarantee that no two scientists were going to have the same combination of given name and family name, then this would be fine, but it is not true—lots of people share the same name. At this point someone might suggest adding in an employee number and referring to the scientists using this. Doing so has some uses, especially if this database were to be connected to their organization's human resources database. However, this is unlikely, and most people don't know their employee number and so getting these might be difficult. It is also just as unintuitive as using the incremental number method. There is also a better option already in this table—the e-mail address. By definition, this will be unique to each scientist, provided, of course that they have an e-mail account. Most scientists now do have these and, if not, they are easily obtained, even if they never use it!

The `Primer` table does not seem to have any natural key in its present form. Eventually this table will also need to be linked to the table `Experiment`. Linking two tables is achieved when two tables share at least one field. In this case neither contains a field present in the other and we therefore need to choose at least one field from one table to place in the other. Here, the `ID` seems like a good choice as the primer sequences will be related to the experimental sequence we are seeking to amplify. This would also allow `ID` to be used as the primary key for the `Primer` table. Once this is done, it can be seen that the two tables now both have `ID` as their key. As all the information in both tables is uniquely identified by the same key, logically all of this information should appear in the same table, although we thought earlier that they should be separate. (There is an argument that the information in `Primer` should, in fact, remain separate because the same primer combination could be used for more than one experiment and, hence, the same information could be repeated many times in the `Experiment` table, which would be undesirable. The final choice would be determined by end use—does each experiment run in this laboratory generally use different primers or not?)

Similarly, no key within `Result` naturally suggests itself and these data are also directly related to the experiment. These fields should, therefore, also be placed within the `Experiment` table. `Experiment` is now a much larger table, as shown in Fig. 2.8.

Conversely, when considering the `Kit` table, an eligible key for the table might be a combination of manufacturer and the kit name (`manufacturer,name`). This works for most of the fields in this table except for those that are related to the supplier—a supplier may provide many makes and versions of kit and, hence, their details are not uniquely identified by a single kit manufacturer and name. This suggests that the supplier details should be brought out of `Kit` and placed in their own table, `Supplier`. As suppliers of similar products should have different names, we will assume that `supplier` will form an adequate key to this new table, as shown in Fig. 2.9.

Experiment

ID
date
time
sequence
purpose
denature_temp
denature_time
anneal_temp
anneal_time
elongate_temp
elongate_time
cycles
completion_temp
completion_time
primer_1
primer_2
primer_conc
design_software
primer_supplier
primer_cost
gel_image
assessment

Fig. 2.8 The new `Experiment` table including fields originally within `Primer` and `Result`. The primary key is shaded in light grey.

However, further consideration of the `Kit` table shows that this primary key is also incorrect. If the same kit is ordered twice, then much of the information within the table will have to be repeated, as this will have a different order number. This demonstrates either that `(manufacturer,name)` is an incorrect primary key, or that this table is still not yet properly designed. The answer is the latter: `order_number` should not be in this table as most of the other information in the table does not depend on the order number. This should therefore be brought out into another table.

The order number does uniquely link to the manufacturer and kit name, and therefore these fields, may also feature in the new table, and thus serve to link the two tables. Furthermore, the order number is naturally assigned to a supplier and this field can therefore appear in the `Supplier` table. The resultant tables and links are shown in Fig. 2.10.

To link `Experiment` to `Kit`, it may be tempting to put the `ID` field into the `Kit` table, but this would break the constraint that all the information in `Kit` should be uniquely identified by `(manufacturer,name)`—the experiment identification number has nothing to do with this. A better choice of fields by which to link the two tables is to do this indirectly through the `Kit_order` table by

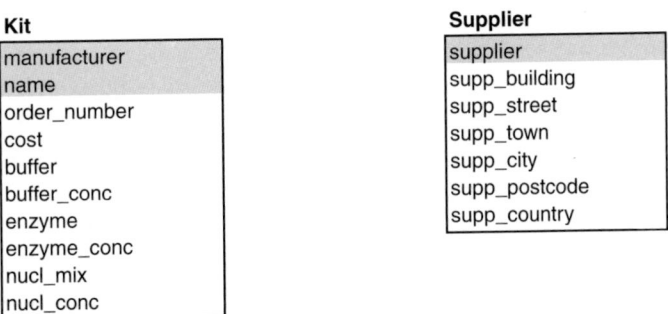

Fig. 2.9 The reduced table `Kit` and the new table `Supplier`. Primary keys are shaded in light grey.

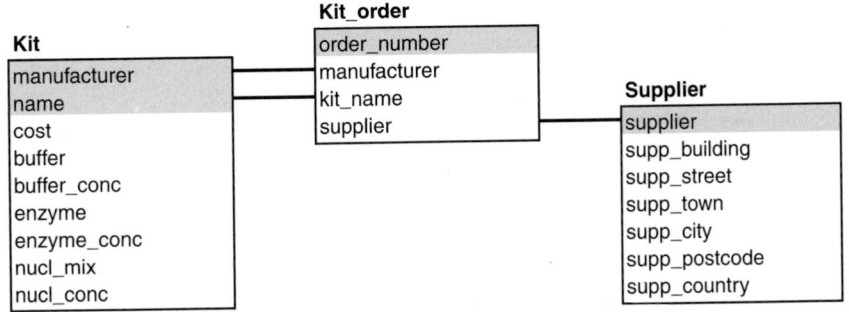

Fig. 2.10 Reconfigured `Kit` table linked through `Kit_order` by `order_number` to `Supplier`. Note that linked fields do not need to have identical names in each table.

placing `order_number` in `Experiment`. This will therefore serve to uniquely identify any kit that is used in an experiment. It is no coincidence that the key to one table forms a good link to another table in this way—they are routes to identify any unique row in their own table and, hence, can be used for a similar purpose in related tables.

Similarly, `Experiment` may be linked to `Scientist` by putting the key of `Scientist, email`, into `Experiment` as well.

Defining relationships between tables

All of the tables in the schema now have keys that may be used to uniquely identify their every row. Each table is also linked to at least one other table. This is the basis of our relational database. This section looks a little more closely at how the relationships between the tables are formed and the terminology that is used to refer to them.

The keys that have been defined above are known as the *primary key* of their respective tables (e.g. the primary key of the `Scientist` table is `email`). A field in a table that links to another table such that any specific value may not be entered unless the same value already exists in the other table is called a *foreign key*. This helps maintain data integrity, and also implies an order for entering data into the tables. Fig. 2.11 shows the complete schema with the primary and foreign keys linked.

Observant readers will notice that subtle changes have been made to two of the field names in this figure. Specifically, the order number added to the `Experiment` table has been called `kit_order_number`, and the `supplier` field in the `Supplier` table has been renamed `supplier_name`. This is because it is not considered good practice to use identical names for linked fields.

A note on many-to-many relationships

When creating your database design using the above method, you should end up with a schema that links a field such that for any one instance of a field in one table, there will be zero, one or many occurrences of that instance in another table. For example, in `Scientist` a scientist's e-mail address will appear once, whereas it may appear zero, one or many times in `Experiment`. In the latter case, this type of relationship may be described as *one-to-many*. If, however, your database design is not yet fully complete, you may find that you have a situation in which many instances of a field in one table might be linked to many instances of that field in another table.

Imagine that we had linked `Scientist` to `Experiment` using the first name of the scientists, rather than their unique e-mail addresses. If 'Bob Andrews' had performed six experiments, his contact details would appear once in `Scientist` and 'Bob' would appear six times in `Experiment`. If 'Bob Barrows' was also in the laboratory group and had performed four experiments, then his contact details would appear once in `Scientist` and 'Bob' would feature an additional four times in `Experiment`. Now, if we had linked the two tables on the first name field, then both instances of 'Bob' in `Scientist` will be linked to all 10 instances of 'Bob' in

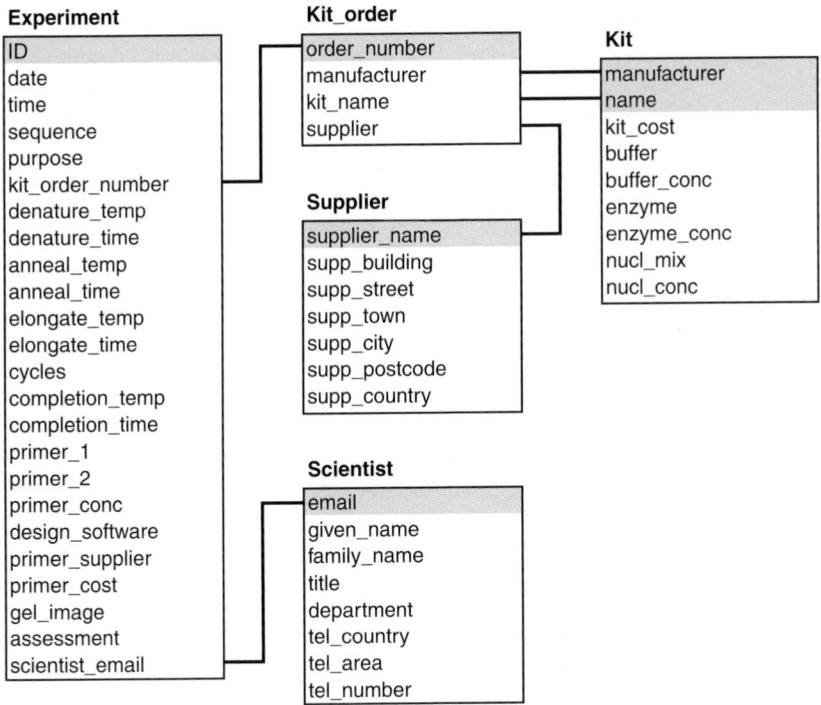

Fig. 2.11 Final schema for the PCR example. Primary keys are shaded in light grey. Links (via shared fields) between tables are also shown. Foreign keys are the fields to which the primary keys are linked.

`Experiment`. This will result in incorrect information being returned and also queries taking much longer to return than they would have done otherwise.

As indicated above, this should not happen in a well-designed schema, and it is hard to see why we would have done anything like this contrived example. It can happen though, especially in more complex databases, so it is always worth checking for any relationships that do not feature a primary key on one side to see whether that may cause a similar problem.

2.2.5 Departure from design

Once you have designed your database you are ready to start implementing it in your preferred RDBMS. As discussed in the introduction to this chapter, it is tempting to dive straight in to typing away at your computer without giving sufficient thought to what it is you wish to achieve. If you approach all new database design on paper, and spend the time and effort to design your database well before reaching for the keyboard, implementing and using your database will be much quicker and a lot simpler.

The next section covers installing a MySQL database server onto your computer, and how to use this to first implement your database, populate it with data, and finally to search through the information stored within.

2.3 Installing and configuring a MySQL server

2.3.1 Download and installation

Getting hold of a copy of MySQL to install on your machine is a simple proc-ess, but can vary depending on the operating system that you are using. If you are using Microsoft Windows or Mac OS X, simply visit the MySQL web site (www.mysql.com), and follow the download and installation instructions for your operating system. The specific version you are looking for—at least as a beginner—is the free 'MySQL Community Server', as opposed to the paid for alternative 'MySQL Enterprise'. Various download options are available for each operating system—for Windows we recommend the `setup.exe` version, which is installed through the familiar Windows installer process. During this process, we recommend you choose a 'standard', rather than 'detailed' configuration, and make sure you tick the box to 'Include Bin Directory in Windows PATH' so you can easily access MySQL from any directory while you are working at the command line.

If you are using Linux, before going to the MySQL website it is best to look into your distribution's package management system, as MySQL is nearly always available for easy installation from there (often this can even be only a couple of mouse clicks for a complete install). In the unlikely event that you cannot find MySQL within your package manager, head over to the MySQL website instead.

During configuration of the MySQL server you will be given the opportunity to set up a password for the *root* user. The root user is effectively the administra-tor of the database server, with a lot more power than regular users. It is good practice to set a root password, as long as it is something you can remember of course!

Once MySQL has been installed, you need to start it from your operating sys-tem's command line (see Appendix A if this is unfamiliar). You can start MySQL by typing `mysql` at the command line and hitting the Enter key. However, if you chose to set up a root user and password during the installation of MySQL, you will instead need to specify these when starting MySQL, by typing the command below and entering the password when prompted.

```
mysql -u root -p
```

Once MySQL has started you will see some information come onto the screen followed by the MySQL user prompt:

```
mysql>
```

You have now moved from the operating system command line to the MySQL command line. Almost all of the commands that you enter into MySQL will be entered at this prompt, so assume that you need to have got to this point before attempting any of the actions described below, unless otherwise stated. Once you've had enough of MySQL, you can close it by typing `quit` (or `exit`) and hitting Enter. If you get totally stuck installing MySQL, head over to www. bixsolutions.net.

2.3.2 Creating a database and a user account

At this point, you will be logged into the MySQL server as the root user. This is a very powerful position to be in and, although it is unlikely that you will do anything to damage anything on your own system, if you were to log into a shared database server within your organization, then this may be a more important issue. In either case, you should create a different user account by which to access your database.

First, you will need a database on which to work. This may be created using the following command:

```
CREATE DATABASE dbname;
```

Here, dbname is any suitable name for your database that you would like to use. (Throughout this chapter we use italics in generic command examples to identify placeholders for parameters that can be passed to the command.) Just as with table names, as discussed above, database names should be descriptive and simple.

Note also the semi-colon (;) that follows the command—this is necessary to tell MySQL that you have finished writing the command. If it is missing you will simply pass on to another line when you hit Enter (the command prompt will change to ->). You can then type in the semi-colon and the command will complete as if it had been written on the one line. This is a useful, although sometimes confusing or annoying, feature as it allows you to split long commands over a number of lines and, therefore, read them back more clearly. SQL conventions are discussed further in section 2.5.

You can now create a user account through which to access your database in preference to the root account. This is done by issuing the following command:

```
GRANT ALL ON dbname.* TO 'username'@'localhost' IDENTIFIED BY
'password';
```

For instance, if you had created a database called sandpit (a name often given to systems intended for playing around in while learning) and wanted to create an account with a user name of 'Ian' and a password of 'BBSbook' you would do this by typing:

```
GRANT ALL ON sandpit.* TO 'Ian'@'localhost' IDENTIFIED BY
'BBSbook';
```

Be careful to get the quotation marks in the right place—note in particular that 'Ian' and 'localhost' are separate entities. The * means that all tables within the database will be covered by the GRANT statement. The term localhost refers to the machine from which you will be accessing the account. If you are working on your own machine and have installed your own MySQL server, this will be fine. However, if you are connecting to a different server from your machine, you will need to put either the full DNS name of your machine here or its IP address (or if you would like your new user to be able to access the database from any other computer—we'll leave you to ponder the security implications of this—you can just replace `'localhost'` with `'%'`). See your database administrator for more information if this is the case for you, as in this instance it is likely they will have to create a user account for you and should then be able to tell you exactly how to access the database server.

Once you hit Enter, MySQL should give a message stating that this operation has completed successfully. It also tells you how long the command took to execute—not very significant for this command, but an indication of how critical performance can be come when databases get large. Following this you should exit MySQL and then reconnect using your new account.

```
QUIT;
```

To reconnect using this new account, you would now type:

```
mysql -u Ian -p
```

and then enter the password (`BBSbook` in this case) when prompted to do so. Note that passwords are case sensitive, even when using MySQL in Windows.

You now have access to your relational database management system (RDBMS), in this case MySQL. There are others available, which we shall discuss briefly in the next section.

2.4   Alternatives to MySQL

MySQL is only one of many RDBMSs available. There are a number of reasons why we have chosen to use it for this book: it is free, widely available and has very large community usage, which means that should you have a question about how to achieve a specific function, or need help solving a problem, almost undoubtedly there will be someone on the internet who has had a similar issue, solved it, and posted the solution.

However, you may well want to consider, or at least feel that we have not just ignored, other available systems. Three of these are discussed very briefly below, but we encourage you to do your own research in this area, with one caveat—comparisons between systems are rife on the internet and many are out of date, so it is probably best to take all you read with a judicious pinch of salt.

2.4.1   PostgreSQL

PostgreSQL is another fully featured open source RDBMS. It is freely available from `www.postgresql.org` in versions for Windows, Linux, and Mac OS. Historically, PostgreSQL has been more feature rich than MySQL. However, there comes a point where the feature set is likely to be more than you really need. There are enterprise installations of both of these open source systems that work extremely well under very high volumes of data and large numbers of concurrent users.

2.4.2 Oracle

Oracle is regarded as the industry standard for database management and has the richest feature set of any current database management system. It is available for many operating systems, including Windows, Linux, and Mac OS. Oracle is often used by the biggest companies as, despite the positive experiences with MySQL and PostgreSQL, it has a reputation as the only choice for supplying the stability, performance, and administrative (recovery) capabilities necessary for a large organization. As an enterprise solution, it is also one of the more expensive options. However, versions of Oracle are available for free from www.oracle.com for you to develop and distribute your own databases. Therefore, if you know that you are going to need to interface with a company instance of Oracle, a good point to start would be to download the most up-to-date, free version you can, and work with this locally until you are ready to hand your database and any associated tools to your database administrator.

2.4.3 Microsoft Access

Microsoft's Access program is present on many computers, but sadly under-utilized in favour of the more approachable Excel spreadsheet package. As a store of data, Excel is extremely limited, and encourages a variety of complex worksheets and formulae to be created to achieve what would be very simple tasks within a database framework.

If you have Access installed on your computer, you may prefer to use this, rather than install one of the other packages suggested here. Furthermore, if you work for a company, MySQL and PostgreSQL may not be on the list of approved software for your work machine. In such cases, Access may be your only choice for a locally installed database server with which to experiment.

Access is a fully featured RDBMS and has the advantage of looking and feeling similar to all other MS Office packages. It also has some advantages over a basic install of MySQL in that it natively features a graphical representation of tables and, hence, implementing database schemas is straightforward as they may literally be 'drawn' into existence. Accessing data stored in the database through Excel to take advantage of the spreadsheet package's features is also very easy. This can also be achieved without too much difficulty using other RDBMSs through a system called ODBC—consult your RDBMS user guide for more information on this topic.

On the negative side, Access is a fairly slow system when compared with standard installations of MySQL, and there are likely to be unacceptable delays when running queries on moderate to large databases or when querying data from a number of linked tables. Furthermore, as a commercial piece of software, Access goes against the open source ethos of the bioinformatics community and ubiquitous availability cannot be assumed because it costs money, and it is only available for Windows.

2.5   Database access using SQL

Structured Query Language (SQL) is, as the name suggests, the language used primarily for querying your database. As this section will show, for almost everything you could want to do with your database the command should be straightforward to generate using just a few simple keywords. As with the structure of the database itself, it is not the implementation that's important, it is the design of your queries that matters. It is also at this stage that the quality of thought behind the design of your database is revealed. A poorly designed creation will result in poor performance when queried, or worse, incomplete or incorrect data being returned by functionally correct SQL commands.

By convention, all SQL commands are written in capital letters. This helps to distinguish them from non-SQL words, such as your table and field names, and as such the convention has been used in this book. However, there is no need to type them in capitals when querying your database if you don't want to—the end results will be just the same.

One common error to watch out for is the use of SQL reserved words (any word in the SQL vocabulary, such as TABLE or VALUES) as the names of your objects, such as databases, tables, and fields. Such usage will confuse the RDBMS and most likely result in it reporting a syntax error that may be hard to find as the query will not look obviously wrong. In such cases look carefully for conflicts between your naming and SQL words.

2.5.1   Compatibility between RDBMSs

In principle, it should be quite easy to move between RDBMSs that support SQL as the database commands and syntax will be the same. So, examples provided in this chapter for MySQL should also work in, for example, Oracle. However, as we have already mentioned, names of data types can differ between RDBMSs. Also, each RDBMS can have additional commands that go beyond standard SQL so care needs to be taken. In particular, we should warn you that the MySQL commands SHOW, DECRIBE, and LIMIT introduced later in this section are not standard SQL commands so may not work in another RDBMS.

2.5.2   Error messages

It is very likely that you will make numerous typing errors when entering commands to the RDBMS. Often the message that is returned can appear exceptionally unhelpful, but there are guiding clues that can help you identify where things went wrong. A very common error message is something like:

```
mysql> SELECT * FROM Supplier WHRE supplier_name LIKE 'Eps%';

ERROR 1064 (42000): You have an error in your SQL syntax;
check the manual that corresponds to your MySQL server
version for the right syntax to use near 'supplier_name like
'Eps%'' at line 1
```

Here, we are informed that there is an error in the SQL syntax. This means that MySQL cannot interpret something that we have typed. The problem might be that we have entered some keywords in an incorrect order, or that we have typed something incorrectly. The error message offers some guidance as to where the problem might lie, in this case just before where we wrote `supplier_name`. If we look in this region, we can quickly spot the typo in the SQL keyword, `WHERE`, here typed `WHRE`. If there is a keyword miss entry, the location may be harder to spot as the error may well be earlier in the query than indicated.

Every RDBMS has a complete listing of error codes and help in interpreting them as part of their documentation. For MySQL, these are in the appendices to the reference manual (`dev.mysql.com/doc/#manual`).

2.5.3 Creating a database

In section 2.3.2 we covered the command used to create an empty database with no tables from which to start. Let's create a database called `PCR_experiment`, in preparation for building a database with the design described in our earlier example. To do this it is necessary to log on to MySQL as `root` and issue the command below. You can then either continue to work in MySQL as `root` (not recommended) or grant another user access to the database as described above, then quit MySQL and log back in using that username.

```
CREATE DATABASE PCR_experiment;
```

Within the RDBMS you may have a number of databases. The first action to perform when preparing to interact with one of these is to tell the RDBMS which one you want. This is accomplished by the `USE` command:

```
USE PCR_experiment;
```

This will change the focus of your commands from the database currently being accessed, if any, to one called `PCR_experiment`.

A newly created database will be empty, with no tables defined and no data present. Before getting data into the database, it is necessary to define tables, for which the simplest generic command is:

```
CREATE TABLE tablename (
  field_1 type_1,
  field_2 type_2,
  ...
  field_n type_n
);
```

Returning to our example database schema, shown in Fig. 2.11, we have five tables to create. We could do this now for each of the tables, but we will also want to enforce the relationships between the tables at this point, for which a little more explanation is required.

2.5.4 Creating tables and enforcing referential integrity

The term *referential integrity* refers to the ability of the database to maintain relationships between the data held in different tables. This is primarily achieved at a design level through the use of the foreign keys discussed previously. Therefore, the responsibility for much of this area rests in your hands, as the database designer.

MySQL supports a number of different table types, of which MyISAM and InnoDB are the most often used, with MyISAM being its default. Different table types impact the way in which a RDBMS handles and stores data within a given database table, and can have effects on performance and functions. We don't need to go into details about this here. Suffice to say that newer versions of MySQL fully support referential integrity when the default MyISAM type is used, so it shouldn't be necessary to specify the table type when defining tables.

There are a number of options that we can include within a CREATE TABLE statement. These include the table type, whether a field can hold a NULL value (whether it can be left empty), and also whether a field is part of a primary key or a foreign key to another table. Bearing in mind that foreign keys to other tables should logically be created after the table to which they refer, the first tables to be created should be those with no foreign keys. In our example, these are Scientist, Kit, and Supplier, created using:

```
CREATE TABLE Scientist (
   email VARCHAR(255) NOT NULL,
   given_name VARCHAR(255),
   family_name VARCHAR(255),
   title VARCHAR(255),
   department VARCHAR(255),
   tel_country INT,
   tel_area INT,
   tel_number INT,
   PRIMARY KEY (email)
);
CREATE TABLE Kit (
   manufacturer VARCHAR(255) NOT NULL,
   name VARCHAR(255) NOT NULL,
   kit_cost DECIMAL(6,2),
   buffer VARCHAR(255),
   buffer_conc FLOAT,
   enzyme VARCHAR(255),
   enzyme_conc FLOAT,
   nucl_mix VARCHAR(255),
   nucl_conc FLOAT,
   PRIMARY KEY (manufacturer, name)
);
```

```
CREATE TABLE Supplier (
  supplier_name VARCHAR(255) NOT NULL,
  supp_building VARCHAR(255),
  supp_street VARCHAR(255),
  supp_town VARCHAR(255),
  supp_city VARCHAR(255),
  supp_postcode VARCHAR(255),
  supp_country VARCHAR(255),
  PRIMARY KEY (supplier_name)
);
```

Note the simplicity of the method by which to create the compound primary key when creating `Kit`. There are other ways to signify which elements of a table are to be included in the primary key, but this method is consistent and clear.

If you wish to check that the tables have been created you can issue the following MySQL command:

```
SHOW tables;
```

If you would like to see more detail about any of the tables, just enter the following command with the appropriate table name:

```
DESCRIBE tablename;
```

These two commands are further described in section 2.5.8.

Now the remaining two tables may be created. There is an order that needs to be followed here too. Consider the relationship between `Experiment` and `Kit_order`. Because `Kit_order_number` in `Experiment` is a foreign key on `order_number` in `Kit_order`, it follows that the table `Kit_order` must exist before `Experiment` can be created.

```
CREATE TABLE Kit_order (
  order_number CHAR(16) NOT NULL,
  manufacturer VARCHAR(255),
  kit_name VARCHAR(255),
  supplier VARCHAR(255),
  PRIMARY KEY (order_number),
  FOREIGN KEY (manufacturer, kit_name)
    REFERENCES Kit(manufacturer, name),
  FOREIGN KEY (supplier)
    REFERENCES Supplier(supplier_name)
);
CREATE TABLE Experiment (
  ID INT NOT NULL AUTO_INCREMENT,
  date DATE,
  time TIME,
  sequence VARCHAR(255),
```

```
    purpose TEXT,
    kit_order_number CHAR(16),
    denature_temp INT,
    denature_time INT,
    anneal_temp INT,
    anneal_time INT,
    elongate_temp INT,
    elongate_time INT,
    cycles INT,
    completion_temp INT,
    completion_time INT,
    primer_1 VARCHAR(255),
    primer_2 VARCHAR(255),
    primer_conc FLOAT,
    design_software VARCHAR(255),
    primer_supplier VARCHAR(255),
    primer_cost DECIMAL(6,2),
    gel_image BLOB,
    assessment TEXT,
    scientist_email VARCHAR(255),
    PRIMARY KEY (ID),
    FOREIGN KEY (kit_order_number)
      REFERENCES Kit_order(order_number),
    FOREIGN KEY (scientist_email)
      REFERENCES Scientist(email)
);
```

Once again, note the simplicity of creating the foreign keys, whereby the field in the table being created is linked, *referenced*, to a field in a previously created table. It is just as simple to link multiple fields, where a compound key is required, as in the creation of `Kit_order`.

AUTO_INCREMENT

You will have no doubt noticed the new command AUTO_INCREMENT in the text used to create the Experiment table. Whenever new data is entered into the table, this command will populate the field ID with a value that is one greater than the previous highest ID in that field. In this way the ID field, which is the primary key of this table, is created automatically, without you needing to know how many entries have been placed in the table before the current one.

2.5.5   Populating the database

All of the tables for this example have now been created and their primary and foreign keys have been defined. The tables are therefore now ready to take in data. This can be done in a number of ways. The simplest, but most cumbersome, is for us to enter the data using SQL from the command line, in a similar manner to creating the tables. This is done using the `INSERT INTO` command—once again bearing in mind that the order in which the tables can be populated is dependent on the structure of the foreign keying. To reiterate, `Experiment` cannot be populated with results from a newly ordered kit (i.e. a kit that is not already in the database) or performed by a new scientist unless their details have already been entered into the relevant tables (`Kit` and `Scientist`, respectively). However, if this information is already in the database, because the scientist has done other experiments and the same kit from a previous order is being used, then data can be entered into `Experiment` as its foreign key conditions will be met.

The generic form of the `INSERT INTO` statement is:

```
INSERT INTO tablename (field_1, field_2,...)
VALUES(value_1, value_2,...);
```

So, to enter a new scientist's details, the following statement could be used:

```
INSERT INTO Scientist (email, given_name, family_name, title,
department, tel_country, tel_area, tel_number)
VALUES ('a.Scientist@example.com', 'Andrew', 'Scientist',
'Dr.', 'Toxicology', 44, 0117, 4960808);
```

Note the single quotation marks surrounding all text entries, but not the numeric entries—this is an SQL convention that should be followed. If you forget, an error will be shown and the command will not complete.

It may seem ridiculous to have to enter all the fields of a table into a command when surely the database system knows that these tables are there. In this case, you would be correct to think this, as we have entered values for all fields in the order in which they appear in the table. Because this is the case, we could shorten the above command to:

```
INSERT INTO Scientist
VALUES ('a.Scientist@example.com', 'Andrew', 'Scientist',
'Dr.', 'Toxicology', 44, 0117, 4960808);
```

This would achieve identical results to the above command, although, if you just tried it you would notice that your database complained. This was because you already had a scientist in the table with an email address of `a.Scientist@ example.com`. This is the primary key for the table and, therefore, all values in this column must be unique—remember the definition introduced in section 2.2.4.

You could try the command using a different email address. Please note though that if you are not the only administrator/designer of this database and you plan to use this shortened form of insert you will need to check that the fields in your database have not changed prior to running your inserts this way as extra or removed fields would cause your inserts to fail (as, indeed, would reordered database fields if someone had rebuilt your table in a different order).

If we wanted to only enter data into some fields of a table, or to enter data in an order that is not identical to that of the table, the field name specification in the `INSERT INTO` command may be used to guide the database—showing it where we want the data entered. For example, if we were to only want to enter a new scientist's email address (required in all circumstances as this is the primary key) and their department, perhaps because they did not yet have a telephone number, we could use the following command:

```
INSERT INTO Scientist (department, email)
VALUES('Systems Lab','a.techie@example.org');
```

In this statement we have only populated two fields and did this in a different order to that in which they appear in the table definition. However, because we explicitly told the database system what we wanted, it will have entered these values into the correct fields. If we wanted to make sure this was so, we would use the `DESCRIBE` command explained later, in section 2.5.8.

Although we can considerably shorten the `INSERT INTO` command by omitting the field names, there will necessarily be a lot of typing to enter the details of just one experiment into the database. In reality, this burden is likely to fall to the people using the system day-to-day and so will be split. Furthermore, the use of forms or well-presented programs used to provide access to the database will eliminate the need for the user to know any of the syntax needed to enter data into the database from the command line. The following chapter, on programming in Perl, and Chapter 5, on integrating these concepts with web-based systems, will allow you to create your own routes by which you and your users can enter data to the database without repeated and excessive typing. Having said that, in many bioinformatics applications, databases are not *populated* (filled) by people at all, but by programs (often written in Perl). A typical example of this is where a database is used to store the results from an automated data analysis pipeline.

For test purposes, it is often convenient to use a *source file* to rapidly populate a database with reasonable quantities of representative data—this is discussed in section 2.5.7.

2.5.6 Removing data and tables from the database

As well as adding data to a database, we might wish to remove data from the database. This might be because there was a user error when populating the system, or, quite likely when designing and testing a system, you wish to reset the database to a blank state. We may wish to remove an entire table from the system or only parts of it. At the most extreme we may want to delete the entire database and start again. Each of these is possible and remarkably simple to achieve and in there lies the rub—once you have done this, there is no going back[2] and the system will not ask if you are sure that you want to do this.

---

2 This is generally the case, although if you use transaction handling (see section 2.5.9) you would be able to recover to the last point at which you confirmed all database changes.

Deleting data from a table

The command below will delete everything from the table *tablename*. The structure of the table will remain intact so that we can enter new data there immediately, but all of the old data will have been removed.

```
DELETE FROM tablename;
```

More selectively, we can use:

```
DELETE FROM tablename WHERE field LIKE 'xyz';
```

This command will delete only those rows of the table for which the condition following the WHERE statement is met. For more discussion of the types of condition that can follow WHERE, see section 2.5.8.

When deleting rows from tables, it should be remembered that there may be foreign keys to those rows from other tables. In these cases, multiple delete statements may be required in order to maintain the referential integrity of the database. If one or a number of rows in one table are foreign keyed to another table, e.g. all of one scientist's Experiment data will be linked to their entry in the Scientist table, then before deleting the parent row, all records in the child table(s) that refer to this key must also be deleted. For example, first delete from Experiment all entries attributed to that scientist before removing the scientist's information from Scientist.

Deleting complete tables

If we want to remove an entire table, i.e. all of its data and its structure and name, from the database, this may be done using the DROP TABLE command:

```
DROP TABLE tablename;
```

Deleting a database

Similarly, an entire database may be removed from the RDBMS using the DROP DATABASE command:

```
DROP DATABASE databasename;
```

2.5.7   Creating and using source files

As we have seen, creating a database can involve a lot of typing at the command prompt. For this reason, it would be useful if, when we do need to replace a database entirely or we want to easily reset all the tables to empty, there were a quick way of doing this that meant we only had to do the majority of typing once. Fortunately, there is, through the use of a *source file*.

Source files are text files that contain SQL commands and/or data that we can call upon from within the database system. The text files should be plain text, which means that to create them we need to use a very basic text editor, such as Windows Notepad, to avoid storing all of the extra formatting information that word processors would place in the document. Section 3.1.2 in the next chapter briefly reviews text editors, should you want to find an alternative to the one that came with your operating system.

To create a simple source file that would create the example database discussed in this chapter, we could just copy the five SQL statements appearing in section 2.5.4 and put them into a `.txt` file. This file, which we call `PCR_database_create.txt`, can be downloaded from this book's companion website, www.bixsolutions.net.

We can use the SQL contained in the source file by using the SOURCE command:

```
SOURCE filename;
```

For example, if we had downloaded the file `PCR_database_create.txt` into the directory `BBSfiles` on our E: drive, the following commands would create all the tables for our PCR database example within the, previously created, database `PCR_experiment`:

```
USE PCR_experiment;
SOURCE e:/BBSfiles/PCR_database_create.txt;
```

A useful file to have handy when building a database that is going to act as the data store for a program that you are designing is a source file to delete all the data from all tables, while keeping the database structure intact. Once again, this is a simple file to create. For this example it would look like this:

```
DELETE FROM Experiment;
DELETE FROM Kit_order;
DELETE FROM Supplier;
DELETE FROM Kit;
DELETE FROM Scientist;
```

This file may be found at www.bixsolutions.net, entitled `PCR_database_clean.txt`.

If we wish to enter a set of data into the database using a large number of INSERT statements, we can do this with a source file too. As the source file just consists of SQL statements, these can be written in exactly the same way as if we were typing them, but with the added advantage that if a mistake is made part way through, the whole series of commands may be run again with little extra effort. A source file to populate the PCR database is provided at www.bixsolutions.net, under the name `PCR_database_populate.txt`. The file populates the database with three entries for scientist, three for supplier, three for kits, four for kit orders, and five for experiments. We recommend you populate the database using this script before proceeding to the examples of querying the database in the next section.

2.5.8 Querying the database

Finally, we come on to accessing the data that is in a database. There are many ways in which to do this and the complexity of the queries may seem daunting at first. However, they are all built up from a few very simple concepts, explained below. The most important thing to keep in mind is to think carefully first about exactly what it is that you want to achieve, and only then to try and write the query for this. As with the design of the database itself, it is the preparation that is they key to getting this right—with solid thinking, the implementation is often straightforward.

SHOW

Once you have focused on the database of your choice (USE *databasename*), you may well want to list the tables present. Here, you can use the SHOW command:

```
SHOW tables;
```

This will produce a list of all the tables present in the database. SHOW may also be used to show all the databases to which you have access in your installation of MySQL, as in:

```
SHOW databases;
```

DESCRIBE

For any table within a database, you may want to see the field names and their associated data types. The DESCRIBE command will return this information.

```
DESCRIBE Scientist;
```

will therefore produce a table of results similar to the following:

```
<mysql> DESCRIBE Scientist;
+--------------+--------------+------+-----+---------+-----+
|Field         |Type          |Null  |Key  |Default  |Extra|
+--------------+--------------+------+-----+---------+-----+
|email         |varchar(255)  |NO    |PRI  |         |     |
|given_name    |varchar(255)  |YES   |     |NULL     |     |
|family_name   |varchar(255)  |YES   |     |NULL     |     |
|title         |varchar(255)  |YES   |     |NULL     |     |
|department    |varchar(255)  |YES   |     |NULL     |     |
|tel_country   |int(11)       |YES   |     |NULL     |     |
|tel_area      |int(11)       |YES   |     |NULL     |     |
|tel_number    |int(11)       |YES   |     |NULL     |     |
+--------------+--------------+------+-----+---------+-----+
8 rows in set (0.00 sec)
```

SELECT

The SELECT command is arguably the most useful, as it allows us to access the data held within the database. Used in conjunction with the other commands described below, it should allow you to access any set of information you require in any order, grouped in any way from any table, or combination of tables.

The format of any SELECT query follows this basic convention:

```
SELECT field FROM Table;
```

So, if we wanted to extract a list of all the scientists' surnames that have performed PCR experiments in the laboratory, we could use the following command:

```
SELECT family_name FROM Scientist;
```

We may select multiple fields in an order that we specify using a similarly structured command, for example:

```
SELECT family_name, given_name FROM Scientist;
```

This returns a table of results that has all the surnames in the first column and all the first names in the second.

Sometimes we may want to return the entire contents of a table, in which case an asterisk may be placed in the *field* position, as in:

```
SELECT * from Scientist;
```

COUNT

Often we will want to know just how many records are going to be returned by a query. To do this, we will use the COUNT command. For example, the command below would return the number of scientists that are present in the Scientist table.

```
SELECT COUNT(*) FROM Scientist;
```

DISTINCT

DISTINCT allows us to specify that we do not want repeated pieces of information to be returned by our queries. This command is often used along with COUNT to give the number of different elements within a table.

```
SELECT COUNT(DISTINCT field) FROM Table;
```

It may also be used to return a list without duplicate entries within fields, such as:

```
SELECT DISTINCT sequence FROM Experiment;
```

This query would return a list of sequences that had been investigated, but each sequence would appear only once, even though it may have been processed under many different conditions or using different PCR kits. The command below would therefore return the number of unique sequences that had been investigated.

```
SELECT COUNT(DISTINCT sequence) FROM Experiment;
```

ORDER BY . . . ASC/DESC

We cannot assume that results will be returned from a query in the order in which they were placed into the database or in an order defined by an index. The ORDER BY command may be used to specify the order in which results are presented to suit the application. For example:

```
SELECT family_name FROM Scientist ORDER BY family_name ASC;
```

This command returns the list of family names of scientists alphabetically ordered, as this is a character-based field. The use of ASC ensures that they are returned in ascending order, i.e. from A to Z. To return them in the reverse order (Z to A), we would use DESC. The same syntax applies when sorting results from numeric fields.

LIMIT n

When creating queries, sometimes we may just want to see a sample of the results that would be produced. This can be quite useful when checking to make sure that the results are of the form that we think they should be. This is especially useful when creating complex queries that we are not quite sure are correct! In such cases, the LIMIT command may be used to return only the number of results that are required. For example, the command below will return the first three results retrieved from the table Experiment.

```
SELECT * FROM Experiment LIMIT 3;
```

Remember that these may not be the experiments numbered 1–3, if we wanted these fields in particular, an ORDER BY modifier would be required, as in:

```
SELECT * FROM Experiment ORDER BY ID ASC LIMIT 3;
```

WHERE

WHERE is an extremely useful command modifier as it allows for highly specific queries to be written, often just the sort of queries that the database was created to allow us to answer in the first place. It is often used to return a set of results for which a certain condition is achieved. For instance, to return from the table Experiment only those results that were generated after a certain date, the following statement could be used:

```
SELECT * FROM Experiment WHERE date > '2008-01-01';
```

This returns all the information about experiments that took place after 1 January 2008—note the use of quotation marks around the date as the date (and time) types are not truly numeric. Numeric comparison symbols other than > may be used. The full list is given in Table 2.5. In the example below, all the experiment information for experiments performed with an annealing temperature set to equal or below 70° would be displayed.

```
SELECT * FROM Experiment WHERE anneal_temp <= 70;
```

Table 2.5 Numeric comparison operators in SQL

Symbol	Description
=	Equal to
<>	Not equal to
>	Greater than
>=	Greater than or equal to
<	Less than
<=	Less than or equal to

For textual and character comparison, we have the LIKE command, an example of which is:

```
SELECT tel_country, tel_area
FROM Scientist
WHERE department LIKE 'Toxicology';
```

This would return the telephone country and area codes for the toxicology department(s). If unsure of the exact string that we are looking for in a textual comparison, a wildcard character, %, can be used. For example:

```
SELECT department, tel_country, tel_area
FROM Scientist
WHERE department LIKE '%tox%';
```

This returns the full name, country and area codes for all departments that contain the string 'tox' somewhere in their name. Note that these comparisons are not case sensitive.

AND and OR

Multiple constraints using the WHERE function may be considered together with Boolean logic statements, such as AND and OR.

For instance, to return all the experimental results performed by a certain scientist (the ubiquitous Darren Oakley) during January 2008, the following statement may be used:

```
SELECT *
FROM Experiment
WHERE scientist_email LIKE 'd.oakley%'
AND date <= '2008-01-31'
AND date >= '2008-01-01';
```

To select all experiments using one of two specific order numbers, we could use:

```
SELECT *
```

```
FROM Experiment
WHERE Kit_order_number = 115
OR Kit_order_number = 121;
```

GROUP BY

Often we may want to view the results grouped by one particular feature of the data. The most common of these are for statistical measures, such as finding the average number of amino acids in all human proteins. This could be done manually by retrieving the sequences of all proteins, summing their lengths, and then dividing by the total number of proteins. Usefully there are a number of GROUP BY functions that allow us to access this sort of information automatically. These include, COUNT, MAX, MIN, AVG, and SUM.

To count the number of experiments that a scientist has performed, we can use:

```
SELECT scientist_email, COUNT(scientist_email)
FROM Experiment
GROUP BY scientist_email;
```

This will return a two column table containing both the scientists' email addresses and the number of times that each of these has appeared in the Experiment table.

However, if we wanted to know the maximum kit cost from each manufacturer, this method could require a lot of manual inspection of the table. Instead, we would use:

```
SELECT manufacturer, MAX(kit_cost)
FROM Kit
GROUP BY manufacturer;
```

This will return a two-column table; the first column containing the name of each manufacturer and the second the cost of their most expensive kit.

JOIN

Up to this point, we have been considering queries against single tables only. However, as has been mentioned previously, one of the most powerful features of a relational database is that all tables are related to one another. If we are to only query single tables, why are these relationships useful? With experience it becomes apparent that the most useful queries involve more than one table and, therefore, the queries that are used to access their data need some way to recognize this. The method by which this is done is called a *join*.

Often a join may be implicit in a SELECT query. Consider the following query.

```
SELECT manufacturer, Kit_order.supplier
FROM Kit_order, Supplier
```

```
WHERE Kit_order.supplier = Supplier.supplier_name
AND supp_city like 'Oxford';
```

This would return all the kit manufacturers that suppliers in the city of Oxford could supply. To break the query down, we have asked for two pieces of information, `manufacturer` and `supplier`, to be returned. Up until now, we have only been querying one table and so only that table has featured after the `FROM` keyword. In this case, we are looking to link this to information from another table, in this case from `Supplier`. Therefore, `Supplier` now features after `Kit_order` in a comma-separated list. We should also be explicit in stating where each field we would like returned is coming from. In the above example, it is obvious that the field `manufacturer` comes from the table `Kit_order` because `manufacturer` does not feature in `supplier`. However, very similarly named fields (`supplier_name` and `supplier`) appear in the two tables, so it is good practice to dictate which table we expect to retrieve this field from. This is done using the dot (`.`) convention, whereby the format `tablename.field` uniquely determines the field we are interested in. Indeed, if we had chosen to give the two supplier fields the same name in both tables, the command simply would not work without specifying both the table and field names in this way.

The `WHERE` statement allows us to join these two tables using their shared field, in this case the field `supplier` in `Kit_order`, which is equivalent to `supplier_name` in `supplier`. This tells the system that every time these two fields are equal, those are the data we are interested in. It is sometimes easy to forget this `WHERE` statement, as it seems obvious to us which two fields in two tables are the same. If you do forget to define this, then every row (n) in the first table will be joined with every row (m) in the second table. This results in a set of information that, if displayed, would have n times m rows. This can be a very large number and is likely to take a long time to run, only to get results that are unlikely to be what you are looking for. We then constrain the query results further to only those suppliers that are based in the city of Oxford.

This type of query features an implicit `JOIN` statement—we have joined the two tables together using their shared field and are expecting only results for which the condition is met. This statement may have been written with an explicit `JOIN` statement as:

```
SELECT manufacturer, Kit_order.supplier
FROM Kit_order JOIN Supplier
ON Kit_order.supplier = Supplier.supplier_name
WHERE supp_city like 'Oxford';
```

This form of `JOIN` is known as an `INNER JOIN`. In set theory terms, it will select the intersection (overlap) of the two tables, with any further constraints applied. Therefore, if there are manufacturers with no suppliers in Oxford, these will not appear. Similarly, if there are suppliers in Oxford who have not sold any PCR kits to this laboratory (say if the `Supplier` table contained all suppliers for all laboratory equipment), they will not appear.

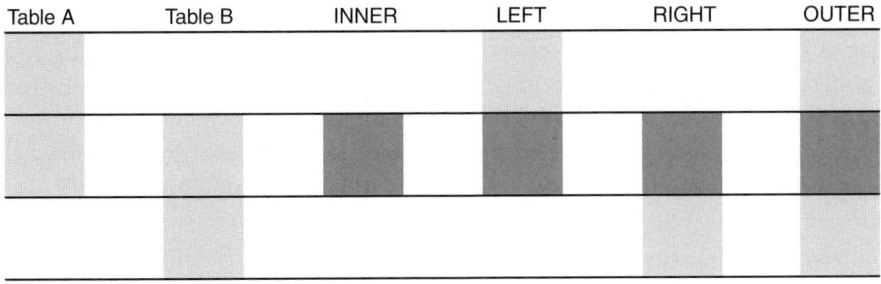

Fig. 2.12 Graphical depiction of the actions of `JOIN` statements. Table A and Table B are joined using the different types of join. The results of these combinations are shown. The `INNER` join results in the union of the two tables where there are equivalent fields in each. The `LEFT` join returns the `INNER` product and the remaining fields from Table A. The `RIGHT` join returns the `INNER` product and the remaining fields from Table B. Finally, the full `OUTER` join returns the contents of both tables, linked where appropriate.

We might, however, want some of this information. For instance, we might want to know details for all of the suppliers of PCR kits in Oxford that we have used plus any other suppliers based in Oxford. For this query we would use a RIGHT JOIN.

```
SELECT *
FROM Kit_order RIGHT JOIN Supplier
ON Kit_order.supplier = Supplier.supplier_name
WHERE supp_city like 'Oxford';
```

In this case, whenever there is a supplier in Oxford that has not yet supplied a kit to the laboratory, columns from `Kit_order` will return `NULL`, otherwise all details will be returned.

It is also possible to use a `LEFT JOIN`, which in this case will give the same results as a `JOIN`, as there are no kit orders that don't have a supplier. However, if we swapped the order of each table name in the query, as shown below, we would get identical results to the previous `RIGHT JOIN` example.

```
SELECT *
FROM Supplier LEFT JOIN Kit_order
ON Supplier.supplier_name = Kit_order.supplier
WHERE supp_city like 'Oxford';
```

It is also possible in some RDBMSs to combine the two forming a full `OUTER JOIN`, but not (simply, at any rate) in MySQL. It is sometimes easier to picture these operations graphically, as in Fig. 2.12.

2.5.9 Transaction handling

As mentioned above, you have complete control over your database when interacting with it either via the command line or through the use of a computer program, as shall be described later. This can often place you within a few mis-placed keystrokes or bad lines of code of disaster. You may mitigate this through a comprehensive backup program, but this would always run the risk of losing the results of valid activity that has occurred between back-ups.

Fortunately, the designers of database management systems also recognize this danger and so have introduced the concept of transaction handling. Simply put, a transaction is any block of database activity, including INSERT, DELETE, SELECT, and any other SQL or other actions. The start of the block is defined using a specific command. At this point all database activity resulting from the commands following the transaction start is not permanently written to the database. Upon reaching the end of the block, a test may be performed, in which a person, or an automated program, checks for errors. If this test is successful then the results from the block are written permanently to the database. If, however, the test reveals some unintended behaviour, the actions of the block are ignored and the database is rolled back to the point at which the transaction block began. In MySQL, this sequence of events is controlled using the commands described below.

AUTOCOMMIT, COMMIT, ROLLBACK

By default, MySQL runs with the AUTOCOMMIT mode turned on. This means that whenever you type or otherwise run a command, the results of this are immediately written to the database. This can be turned off using:

```
SET AUTOCOMMIT=0;
```

Once AUTOCOMMIT has been turned off each command needs to be followed by a COMMIT statement in order for its effect to be written to the database. For instance, if you wanted to remove some of the rows from a table, you may have entered the following command:

```
DELETE FROM Experiment;
```

You then realize that what you really meant to do was only delete certain rows from the table that were entered by one particular scientist. If AUTOCOMMIT was on, as it would be as standard, then it is now too late; all the rows are gone. However, if you had turned AUTOCOMMIT off and had not issued a COMMIT statement, the choice is yours. In this case, you could ROLLBACK the statement:

```
ROLLBACK;
```

The database is now exactly as it was before you issued the DELETE statement. You may now enter the correct statement:

```
DELETE FROM Experiment
WHERE scientist_email LIKE 'i.shadforth@bixsolutions.net';

COMMIT;
```

The first statement is executed and then written to the database. You may enter any number of commands before issuing a COMMIT statement. All will then be permanently written to the database or rolled back if you choose.

AUTOCOMMIT may be turned back on again using the command:

```
SET AUTOCOMMIT=1;
```

START TRANSACTION...COMMIT

You may wish to enter a block of commands that you wish to try out without setting AUTOCOMMIT to off. To do this, start the block with START TRANSACTION. This will temporarily suspend AUTOCOMMIT, which will be reinstated at the end of the block, as indicated by your use of either a COMMIT or a ROLLBACK.

```
START TRANSACTION;
DELETE FROM Experiment;
DELETE FROM Scientist;
COMMIT;
```

Note that when a START TRANSACTION command is issued, this implicitly issues a COMMIT command, finishing any previous transaction that had not been committed or rolled back.

2.5.10   Copying, moving, and backing up a database

We will often want to backup or move a database from one machine or location to another. To achieve this, MySQL has a simple set of commands.

The first of these, to back-up your database, should be invoked from outside the MySQL environment, so type exit to leave MySQL and return to the normal terminal prompt. In Windows, to back-up your database to a text file, which will contain all the information needed to recreate the database, including table structures and data, type the following and enter the password when prompted.

```
mysqldump -u username -p databasename > c:\directory\
backup.txt
```

If you have opted not to use a password for your chosen user account, then don't type the -p switch.

You will find your output file in the specified directory. If you are using Linux or Mac OS, the format of this command is similar, but navigate from a suitable point, for example:

```
mysqldump -u username -p databasename > /usr/mydirectory/
backup.txt
```

If you use a text editor to look at the file produced by mysqldump you will see that it is essentially a series of MySQL statements that define the database and, if it contained data, populate it. The database can therefore be reinstated on any MySQL server by using this file with the SOURCE command. To do this, you would need to start MySQL then first CREATE (or DROP and then CREATE) your blank database, change focus to that database with USE, and then use SOURCE to execute the SQL commands in the backup file:

```
SOURCE c:\directory\backup.txt;
```

This will drop all existing tables in your database, recreate them, and then populate them with any stored data.

2.6   Summary

This chapter has dealt with the basics of building databases, starting with design—which is the most important factor—through to getting your hands on a suitable system, creating, populating, and finally querying your data. This is a large topic, and there is only space in this book to cover the basics of database design, creation and use. There are many excellent books available that will guide you through more advanced topics, as referenced through the chapter. However, one that we would like to recommend in particular at this stage, for those using MySQL, is the *MySQL Cookbook* (DuBois, 2006). Having used this chapter to grasp the basics of MySQL and database design, you will find *MySQL Cookbook* is an excellent reference for ways in which to perform almost anything you might want to do with MySQL. There are similar works available for other RDBMSs and also for SQL in general, all of which should be accessible after working through this chapter.

It is likely that you will not want to interact with your database system directly once you have designed and built it, and you will almost certainly not want other users of your database to have to log in to the command line directly. There are also lots of tasks for which manual entry of data at the command line would be a bore. This is why all the popular bioinformatics databases mentioned in the previous chapter are accessed via a more intuitive web-based interface—with no knowledge of SQL required. This ease of use is achieved by producing a database front end, essentially a program that sits between the database server and the user. In bioinformatics, such interfaces are often written using Perl, which is the subject of the next chapter.

References

Codd, E. (1970). A Relational Model of Data for Large Shared Data Banks. *Communications of the ACM*, **13**(6): 377–387.

Connolly, T. & Begg, C. (2003) *Database Solutions: A Step-by-Step Approach to Building Databases*. Addison-Wesley: Boston, USA.

DuBois, P. (2006). *MySQL Cookbook*. O'Reilly: Sebastapol, California, USA.

Hernandez, M. (2003) *Database Design for Mere Mortals: A Hands-On Guide to Relational Database Design*. Addison-Wesley: Boston, USA.

Simecek, N. (2007). *Development of a database with web-based user interface for taqman assay design*. MSc Thesis, Cranfield University.

Stephens, J. & Russell, C. (2004) *Beginning MySQL Database Design and Optimization: From Novice to Professional*. Apress: Berkeley, California, USA.

CHAPTER 3

Automating processes using Perl

Being able to program was once a prerequisite for doing bioinformatics, simply because there was very little bioinformatics software available. Although the situation is now different, with freely available bioinformatics tools being released all the time, being able to write your own software is still invaluable for all but the simplest bioinformatics tasks. Not only does programing give you the flexibility to produce novel tools, it crucially allows you to automate processes, which overcomes the bottleneck of manual analysis that typically occurs when data throughput increases. Programing can also be used to link existing tools together, to create powerful data analysis pipelines.

There is an array of programming languages available that can fulfil the requirements above, but the programming language of choice when it comes to bioinformatics tasks is usually Perl (Practical Extraction and Retrieval Language). This is due to Perl's specific strengths—a very quick learning curve, relatively easy to read syntax, ability to add extra functionality by installing third party modules, and very accomplished text manipulation abilities. Perl is now engrained in the bioinformatics community, with some major organizations using it as their standard development tool, and there are vast amounts of Perl code out there for you to incorporate into your own programs. If you have any doubts as to Perl's importance, we recommend the paper *How Perl Saved the Human Genome Project* by Lincoln Stein (an archived copy can be found at www.foo.be/docs/tpj/issues/vol1_2/tpj0102-0001.html).

In this chapter we cover the basics of Perl programming, particularly those of specific relevance to bioinformatics. The level of detail in each section is limited to allow the maximum number of individual bioinformatics-related topics to be covered. If we were to cover everything in depth, we would need a separate book for Perl, and there are already plenty of good Perl programming books out there (Wall *et al.* 2000; Tisdall 2001, 2003). There are also many excellent Perl resources on the web. As such, we cover the basics and give you enough information to enable you to get on with the technologies that we cover.

3.1 Downloading and installing Perl

Before getting started programming in Perl, you will need to have the Perl interpreter installed on your computer. The interpreter is what actually runs Perl programs, so although you could technically write a Perl program without it, you
wouldn't be able to see what that program does. If you're using Linux or Mac
OS X, you already have it installed as it comes as part of the operating system.
In order to confirm this and to find out which version of Perl you have, go to
your operating system's command-line (see Appendix A) and type the following
(followed by the Enter key):

```
perl -v
```

You should then be greeted with output similar to the following:

```
This is perl, v5.8.8 built for darwin-2level
Copyright 1987-2007, Larry Wall
Perl may be copied only under the terms of either the
Artistic License or the GNU General Public License, which may
be found in the Perl 5 source kit.
Complete documentation for Perl, including FAQ lists, should
be found on this system using "man perl" or "perldoc perl".
If you have access to the Internet, point your browser at
http://www.perl.org/, the Perl Home Page.
```

This indicates that you have Perl version 5.8.8 installed on your system. If you
would like more details on your Perl install, you can use the following command
(note the uppercase V):

```
perl -V
```

This will then give you full details of how your version of Perl was built and
where you can find all of the Perl libraries on your system (this is good to know
if you ever have trouble with Perl modules from external sources such as CPAN,
which is introduced later in this chapter).

3.1.1 Getting Perl on Windows

The above commands will also work on a Windows based computer, but only if
you have the Perl interpreter installed. Perl is not automatically installed as part
of the operating system, so unless somebody has already done it for you, you will
need to download and install it. The easiest way to do this is to use ActivePerl.

Head to www.activestate.com/store/activeperl and download the latest
ActivePerl Windows .msi installer (click to download ActivePerl, and then click
the MSI option in the list of downloads for the latest version). ActivePerl is free
to download and use. You may be given the opportunity to enter your contact
details, but this is optional and you can continue direct to the download. As long
as you have administrator permissions on your system, all you have to do is open

the downloaded package and go through the usual Windows install procedure. We recommend accepting the default installation options unless you have a very good reason not to.

3.1.2 Before getting started

Before embarking on understanding and programming in Perl, there are two things to get ready beforehand. A Perl program is just a list of commands in a plain text file, so the first thing we need is a text editor in which to write programs. There are many different text editors available for the various operating systems. There is no 'best' editor and, in the end, it comes down to what you feel comfortable working with. Below is a list of some of the text editors that we recommend for Perl programming, organized by the operating system they support:

- Windows:

  - *Programmer's Notepad* (www.pnotepad.org): a free, open source, text editor with special features for programmers. Suited for Perl, but also useful for many other programming languages.

  - *SciTE* (www.scintilla.org): another free, open source programming editor suited to Perl programming. Like the Programmer's Notepad, this editor is also useful for other programming languages.

  - *Komodo* (activestate.com): a programming editor developed specifically for dynamic languages such as Perl, Python, and Ruby. A slimmed down (but still very good) edition of this editor (Komodo Edit) is available for free. The full Komodo IDE with a built-in debugger and other useful tools is a commercial package, for which payment is required.

  - *Emacs/XEmacs* (www.gnu.org/software/emacs and www.xemacs.org): users of Unix systems will no doubt be familiar with these two editors, which have been ported to Windows. Emacs and XEmacs are free, open source, and highly customisable text editors that have a very long history in the Unix/Linux world.

- Mac OS:

  - *TextMate* (macromates.com): a programming editor useful for most programming languages. This editor is also highly expandable and customisable through the use of plug-ins. The only downside of TextMate is that it's not free, but it is very reasonably priced.

  - *TextWrangler* (www.barebones.com): a free text editor that is suited for programming in many different languages. If you grow to like this editor, there is also a commercial product available with extra features called BBEdit.

  - *Affrus* (www.latenightsw.com): a commercial programming editor designed specifically for Perl, with a built-in debugger and many other useful tools.

  - *Emacs* (homepage.mac.com/zenitani/emacs-e.html): this is the same Emacs text editor as described above, this time ported to the Mac.

- *Komodo* (activestate.com). This is the same as the Windows version.

- ◆ Linux

  - *gedit* (www.gnome.org/projects/gedit): the default text editor for the Gnome desktop environment. This is a basic, general-purpose, and easy to use text editor.

  - *Kate* (kate-editor.org): the default text editor in the K desktop enviroment (KDE). Like gedit, this is also a basic, general-purpose and easy to use text editor.

  - *SciTE* (www.scintilla.org): this is the same as the Windows version.

  - *Emacs/XEmacs*: these are the same at the Windows versions.

  - *Komodo* (activestate.com): this is the same as the Windows and Mac versions.

In addition to the editors listed above, if you're already a programmer using the Eclipse development platform (www.eclipse.org), you will be happy to know that Eclipse can also be used for Perl. Perl support can be added to Eclipse by installing the EPIC plugin (e-p-i-c.sourceforge.net).

If forced to recommend just one of the above editors for this book, we would probably opt for Komodo Edit, as it's free, available for all the major operating systems, and as well as being suitable for Perl, it can also be used with R, HTML and XHTML, which we cover in later chapters.

Once armed with one of these text editors, the final thing that you need to be familiar with for Perl programming is the command line. If you're not familiar with the command line, we would refer you to Appendix A. Particularly important is which directory (or folder) you're positioned in (i.e. in a Windows XP command-line you will automatically be positioned in `C:\Documents and Settings\UserName\My Documents`; on a Mac `/Users/UserName/`; on Linux `/home/UserName`). If you save your Perl programs anywhere other than your home directory, you must change your directory in the command line (using the `cd` command) to wherever you have saved your programs in order to run and use them.

3.2   Basic Perl syntax and logic

To get started, let's write a simple Perl program and see what happens. Open up your selected text editor and type the following code and save it as a file called `hello_world.pl`:

```
#! /usr/bin/perl
# A Perl 'Hello, world!' program
print "\nHello, world!\n";
print "=============\n";
```

Now, open up your command line terminal (ensuring that you have moved into the directory where you're saving your Perl scripts) and type the following:

```
perl hello_world.pl
```

If all went well, you should now have the famous words 'Hello, world!' (minus the quotes) printed to the screen in your terminal window. If not, and you get an error message instead, check the code above to see if you have mistyped something. In particular, make sure that you are using the right types of quotes in the `print` statement, and note that Perl is case-sensitive, so `print` is not the same as `PRINT`, or even `Print`.

So, what went into that first program?

The first line in the program is known as the *shebang*—this is a special command required to tell the operating systems what is going to run the script (in this case, Perl) and it always starts with `#!`. The shebang also tells the operating system where to find the Perl interpreter—in this example we assume it's in the `/usr/bin` directory (a common location for Perl in Linux and Mac OS). If you received an error saying that Perl was missing or not found, you should check to see where Perl is installed and change the shebang as appropriate. In rare cases, the Perl interpreter is installed at `/usr/local/bin/perl`, so that would be something to try. In Windows, Perl will most likely be found in `C:\Perl\bin`, but you will notice that the program works in windows regardless of what the shebang says. This is because the shebang is not always required in non-Linux environments. However, we strongly recommend specifying the shebang anyway, because it is needed in Windows in some situations (e.g. when used with Apache as described in Chapter 5).

The second line of the program is a comment. Comments are lines or statements in programming code that are not read by the computer, they are just there to help you, the programmer, or any programmer who carries on your work, to annotate and make notes within the program code. In Perl, comments are defined with the use of a # symbol, and all text to the right of the # symbol until the end of the line is ignored by the Perl interpreter. (NB: This should not be confused with the shebang—`#!`—they are different beasts.)

The third line of the program is a `print` statement—the first bit of the program that actually does something. Print statements are a way in which a program can let its users know what is happening. It is also a handy way of giving output from your script, including diagnostic information during program development and debugging. In the most basic form that we have used here, anything contained within the quotes is printed to the command line. Well, not quite everything is printed—for example, the `\n` construct is a special code telling Perl to start a new line of text. Many such codes are available, and we shall cover more of these and their uses later.

The last line of the program is just another `print` statement, included to add some rudimentary underlining to our message. The reason we included this was to demonstrate a very basic principle common to most programming languages—programs generally run from the top of the code to the bottom. Indeed, simple programs like this one are sometimes referred to as *scripts*, as they are little more than lists of actions to be performed one after the other. However, we will see later in the chapter that Perl supports control structures that facilitate a much more complex program flow.

Note that the end of each Perl command must be denoted by a semicolon (*;*) character. Failure to do this will result in errors when you try to run the program, which often catches out beginners (and even some more experienced coders when they're up against a deadline!). The semicolon is needed because in more complex programs, commands may extend over several lines, so we need a way of telling the Perl interpreter where the command ends. Because comment lines beginning with # are ignored by Perl, they do not require a semicolon.

To avoid repetition, from here on we shall not mention or print the shebang, or other starting code, for our smaller examples. So, if you create new files to test the many snippets of code presented throughout this chapter, don't forget to add in the shebang, a quick comment to say what the program does, and to save the code with an appropriate name ending in .pl, so that it is recognized as a Perl program. In longer examples, where we provide programs, we have included the standard Linux shebang. If you're using Windows, you should really change it to point to wherever you installed Perl.

3.2.1 Scalar variables

Bioinformatics is all about data, so being able to manipulate data within our programs is essential. As we've seen in previous chapters, databases and files are used for long-term data storage. In programming, we have the additional concept of *variables*, which are objects within a program within which data can be stored temporarily while the program works with it.

A scalar variable is the simplest type of data that Perl handles. This is typically a single number (e.g. 465 or 1.25) or strings of characters (e.g. 'carbon dioxide' or 'ATGGGCCGAT'). In most other programming languages numbers and strings are handled separately (even different types of numbers are handled differently), in Perl, however, they are all treated nearly identically. Scalar data in Perl is indicated through the use of the dollar symbol in front of the variable name—i.e. $sequence is a scalar variable called 'sequence'.

Assigning values to scalar variables

One of the most basic operations for scalar variables is *assignment*—giving the variable a value. To do this we use the equals sign (=).

```
$num = 24;        # give variable $num, the number value 24
$dna = 'ACTG';    # give $dna the string value ACTG i.e. the string
                  # between the inverted commas
$bar = $num * 2;  # makes $bar now equal to the value of $num (24)
                  # multiplied by 2 (48)
$bar = $bar + 12; # make $bar equal to $bar (48) plus 12 (60)
```

From the examples above, you can see that we assign the variable named on the left, with the value defined on the right. Also, the last two statements show that it's possible to overwrite variables with new values, even using the same variable that we are about to replace (as in the last line where we use $bar twice). Operations like this are quite common, so common, in fact, that there are useful shortcut operators that help us do this. A few examples of these are shown below:

```
$foo = 5;           # make $foo equal to 5
$foo = $foo + 5;    # this is one way of increasing $foo by 5
$foo += 5;          # this is another way of doing it!
$bar = 5;           # make $bar equal to 5
$bar = $bar * 2;    # this multiplies $bar by 2
$bar *= 2;          # so does this!
```

This is not just applicable to numbers; similar operations can be carried out on strings. One such operation is using the concatenate operator, a dot symbol (.)—this gives us the ability to append one string onto the end of another string.

```
$dna = 'ACTGATCG';      # define a DNA sequence
$dna = $dna . 'AAAA';   # add a poly-A tail to our sequence
$dna .= 'AAAA';         # another way of adding the poly-A tail -
                        # the string is now ACTGATCGAAAAAAAA
```

Special attention for strings

Assigning numbers to scalars is quite straightforward—you just use an equals sign, followed by the number. Strings, on the other hand, need a little extra care in that they need to be surrounded by quotes to let Perl know the start and the end of the string. Furthermore, different types of quotes are used depending on how you want Perl to treat the string.

Single-quoted text is the simplest way of defining a string in Perl—the string is read exactly as typed into the variable, as shown in the examples in Table 3.1. With single-quoted text the only real considerations that you must make are for the quote (') and backslash (\) characters. The backslash character is used to cancel out special characters in strings, as we have seen below to get a quote character (') in one of our strings we had to use \' within the string assignment, otherwise the string assignment would stop at the quote. Similarly, to get a backslash character at the end of a string, this must also be preceded by another backslash (otherwise it would cancel out the closing quote!).

Table 3.1 Perl strings and their appearance when printed with single quotes

Code	Output
`'ACTG'`	ACTG
`'Homo Sapiens'`	Homo sapiens
`'The Human\nGenome Project'`	The Human\nGenome Project
`'The Human Genome Project\'s Website'`	The Human Genome Project's Website
`'\\\\servername\\path'`	\\servername\path
`'Human\tand\tMouse'`	Human\tand\tMouse

Double-quoted text is another method for assigning text to variables in Perl. This is slightly more advanced than the single-quote method shown previously in that we can utilize special text characters and even other variables within our variable assignment. Examples of this can be found in Table 3.2. As you can see, the backslash character has more power within double-quoted strings. There are many of these special characters that are quite useful—some of the more relevant are listed in Table 3.3.

Some useful scalar operations

As with other programming languages, Perl has many built-in functions and operators for manipulating variables of different types. Before we move on to explaining some of these, let's pause for a moment to explain what functions and operators are, and how they relate to each other. Functions (often also known as sub-routines, methods, procedures or sub-programs) are small portions of code that you can call upon for performing a specific task. An example of a function that you have used already would be `print`—this is a function that is used for generating output from a program. Operators on the other hand are a specific subset of functions that are typically used in direct manipulation of variables, examples of which would be arithmetic operators (+, −, etc.) and string operators,

Table 3.2 Perl strings and their appearance when printed with double quotes

Code	Output
`"ACTG"`	ACTG
`"ACTG\nACTG"`	ACTG ACTG
`"Human\tand\tMouse"`	Human and Mouse

Table 3.3 Some of the most important special characters in Perl

Character	Meaning
`\n`	Newline
`\r`	Return
`\t`	Tab
`\\`	Backslash
`\'`	Single quote
`\"`	Double quote
`\l`	Lowercase next letter
`\L`	Lowercase all following letters until `\E`
`\u`	Uppercase next letter
`\U`	Uppercase all following letters until `\E`

such as the assignment operator (=) and substitution operator (s), which we will come to later.

Two useful functions that are worth committing to memory are `chomp()` and `chop()`. These two functions perform similar operations, namely removing characters from the end of strings. However, there is one very important difference: `chomp()` will remove the end character from a string if—and only if—it is a newline (\n) character; `chop()`, on the other hand, will remove the end character from a string no matter what it is. Although these might not seem immediately useful, you will find `chomp()` invaluable later when we start receiving input from the command-line and reading in files, as these always have newline characters at the end of them. Unhandled, these could cause unexpected results from your programs.

More information about `chop()`, `chomp()`, and indeed any other aspect of Perl can be found by searching the official Perl documentation (perldoc.perl. org). This excellent resource details every standard Perl function and operator, complete with example code.

String substitution

Another essential string operator is the substitution operator, s. This can be used to swap a specific segment (that you define) of your string to something else. A simple example is given below:

```
$string = 'I like Perl';  # create a new string
$string =~ s/like/love/;  # substitute the word 'like' for 'love'
print $string;            # would give: I love Perl
```

In the above snippet of code we created a new string and then substituted one of the words in the string. The generic syntax for using the substitute operator is shown below—as in the previous chapter italics are used to indicate placeholders for parameters that you need to specify:

```
$string =~ s/string_to_replace/replacement_string/modifiers;
```

Simply, we have our string variable, followed by =~ (this indicates that we are doing a pattern match operation), then the substitution operator, which contains the part of our string that we are trying to match, followed by what we are going to replace it with (surrounded and separated by forward slashes). At the end of this we also have a position for optional modifiers to affect our substitution. Examples of two such modifiers are the letters i and g, which respectively imply that our match is to be case-insensitive and global. A global substitution means that the substitution would happen on every occurrence of the match—not just the first match that is found.

Here is another example of the substitution operator in action. In the following example we try to determine the reverse compliment a DNA sequence:

```
$dna = 'ACTGACC';       # assign DNA sequence to a string
$dna =~ s/A/T/ig;       # swap all the A's for T's
```

```
$dna =~ s/T/A/ig;        # swap all the T's for A's
$dna =~ s/C/G/ig;        # swap all the C's for G's
$dna =~ s/G/C/ig;        # swap all the G's for C's
$dna = reverse($dna);    # reverse the sequence
print $dna;              # output result
```

If you run this code, you will get the result CCACACA, which is not actually the reverse compliment of the sequence we started with. This demonstrates an important limitation with the substitution operator—if you want to perform more than one substitution at a time (in this example we want to do four), it might not work in the way you expect as the substitutions happen in the sequence they are written, resulting in a chain where each substitution operates on the result of the previous one, giving an undesired result.

The good news is that this type of operation is possible in Perl, we just have to use another function. This is known as the *transliteration* function, or `tr` for short. The `tr` operator has a syntax structure almost identical to `s`:

```
$string =~ tr/string_to_replace/replacement_string/;
```

The main difference between transliteration and substitution is that the transliteration operator acts on individual characters at the same time—whereas the substitution operator acts on the contents of the first set of slashes as a whole.

Therefore, in the case of our reverse compliment problem, our code would look like this:

```
$dna = 'ACTGACC';                    # create our DNA string again
$dna =~ tr/ACTGactg/TGACtgac/;       # change all the bases at once
$dna = reverse($dna);                # reverse the sequence
print $dna;                          # output result
```

This time we get the intended result, GGTCAGT. There are many more string manipulation operations in Perl, which we shall come back to later in the chapter.

Printing strings

One other common activity that you often want to perform with string-based variables (or, indeed, any of the variable types that we cover in this chapter) is that of printing them out to the screen for the users of our programs to see. This is achieved with the `print` function that we met in the first example. Examples of this are shown below:

```
$dna = 'ACTGACC';
print "$dna \n";      # This prints ACTGACC followed by a new-line
print $dna . "\n";    # This prints the same as above print
print '$dna \n';      # This prints $dna \n
```

This shows that once more the choice of quotes used to surround a string can have an impact on the resulting output. If we use double quotes in our `print` statements, variables can be used intermixed with other text and special (i.e. newline) characters, and upon printing, the value of the string variable will be printed, not the name of the string. If, however, we were to use single quotes, the text inside the quotes will be printed—no variables or special characters will be interpreted. The last thing that we would like to note here is the use of the concatenation operator (.) in the second print statement. If you prefer to clearly detach your variables from text in your code (this can aid in the readability and cleanliness of your code), you can use the concatenation operator to join variables with text strings in a single `print` statement. Here is a typical example of this in use:

```
# Demonstrates concatenation operator in print statements
print "This is our DNA string: " . $dna . "\n";
```

This would then print the text 'This is our DNA string: ACTGACC' followed by a newline character to the console.

3.2.2 Arrays

An array may simply be considered as a collection of scalars—we can loosely think of them as a list of scalar variables that can contain any type of scalar variable described previously. An important difference between Perl and other languages is that different data types (e.g. string and numbers) can be mixed together in a single array. Figure 3.1 shows a pictorial representation of a Perl array.

Creating and assigning values to arrays

As with many things in Perl, there are several ways to create and populate arrays. Here are some examples:

```
@dna_seqs = ("ACTG", "CCGGC", "CGCGC");  # a 3-element array
@more_dna = qw(ACTG CCGGC CGCGC ATGAAA); # a 4-element array
```

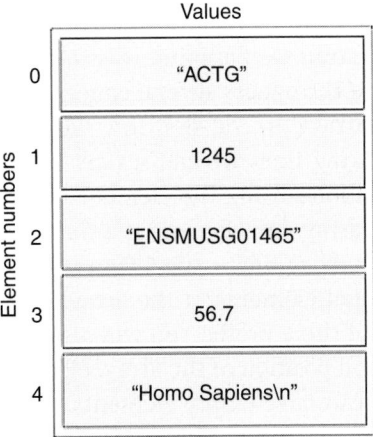

Fig. 3.1 A Perl array containing five elements.

```perl
@other_array = ();                      # create an empty array
$other_array[0] = 'ACTG';               # add 'ACTG' as the 1st
                                        # element in array
$other_array[2] = 'ENSMUSG01465';       # 'ENSMUSG01465' comes next
$other_array[3] = '56.7';               # then '56.7'
```

As you can see from the above examples, assigning values to arrays uses the same assignment operator (the equals sign) as used with scalar data. The most obvious difference is the use of the @ symbol to represent an array instead of the $ scalar indicator.

Let's look at these examples more closely, step-by-step:

```perl
@dna_seqs = ("ACTG", "CCGGC", "CGCGC");
```

This line of code creates a three-element array called @dna_seqs. The assignment of values to the array is done with the use of the brackets surrounding the new contents of the array, and each individual element is surrounded by quotes and separated by a comma. The next example uses a different approach, to populate another array, @more_dna.

```perl
@more_dna = qw(ACTG CCGGC CGCGC ATGAAA);
```

The assignment for this is slightly different as there are no commas or quotes used within the braces—the elements are separated by white space—this is the syntax defined by the qw() function preceding the braces; specifically, the qw() function takes a list of space-separated values and returns the same list, comma-separated, with each element surrounded in quotes:

```perl
@other_array = ();                      # create an empty array
$other_array[0] = 'ACTG';               # add 'ACTG' as the 1st element in
                                        # array
$other_array[2] = 'ENSMUSG01465';       # 'ENSMUSG01465' comes next
$other_array[3] = '56.7';               # then '56.7'
```

The above code demonstrates yet another way to create and populate an array. It seems long-winded, but introduces several concepts that are useful when writing programs that use arrays. In the first line we name and create an empty array, then on the following lines we add scalars to individual elements of the array using list interpolation—using the element numbers to enter scalars into specific elements of our array one element at a time. Note one of the important character changes in the above lines—the $ sign is used instead of the @ sign as we are accessing individual elements of the array. The individual elements are scalars—hence, the use of the $ prefix. You will also notice that we neglected to put anything in the second position of the array, element number 1. This is not a problem because arrays can have empty elements. Accessing this array element will return a null value, which will behave differently depending on context. Finally, note that the numbering of elements in array starts at zero.

Printing and retrieving data from arrays

Having created and populated an array, it's quite natural that we will want to get some information back out of it. If you wish to copy a specific element of an array and put it into its own scalar variable, this is as simple as the following line of code:

```
@dna = ("ACTG", "CCGGC", "CGCGC");
$sequence = $dna[2];
```

This assigns the contents of the third element of the array to the scalar variable called $sequence. However, we need to note here that we have not done anything to change the third element of the array—it's still there, we have merely copied it. We shall discuss *removing* elements from arrays shortly.

As well as getting data out of arrays and into scalar variables, you might just wish to print either an element of an array or the array as a whole. This is really quite simple, but there is one small warning that needs to be given: Consider the snippet of code below:

```
@dna = qw(ACTG GGCG AAAA TTTG);
print "Here's a single element:\n";
print $dna[2] . "\n\n";
print "Here's the whole array:\n";
print "@dna\n";
```

This will give the following output:

```
Here's a single element:
AAAA

Here's the whole array:
ACTG GGCG AAAA TTTG
```

The above code demonstrates a two different ways in which we can print out data from within arrays. The first section prints a single element on its own, concatenated with two line breaks—you will also notice that we left the array element to print outside the quotation marks, as mentioned when we covered printing string variables earlier, this is not entirely necessary and we could have used the following to get the same effect:

```
print "$dna[2]  \n\n";
```

The second print statement in the example shows how to print out a whole array. By placing the array within quotation marks, each element of the array has a space between them which makes the output very readable.

Special array operators

Arrays are slightly more advanced data types than scalars and there are a number of special operations that can be performed on them. Functions to perform these operations include pop(), push(), shift(), and unshift(). These allow us to add and remove data from the beginning and end of an array:

```
@array = qw(0 1 2 3 4 5 6 7 8 9 10);
$scalar = pop(@array);      # remove the last element from @array (10),
                            # and put it in $scalar
$scalar = shift(@array);    # remove the first element from @array (0),
                            # and put it in $scalar
push(@array,'ACG');         # 'ACG' is added to the end of @array
unshift(@array,'CGC');      # 'CGC' is inserted at the beginning of @array

# @array now contains ('CGC' 1 2 3 4 5 6 7 8 9 'ACG')
```

Using combinations of `pop()`, `push()`, `shift()`, and `unshift()` it is possible to quickly and easily add or remove data from either end of arrays.

There are two more array functions that are especially useful for the conversion of data. The first of these is the `split()` function—this allows us to create an array from delimited data. Common examples of delimited data are comma- (known as `.csv` files) and tab-separated data.

An example of using the `split()` function follows:

```
$genestring = "ENSG00000058668, ENSG00000047457, ENSG00000067715";
@array = split(",",$genestring);
```

Although this is not something you would ever want to do in practice (why would we create a string on one line, only to split it on the next?), it does show how it works. The `@array` variable returned by this code contains three elements taken from the above string. A more common use of this would be to read data from a file. Getting data in and out of files is covered later in the chapter.

The generic syntax for the `split()` function is:

```
array_variable = split("delimiter",scalar_variable_to_split)
```

What if we have an array that we wish to print out to the screen or a file as comma separated or tab/space separated data? This is essentially the opposite of the `split()` function—implemented in Perl as the `join()` function. Here is the syntax for the join function followed by a quick example:

```
scalar_variable = join("delimiter",array_to_convert)

@genearray = qw(ENSG00000058668 ENSG00000047457 ENSG0000006771);
my $output = join(",",@genearray);
print $output . "\n";
```

As you can see from the above code, the syntax for `join()` is essentially the same as `split()`.

One final useful array operator we would like to cover is `scalar()`, which is used to find out the size of an array, and can be used as follows:

```
@codon = qw(ACT CCG GGC AAA);
print "Our codon array has " . scalar(@dna) . " elements\n";
```

If you put this code into a file and run it, you will get the output 'Our codon array has 4 elements' which is correct and as we expected. However, it's worth noting that the function `scalar()` counts the elements of our array starting from 1, which is different from the actual number assignment of the elements (array numbering starts at zero remember). This is important as we use the number of elements in an array to control loops and other control structures later in the chapter.

3.2.3   Hashes

The final Perl data structure that we want to highlight is the hash. A Perl hash is similar to an array in that it is a list of scalar variables, the difference is that a hash is not a number indexed list—the values within a hash are indexed using *names*. These names are more correctly referred to as *keys*. They are unique string variables that are completely arbitrary in form, i.e. they can be anything you like.

Figure 3.2 shows a hash containing five scalar variables that can be accessed using the given example keys. To create this hash in Perl:

```
# Please note - the extra spacing is optional...
%genbank_record = (
  'Official Symbol'      => 'BRCA1',
  'Official Full Name'   => 'breast cancer 1, early onset',
  'Primary Source'       => 'HGNC:1100',
  'Gene Type'            => 'protein coding',
  'Organism'             => 'Homo sapiens'
);
```

The declaration of a hash and its structure is clearly different to that of a scalar or array variable. The first, and possibly most important, difference is the change

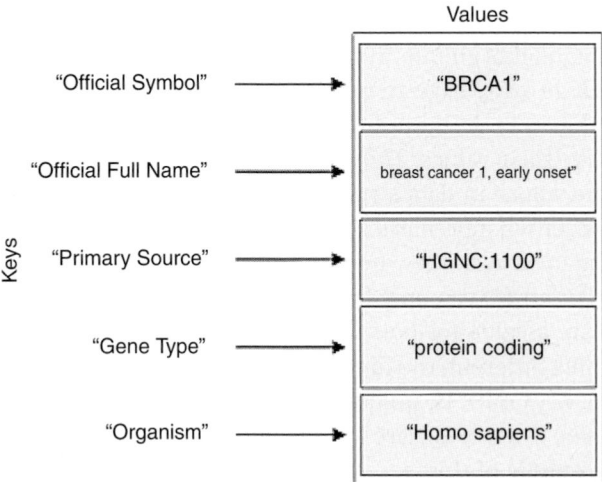

Fig. 3.2 A Perl hash containing five key/value pairs.

in symbol to represent this type of variable; a percentage sign (%) is used to represent hashes. The other main difference is the way in which we put data into our hash. As we are no longer dealing with a single scalar or an ordered list of scalars we need a more structured approach. Assigning the key/value pairs is done using the => construct, with the key on the left, and the value on the right.

The above example is not the only way to create a hash, (as with most things in Perl—there is more than one way to do it), but it is the simplest to understand. We could have done the following:

```
%genbank_record = ( 'Official Symbol', 'BRCA1', 'Official
Full Name', 'breast cancer 1, early onset', 'Primary Source',
'HGNC:1100', 'Gene Type', 'protein coding', 'Organism', 'Homo
sapiens' );
```

In the above we have the key, followed by the value on the same line, then followed by the next key/value pair. The above code will give you exactly the same hash in the end—but it's by no means as easy read, especially for larger hashes.

Like arrays, hashes do not need to be completely filled from the beginning—we can declare an empty hash, and then add/remove values as and when we wish. An example of this is shown below.

```
%rna_triplets;                  # declare empty hash

$rna_triplets{'UAG'} = 'stop';  # This adds the key/value of UAG/stop
$rna_triplets{'GCC'} = 'Ala';

delete $rna_triplets{'UAG'};    # deletes the UAG/stop entry
```

As you can see, adding and removing elements to and from a hash is quite similar to an array, we just use the scalar key to assign the value, instead of the number index used in arrays, and curly braces ({ }) are used instead of square brackets. Also like arrays, the individual elements of the hash are scalars (denoted by the $ symbol). This highlights an important consideration—hashes are unordered lists. The elements of an array have an order to them ranking each element from zero to the size of the array. In hashes there is no order to the keys as they are completely arbitrary scalar values. This will be important later when we cover looping through the values in data structures. In arrays we would loop through the array in a set order whereas hashes will give a random order.

One last thing to be aware of when considering the similarities between hashes and arrays is that arrays can only have one value for each element within them. So, if you declare a value for position [2] of an array, then re-declare that again later as something different, the first value will be overwritten. Hashes are exactly the same—your keys must be unique within the hash (as the numbers within the array are unique). If we re-declare a value within a hash, we overwrite the original value. An example of this is:

```
@ala_triplets = qw(GCU GCC GCA);
```

```
$ala_triplets[1] = 'GCG'; # This replaces 'GCC' with 'GCG'

%genetic_code = (
  'GCU' => 'Ala',
  'AAA' => 'Ala',
  'GCA' => 'Ala'
);
$genetic_code{'AAA'} = 'Lys';  # We replace 'Ala' with 'Lys'
                               # as this is the
                               # correct translation.
```

As you can see, replacing elements of a hash or array is easily accomplished, but this can also lead to accidental replacements that can be hard to spot.

Getting data out of hashes

As we have shown, getting data into a hash is analogous to getting data into an array. Getting data back out of a hash is equally straightforward.

```
%genetic_code = (
  'GCU' => 'Ala',
  'AAA' => 'Lys',
  'GCA' => 'Ala'
);
print $genetic_code{'AAA'}; # This prints the value 'Lys'
$alanine = $hash{'GCU'}; # Makes $alanine equal 'Ala'
```

The above code shows just how easy it is to get data out of a hash if you know what the keys are. However, what happens if you do not know what the keys for your hash are? This can happen when you load data into a hash dynamically within your program. Thankfully, Perl's keys() function is there to get this information for you.

```
@keys_from_my_hash = (keys %hash);
```

The keys function takes all of the keys from the specified hash and returns an array of the values that it has found. This then allows you to gain access to all elements of a hash in an ordered manner.

Finally, keys() also has a complementary function, values(), which returns all of the values in a hash. This may be useful in certain circumstances, i.e. when you would just like to know the values stored within a hash and are not particularly worried about the keys associated with them.

```
@values_from_my_hash = (values %hash);
```

The scalar, array, and hash are all you will ever be likely to need in a Perl program to store and handle data. We will come back to data structures later in the chapter through the use of references, but for now we will move on to controlling the flow of our programs.

3.2.4 Control structures and logic operators

So far our Perl programs have been limited to simple *scripts*—lists of commands that execute in the sequence that they appear in the file. Scripts like this are good for automating otherwise tedious sequences of command line input, but to produce real programs with more complex behaviour and the ability to respond to user interaction, we need to be able to implement loops and conditional statements to control the flow of our programs.

IF, ELSIF and ELSE conditionals

The first control structures that we are going to consider are the `if`, `elsif`, and `else` control structures. These are used where you want a program to do something specific based on a test, if that test is not met, you might want the program to do something different. This is why we refer to them as conditionals—they allow your program to do different things based on a set of conditions that you define. That may sound complicated if you haven't done programming before, but be assured they are not complicated, and will become second nature to you after your first couple of programs as they will most likely be in all of your Perl programs. The reason for this is that conditionals allow our programs to respond differently according to the data they receive, or interactions with the user. Here is an example of how we might use an `if` conditional:

```perl
$species = 'Human';

if ($species eq 'Human') {
  print "Your species is Human";
}
```

As you will see in the first line of the above code, we create a new string variable that has the value 'Human'. The next line begins with the function `if` followed by a test—in this case `$species eq 'Human'` —this is a string comparison testing whether our variable is the same as 'Human', this is then followed by an opening brace. If the condition is met (i.e. if `$species` is exactly the same as 'Human'), the code in between the braces following `if` will be executed. If, however, the test does not return true (i.e. if `$species` is not equal to 'Human'), nothing will happen, the block of code defined by the braces (controlled by the `if`) will be ignored. Let's expand on this example:

```perl
$species = 'Mouse';
if ($species eq 'Human') {
  print "Your species is Human";
} elsif ($species eq 'Mouse') {
  print "Your species is Mouse";
}
```

In this example we introduce an extension to the `if` conditional—an `elsif` conditional. This is used in combination with `if` conditionals to give you more options within your programs. The conditionals are evaluated sequentially as we move down the program (as with everything else in Perl), therefore, the `if` conditional is evaluated first. If this condition is met, the code block associated with it will be executed, however, if it is not met, the conditional will continue onto the `elsif` block and this will be evaluated as if it was another `if` conditional. However, what about when none of our conditionals are evaluated as true? In the above example, if `$species` was not either 'Human' or 'Mouse', the program would simply skip over the conditional blocks and move on, sometimes we need a back-up plan. Let's expand on this idea once again:

```
$species = 'ZebraFish';

if ($species eq 'Human') {
  print "Your species is Human";
} elsif ($species eq 'Mouse') {
  print "Your species is Mouse";
} else {
  print "Your species is not Human or Mouse!";
}
```

In the above code we introduced the `else` conditional. This conditional is used with other conditionals to offer alternatives for execution should the previous conditionals fail (the `if` and `elsif`). In the above section of code we once again create our variable `$species` and have the same `if` and `elsif` conditionals, and braced code blocks. However, this time the value of `$species` is not equal to 'Human' or 'Mouse', (it is set as 'ZebraFish'); therefore, the tests following the `if` and `elsif` statements will not return true, and the code blocks within the braces will not be executed. As the `if` and `elsif` statements are followed by an `else` conditional—it's this code block that is executed in this case, so the output of this piece of code would be the line 'Your variable is not Human or Mouse!' printed to the command-line. Table 3.4 shows other comparison operators that can be used in conditional tests.

More advanced conditionals

The `if`, `elsif`, and `else` conditionals are fairly simple, but very useful. However, what if we want to test for more than one condition simultaneously? You could simply string together lots of `if` and `elsif` conditionals, but sometimes this can seem like a lot of work for simply testing a few variables and the code can become difficult to read. On occasions such as this there is a potentially more efficient option that is to combine a series of tests using logical operators, such as and (which can also be shown as `&&`) or or (which can also be shown as `||`). Here is an example of such a use:

```
my $test_var = 18;

if (($test_var > 12) && ($test_var < 24)) {
  print "Your variable is between 12 and 24!";
}
```

Table 3.4 Common comparison operators for numbers and strings. When using comparison operators with strings the terms 'less than' and 'greater than' to refer to alphabetical order in the sense that 'a' is less than 'b' in value as it comes earlier in the alphabet. Note that upper case letters are considered to be 'less than' their lower-case counterparts, i.e. 'A' is considered less in value than 'a'

Test operator		Description
Numbers	**Strings**	
==	eq	Equal
!=	ne	NOT equal
<	lt	Less than
>	gt	Greater than
<=	le	Less than or equal
>=	ge	Greater than or equal

The above test would look to see if our variable ($test_var) had a value between 12 and 24, as we test that the variable is above 12 and below 24. The basic rule of thumb when stringing together multiple tests is that all of the tests must be surrounded by a pair of brackets and each individual test must be surrounded by their own set of brackets. There is no limit on the number of tests that you can string together, you can use as many as you need.

Creating loops with FOR, FOREACH and WHILE

The next set of control structures that we are going to look at are loops. These are used in programs when you want to repeat an action multiple times and are features of most programming languages. There are two different flavours of loop that can be used for different tasks; these are loops that are carried out for a defined number of iterations and loops that repeat until a certain condition is met.

The first class of loops (those that repeat for a defined number of iterations) includes `for` and `foreach` loops, which are particularly useful if you have a list of variables (either in an array or hash) and you would like to perform an operation on each element of the list. Let's start by looking at an example using a `for` loop:

```
@array = qw(one two three four five); # create a five element
                                       # array

for ($i=0; $i<scalar(@array); $i++) {
  print "We are looking at: $array[$i] \n";
}
```

In the above snippet of code we establish our for loop with the `for` statement, and iterate through each element of our array and print the contents of each element of the array. To explain this more clearly, consider the generic syntax of a `for` loop in slightly more detail:

```
for (iterator_variable; final_test; change_to_iterator) {
  operations_to_perform_upon_each_iteration;
}
```

So, the definition of a `for` loop is split into three parts. We first define an iterator variable (in the example above this was `$i`), this variable contains a count of how many times we have been through the loop. The second parameter is the test to determine when we stop going through the loop. In the above example we first calculate the size of our array (using the `scalar` function) and state that we should keep going through the loop while `$i` is less than the size of the array. When `$i` is equal to the size of the array, or greater, the `for` loop will no longer be run and the program will continue onto the next section of code. It might seem more logical to use <= instead of < in our example to be sure not to miss the final array element, but the `scalar()` function gives the length of an array as if we had started counting from one, while we know arrays begin from zero (as does our iterator). So the use of < in the example stops us trying to use a nonexistent array element.

The final parameter that we set in the `for` loop is the amount that we increment our iterator variable with each iteration of the loop. In this example we increment our variable by one as the command `$i++` is equivalent to `$i = $i + 1`, and we want to access each element of our array. However, we are not restricted to incrementing iterators by one—sometimes it might be desirable to only look at every other element of the array, so you could simply put `$i + 2` at the end of the `for` loop definition.

The next type of loop that we are going to look at is the `foreach` loop. This is a more specialized version of the `for` loop, designed specifically for the common task of working with arrays. Basically, the `foreach` loop is used to iterate over each element of an array—hence, the name `foreach`—you can think of it as meaning: '*for each* element of this array, do this'. Here is an example of how we could use a `foreach` loop to do the same as the previous example:

```
@array = qw(one two three four five);

foreach $element (@array) {
  print "We are looking at: $element \n";
}
```

The above does exactly the same as our previous for loop, but the code is more concise and easier to read. Let's just look at the syntax of the `foreach` loop and explain exactly what is going on:

```
foreach element (array) {
  operations_to_perform_upon_each_iteration;
}
```

The major difference here between `for` and `foreach` loops is that `foreach` loops do not have an iterator variable; instead, they have a variable that gets assigned the element value of the array at that the loop is currently working on. In the above example, we call this variable `$element` and treat it as a normal scalar variable (as that it exactly what it is). Using the `foreach` loop makes moving through each element of any given array a very simple process.

However, there is one last thing to note about `foreach` loops—the element variable that we defined before as `$element` is an entirely optional argument in `foreach` loops. If you choose not to set a name for the element variable, Perl will use its default variable: `$_`. Here, is an example of the use of `$_`:

```perl
@array = qw(one two three four five);

foreach (@array) {
  print "We are looking at: $_ \n";
}
```

As you can see, this example is identical to the previous one, we just use `$_` to access the element of the array that we are looking at instead of declaring another variable.

You may now be wondering why you would declare a named variable when you don't have to. However, there are instances when it is of benefit to name our variables, such as nested loops (one loop within another), as it makes it clear to us which array element we are looking at. Here is an example of how we would use nested loops (loops within loops) to print out a list of letter/number co-ordinates (possibly useful for indexing items in a grid):

```perl
@columns = qw(A B C D E F G);
@rows = qw(1 2 3 4 5);

foreach $row (@rows) {
  foreach $column (@columns) {
    print $column . $row . ' ';
  }
  print "\n";
}

# This produces the following output:
#
# A1 B1 C1 D1 E1 F1 G1
# A2 B2 C2 D2 E2 F2 G2
# A3 B3 C3 D3 E3 F3 G3 etc...
```

As you can see above, if we are using more than one loop structure, it is beneficial to name the variables for each loop as it makes it clear which variable is which. In fact, the arrangement we have demonstrated here is impossible to do without naming the loop variables, as the `$_` from the outer loop will be overwritten within the inner loop.

The next type of loop that we'll consider is the `while` loop. The main difference between this type of loop and the previous kind is that the previous loops (`for` and `foreach`) iterate a given number of times—defined either by your constraints in a `for` loop, or the size of your array in a `foreach` loop—whereas `while` loops do not have a set number of iterations. They are based on a logic test that you define (using the same syntax as the `if`/`else` conditionals earlier), and they keep going until the condition that we have defined is met. The generic syntax of a `while` loop is:

```
while (test_case) {
  operations_to_perform_upon_each_iteration;
}
```

Let's now look at a quick example of a `while` loop in use:

```
$test_var = 12;
while ($test_var < 45) {
  print "Variable is $test_var \n";
  $test_var = $test_var + 10;
}

# This will produce the following output:
#
# Variable is 12
# Variable is 22
# Variable is 32
# Variable is 42
```

As you can see from the example above, the `while` loop will keep repeating until the condition that we define at the beginning of it is met—this can be useful if you have no way of knowing how many times you need a loop to repeat, but you can set a goal or condition that you need to meet—the only thing that you need to watch out for is initiating an infinite loop. This occurs when your loop conditional is never met (i.e. if our `$test_var` in the example above never becomes greater than 45), the loop will never exit, and your program will never complete. This is why programs sometimes appear to 'hang' or 'freeze'—they are trapped in an infinite loop. Provided you look out for instances such as this when you use a `while` loop they can be an indispensable tool.

3.2.5 Writing interactive programs—I/O basics

In this section, we will introduce ways in which you can make your Perl programs interact with users—this is a particular subset of I/O (input/output) functionality. I/O also includes dealing with files, which is covered later, in section 3.6.

So, say you have created a program to reverse compliment a DNA string, as we did earlier in the chapter. Here is a program to do this:

```
#! /usr/bin/perl
```

```perl
# Program to convert a DNA string to its reverse compliment

# Our DNA string
my $dna = 'ACTTTTGGGGCCCCAATGCATTTTAAAAA';

# First we reverse the DNA
my $revcom = reverse $dna;

# Now translate the DNA bases
$revcom =~ tr/ACGTacgt/TGCAtgca/;

# Then print out the results
print "Original DNA string: " . $dna . "\n";
print "Reverse compliment: " . $revcom . "\n";
```

In this example, the DNA string to reverse compliment is defined at the top of the program. However, what if we want to work out the reverse compliment of another DNA sequence? Simple, we just change the DNA sequence within the program. What happens though if we would like to do this quite a number of times, or even as part of another program and call this program automatically from the command line? Having to go into the program and edit the sequence is fiddly, and we run the risk of accidentally modifying another part of the program in the process and introducing an error. This is where we can increase the functionality of our program by taking input from the command line.

There are two ways in which we can take command line input from users—real-time interaction and at run-time. By real-time interaction we mean that our program will ask the user for input as it runs, so when we need to get our DNA string, we get our program to pause and ask the user for a DNA string. This approach is useful for scripts that you would like other people to use as you can prompt for input as it is needed. When we say run-time input we mean that we declare all of our input for the program up front, as we run the program. This can be useful for users of your scripts as it means that they no longer have to edit program code to change variables, but the real benefit of run-time input is that no interaction from the user is needed from there—so if the program takes a long time to run, the user can just start the program off and walk away. If the input method is interactive, the user will need to sit there and watch the program run as they wait for the next input stage. Here is how we would use the interactive input method:

```perl
#! /usr/bin/perl

print "What is your name?\n";    # Ask the user their name
$name = <>;                      # Get the user to type an answer
chomp($name);                    # Remove the newline
print "Hello $name!\n";          # Say hello
```

In the above example we show you how easy it is to ask the user for input—you simply declare a new scalar variable and mark the contents as <>, this makes

Perl wait for the user input. You can do this for as many variables as you like in a given program—there are no limits to its use. You will also notice the use of the chomp() function that was discussed earlier in the chapter—chomp() is used to remove a newline character from the end of a string. The reason for this is that the user must hit the Enter key to signify that they have finished typing, a side effect of this is that a newline character is appended to the end of the input. Because this could potentially cause problems later on if we were using the input for something more significant than printing back to screen, we use chomp as a matter of course.

That is pretty much all there is you would ever really want to know about interactive input, now let's have a look at using run-time inputs that are passed to Perl as command line parameters. Command line parameters are pieces of data that you type as part of the Perl command to run your program. Consider the program below:

```
#! /usr/bin/perl

# Make sure that we have some command-line arguments
unless (@ARGV) {
  die "No input given!";
}

# Do something with our input . . .
print " Your first input was $ARGV[0]\n";
print "Your second input was $ARGV[1]\n";
```

If you save this program as input_example2.pl and run it with the following command:

```
perl input_example2.pl ACTGGG DNA
```

You will then get the following output to your screen:

```
Your first input was ACTGGG
Your second input was DNA
```

This shows how you can accept command line parameters in your Perl scripts. The first thing that we must understand is the way in which Perl handles command line input. Simply, your scripts can accept parameters separated by spaces, which are then passed into your Perl program as elements of the special array @ARGV. In the first section, we use an unless conditional to determine if we have any command line parameters being passed to the program—if no parameters have been passed, then @ARGV would not exist and our program would then exit. This premature exiting of the program is achieved using the die function, which is a handy way of making the program stop wherever it is, write the specified message to the screen, and return control to the command line. If one or more parameters have been passed, we then simply print out the first two elements of @ARGV to screen.

This is a very basic example of what we can do with command line input serving only to demonstrate the concept and syntax. In reality, there would be little point in writing the parameters back to the screen—more typically the input would be tested in a conditional statement to determine the behaviour of the program, or used to pass a file name or analysis parameter to the program.

As an example, let's return to the reverse compliment program shown at the start of this section. We said that it would be beneficial for our users to not have to edit the Perl program each time they wish to run another DNA sequence through it. Well, now that we know how to get Perl to accept input from the command line (i.e. the DNA sequence to process), we can modify the program accordingly:

```perl
#! /usr/bin/perl
# Program to convert a DNA string to its reverse compliment

# Get the input string
unless (@ARGV) {
  die "You need to pass me a DNA sequence!";
}

# Our DNA string
my $dna = $ARGV[0];

# First we reverse the DNA
my $revcom = reverse $dna;

# Now translate the DNA bases
$revcom =~ tr/ACGTacgt/TGCAtgca/;

# Then print out the results
print "Original DNA string: " . $dna . "\n";
print "Reverse compliment: " . $revcom . "\n";
```

Basically, the only difference is that we first make sure that there are command-line arguments being passed to the program, then we make whatever the first variable the user gives us into our variable $dna, therefore completing our program. If you want to try this program out without typing it in, you can download it from www.bixsolutions.net (it's called revcomp.pl).

This is all we want to cover about getting information from your users for now. If a program needs large amounts of input, such as whole protein sequences or a long list of gene IDs, expecting the user to enter the data by hand is not really feasible, and we would look to load the data from a file or database instead. This is discussed later (in sections 3.6 and 3.9, respectively). Where user input remains essential, we may spare our users the discomfort of the command line by building a web-based front end through which users can interact with our programs—this is explained in Chapter 5. First, we shall look at some good bits of advice to consider as our programs begin to get slightly bigger and more complex.

3.2.6 Some good coding practice

We have shown thus far the basics of Perl programming and, we hope you will agree that it's really not too difficult to get along with. However, as Perl is a straightforward language that allows you many different ways to do things, mistakes can easily be made. We would therefore like to take a little time to introduce a few recommendations, based on our experience, that will help you avoid common pitfalls as you develop increasingly complex programs.

Use strict

There are several built-in modes (more correctly called *pragmas*) within Perl that assist you in making sure that your code is as *clean* as it can be. By clean, we mean that it's likely to be free of simple errors. Switching on these pragmas can result in Perl throwing up more error messages, which although somewhat off-putting, are of great value as they alert you to potential problems with your code. The first pragma we recommend is called `strict`. In order to use `strict`, we have to add the following to the top of our Perl programs (just under the shebang line):

```
use strict;
```

So what does `strict` do? Basically, `strict` forces you to code your Perl programs better as it checks for unsafe constructs and enforces variable namespacing (also known as the *scope* of a variable). So what is an unsafe construct and namespacing?

Up until now, whenever we declared a variable we have been declaring *global* variables. This means that when we have subroutines (reusable pieces of code, sometimes called functions—we cover these in section 3.4) in our scripts, if they contain a string, array, or hash that matches the name of one of your variables, they will overwrite your original variables without warning. This is why we use `strict`; with the `strict` pragma in use in our program the global variable would not be replaced by another variable of the same name, instead it would be temporarily put to one side, whilst a *private* variable would be used within the function. Once the function has completed, your global variable would once again be available, unchanged from its previous state. We shall go into more detail about this when we look at subroutines later.

In order to be able to get away from using global variables (and for our programs to work whilst the `strict` pragma is in use), we need to use the `my` operator when we define our variables. The use of `my` declares a variable as a *local* variable (private) and is enough to satisfy the needs of the `strict` pragma. Some examples of this are shown below.

```perl
my $dna_string = 'ACTG';

my @asn_codons = qw(AAU AAC);

my %genetic_code = (
  'AAU' => 'Asn',
```

```
  'GCU' => 'Ala',
  'GAU' => 'Asp'
);
```

We shall be using this form of variable declaration as well as the `strict` pragma throughout the rest of this chapter. We would recommend that you never write another Perl program without using `strict`.

Warnings and diagnostics

Two other pragmas that are commonly used to assist you in writing your code are `warnings` and `diagnostics`. They can be included in your program in the same way as `strict`, by adding the following lines to the top of your code:

```
use warnings;
use diagnostics;
```

These two pragmas aid in the writing of problem free code and debugging code that is not behaving as you intended. The `warnings` pragma specifically gives you a text warning while your code is running at the command line whenever it finds something that is potentially wrong with your code. On the other hand, `diagnostics` only does something when your program goes wrong—it adds additional explanation to Perl's standard error messages and even suggests possible fixes to your code when an error occurs. Most of the time people only tend to use the `strict` and `warnings` pragmas, but if you are having problems debugging a particularly difficult bit of code, `diagnostics` can be invaluable in pointing you in the right direction.

Variable naming and commenting

Our last tip is really just a piece of advice for the way in which to program. Basically, as with naming elements of a database, when naming your variables and programs, use common sense and give them names that relate to their function. This will aid you in the long run by allowing you to walk away from a program for quite some time, and the next time you come to it you will not have to figure out what test_script1.pl does or what information is contained in $string1. Here is a quick list of recommendations.

- When you name your program—name it according to its function. For example, if it's a program for parsing BLAST results, call it `parse_blast_results.pl` or something similar.

- When you name variables, name them sensibly—$a or $string1 means nothing when you have forgotten exactly how your program worked. For example, if you have a string that is to contain a DNA sequence, call it $dna, or something more specific if possible.

- This will make more sense after reading the next section, but is more appropriately mentioned here. When naming and using references, the following tips can make your code a lot more readable:

- Always name your reference $something_ref—the important part here is the _ref at the end, this immediately lets you know that this is a referenced variable and not just another scalar.

- If you have a reference to an array or hash, precede the variable name with either an a_ for an array reference or a h_ for a hash. If you have more complex data structures, such as a reference to an array of hashes, use a combination of the two—i.e. ah_ would indicate an array of hashes, whereas hh_ would indicate a hash of hashes. Using this naming scheme can help you keep track of what is going on in the complicated soup of variables that you may find in a large and complex Perl program.

Following these guidelines—using the strict, warnings, and diagnostics pragmas, and applying some common sense when it comes to naming things can greatly help you in writing your code, and make it understandable to other people, or even yourself when you have been away from your program for a while. Finally, it's always good practice to insert copious comments in your programs as you write them—it may slow you down slightly, but could save hours later when you need to return to the code to unravel how it works.

3.2.7 Summary

That bring us to the end of our coverage of the basics of syntax and logic for Perl. Since this has been a pretty big section, let's quickly recap the main points:

- The basics of putting together a Perl program. Remember to use the appropriate shebang so the operating system can find the Perl interpreter, and save your scripts with a .pl file extension.

- There are three different types of data structures/variables available in Perl:

  - The scalar (a number or string).

  - The array (a number indexed list of scalars).

  - The hash (an unordered list of scalars arranged in key/value pairs).

- Control structures like loops including for, foreach, and while, and conditional tests using if, elsif, and else, combined with logic operators are the building blocks for programs that can automate tasks, respond to user input and perform many other useful functions.

- Input can be provided to Perl programs by the user interactively or via command line parameters.

- Finally, we provided some basic advice to keep in mind when writing your Perl programs to try and keep things as understandable as possible.

If you understand these concepts, you can start writing original programs in Perl right away. Indeed, most of these concepts are common across all major programming languages, so if you decide to move on to another language such as Java or C++ you will find you have a slight head start. In the remainder of this chapter, we focus on some more advanced topics, most of which are specific to Perl, and all of which are useful in bioinformatics.

3.3   References

A reference is a pointer to a variable, it is not actually a variable itself—it just points to a variable that already exists. If you're from a Linux background, think of references as Perl's equivalent of symbolic links. If you're from the Windows world, think of them as a shortcut—both of these appear to the file system as a basic file, but instead they just point to another file—Perl references act in the same way. They therefore appear to your code as scalar variables, although they are merely pointing to another variable.

   As we've seen, scalars, arrays, and hashes are great for storing the data within simple Perl programs, so why do we need references? Essentially, references are used to extend the existing data structures—to make more complex arrangements possible that are not permitted with the standard variables. Such situations occur frequently in bioinformatics, hence the importance of learning this skill. The best way to understand this is with a few good examples.

3.3.1   Multidimensional arrays

For our first example, what if we wanted to store information that would be best arranged in a two dimensional array (e.g. a set of experimental results, like you would normally record in a tabular form)? Maybe we could try this:

```
my @array1 = qw(24 48 56 12);
my @array2 = qw(25 48 55 12);
my @array3 = qw(23 49 54 11);
my @array4 = qw(24 48 55 12);
my @twodarray = (@array1, @array2, @array3, @array4);
```

   If you put the above code into a program and try running it, it appears to work; no errors are given and our array is populated; however, all is not quite as well as it seems. If you check this array using the debugging technique in section 3.3.3 (`Data::Dumper`), you would find that we have not actually produced a two dimensional array, just one long list (single dimension) array made up of the elements of each of the arrays we placed into it. This is not what we intended and will not be useful to us. To get round this problem we need to use references:

```
my @array1 = qw(24 48 56 12);
my @array2 = qw(25 48 55 12);
my @array3 = qw(23 49 54 11);
my @array4 = qw(24 48 55 12);

# This is how we create a reference to a variable - by using
# the '\' character. You must remember that
# references appear as scalar variables though.
my $a_array1_ref = \@array1;
my $a_array2_ref = \@array2;
```

```perl
my $a_array3_ref = \@array3;
my $a_array4_ref = \@array4;

my @twodarray = ($a_array1_ref,$a_array2_ref,$a_array3_ref,
$a_array4_ref);
```

The above code gives the desired result, thanks to the use of references to the arrays that contain our data. To the @twodarray variable these appear as scalars and are therefore permitted to create the array. This is quite a bit of extra code to write at the moment (as we have to first declare our array, then our reference), and might put some of the more lazy programmers off the idea of references. Thankfully, as with all things in Perl there is more than one way to do it, so below are a couple of other ways we could have done the same. The way in which you use references is up to you—basically choose the method that makes the most sense to you.

```perl
my @array1 = qw(24 48 56 12);
my @array2 = qw(25 48 55 12);
my @array3 = qw(23 49 54 11);
my @array4 = qw(24 48 55 12);
my @twodarray = (\@array1, \@array2, \@array3, \@array4);
```

In the above example we reference the arrays containing our data within the declaration of the @twodarray, this removes the extra effort of declaring our references explicitly and should make the code slightly easier to read. You can however take this even further.

```perl
my @twodarray = (
  ["24", "48", "56", "12"],
  ["25", "48", "55", "12"],
  ["23", "49", "54", "11"],
  ["24", "48", "55", "12"]
);
```

In the above we have taken our example to the most extreme and compact form possible, (without making the @twodarray a reference itself). In this instance, we do not even create our arrays beforehand and reference them—they are created *in situ* as anonymous arrays. Because these arrays don't have names, it is impossible to access them elsewhere in the program, but this is fine if we have no intention of accessing them individually. The square brackets surrounding the values tells Perl that we are creating a reference to an array.

Once we have a two-dimensional array like this, we need to access the data contained within the structure. To do this we must remember that we are using referenced data (it's not the actual variable, but just a pointer to it), so to gain access to the data that we have referenced, we must first *de-reference* it. This can be achieved as follows:

```perl
# We have already created our @twodarray (using one of the methods
    above),
```

```perl
# so no need to show this again...

# Here we extract some single values

print "Patient1, var2: " . $twodarray [0]->[1]; # This will print '48'
print "\n";
print "Patient4, var3: " . $twodarray [3]->[2]; # This will print '55'
print "\n";

# Or we could just extract and dereference a whole array...

foreach (@twodarray) {
  # This is how we de-reference a whole array
  my @patient_data = @{$_};

  foreach my $var (@patient_data) {
    print $var . ' ';
  }

  print "\n";
}
```

In the above code we show how we can access the data within the multidimensional array that we created before (in any of the three examples—they all create the same final data structure), this is done by the process of de-referencing our data structure. The easiest way we can explain how this works is this:

- In a normal array, we access each (scalar) element of the array by using the index value of the element we want to retrieve—e.g. $array[1] gives us the second element in an array.

- In a referenced array we access data in the same way (using the index value), and then de-reference the scalar value by either using arrow symbols (->), or by using a double dollar symbol ($$). For example, $array_ref->[1] returns the second element from an array reference and $$array_ref[1] does the same.

The other method of de-referencing that we show above is where we de-reference a whole array at once, this is achieved by surrounding the array reference with @{ }. Finally, here is a brief example of how we would go about creating and accessing our data if we wanted to store all of the data within a reference (a reference to an array of arrays).

```perl
# Create our initial data structure as a reference...
my $aa_2d_array_ref = [
        ["24", "48", "56", "12"],
        ["25", "48", "55", "12"],
        ["23", "49", "54", "11"],
        ["24", "48", "55", "12"]
];

# And to access the data within...
print "Patient1, var2: " . $aa_2d_array_ref->[0]->[1] . "\n"; # '48'
print "Patient4, var3: " . $aa_2d_array_ref->[3]->[2] . "\n"; # '55'
```

```
# Or... (note the double '$$' to de-reference our data)
print "Patient1, var2: " . $$aa_2d_array_ref[0][1] . "\n"; # '48'
print "Patient4, var3: " . $$aa_2d_array_ref[3][2] . "\n"; # '55'

# Or access the whole structure...
foreach my $a_patient_ref (@{$aa_2d_array_ref}) {
  foreach my $measurement (@{$a_patient_ref}) {
    print $measurement . ' ';
  }
  print "\n";
}
```

3.3.2 Multidimensional hashes

We have looked at multidimensional arrays in our previous example; now what if the data that you want to handle is slightly more complicated, such that it would be more ideally handled within a hash or even tree-type structure?

First, let's have a look at how you could create a hash containing arrays (as references) for the value part of each key/value pair. This uses the same techniques as in our previous example.

```
my %exp_results = (
  'patient1' => ["24", "48", "56", "12"],
  'patient2' => ["25", "48", "55", "12"],
  'patient3' => ["23", "49", "54", "11"],
  'patient4' => ["24", "48", "55", "12"]
);

# Now to retrieve some data...
print "Patient1, var1: " . $exp_results{patient1}->[0] . "\n";
print "Patient4, var3: " . $exp_results{patient4}->[2] . "\n";
```

The following code shows how to create the initial hash as a reference too:

```
my $ha_exp_results_ref = {
  'patient1' => ["24", "48", "56", "12"],
  'patient2' => ["25", "48", "55", "12"],
  'patient3' => ["23", "49", "54", "11"],
  'patient4' => ["24", "48", "55", "12"]
};

# Now to retrieve some data... (using '->' to de-reference)
print "Patient1, var1: " . $ha_exp_results_ref->{patient1}->[0] . "\n";
print "Patient4, var3: " . $ha_exp_results_ref->{patient4}->[2] . "\n";

# Or... (note the use of the '$$' again)
print "Patient1, var1: " . $$ha_exp_results_ref{patient1}[0] . "\n";
print "Patient4, var3: " . $$ha_exp_results_ref{patient4}[2] . "\n";

# Or access the whole hash...

# Just like 'normal' hashes, the keys function gives us the
# keys for a referenced hash - we just need to de-reference it first
```

```perl
foreach my $patient (keys %{$ha_exp_results_ref}) {

  print $patient . "\n" . "\t";

  # Now we can access all of the measurements in the inner array
  # reference by de-referencing it...

  foreach my $measurement (@{$ha_exp_results_ref->{$patient}}) {
    print $measurement . ' ';
  }

  print "\n";

}
```

As before, we created a reference to an anonymous array by creating our initial array reference using square brackets and we have also shown above that it's possible to directly create a reference to an anonymous hash by simply using curly braces. So, the rule for creating references to anonymous data structures is: square braces for an array reference; curly braces for a hash reference.

Having seen that we can put arrays within hashes through the use of references, let's have a quick look at an example of how we would embed numerous hashes inside another hash (again using references). This is one of the most complicated examples in this chapter, so it's worth taking time to understand it.

```perl
my $hh_exp_results_ref = {
  'patient1' => {
    'var1' => 24,
    'var2' => 48,
    'var3' => 56,
    'var4' => 12
  },
  'patient2' => {
    'var1' => 25,
    'var2' => 48,
    'var3' => 55,
    'var4' => 12
  },
  'patient3' => {
    'var1' => 23,
    'var2' => 49,
    'var3' => 54,
    'var4' => 11
  },
  'patient4' => {
    'var1' => 24,
    'var2' => 48,
    'var3' => 55,
    'var4' => 12
  }
};
```

```perl
# Now to retrieve some data...
print "Patient1, var1: " . $hh_exp_results_ref->{patient1}->{var1} . "\n";
print "Patient4, var3: " . $hh_exp_results_ref->{patient4}->{var3} . "\n";

# Or access the whole hash...

# Just like 'normal' hashes, the keys function gives us the
# keys for a referenced hash - we just need to de-reference it first

foreach my $patient (keys %{$hh_exp_results_ref}) {

  print $patient . ":\n";

  # Now we can access all of the keys to the measurements in
  # the inner hash reference by de-referencing it...

  foreach my $measurement (keys %{$hh_exp_results_ref->{$patient}}) {
    print "\t" . $measurement . ": ";
    print $hh_exp_results_ref->{$patient}->{$measurement} . "\n";
  }

  print "\n";

}
```

The above code looks pretty scary at first, but all we have done is to put together each of the things that we have done previously. We first create a hash reference (using curly braces), and then the values in the key/value pairs for this reference are more hash references—this gives us a tree-like data structure that could be quite useful when building real bioinformatics solutions. Below this we just dereference the outer hash so that we can access the keys of the hash, and then do the same for each of the inner hash references.

The only data structure we have not shown an example of within this section is referenced hashes embedded within an array. Here is a quick example that should not really need any explanation, but shows a way we could handle related data from multiple experiments.

```perl
my $ah_exp_results_ref = [
  {
  'patient1' => ["24", "48", "56", "12"],
  'patient2' => ["25", "48", "55", "12"],
  'patient3' => ["23", "49", "54", "11"],
  'patient4' => ["24", "48", "55", "12"]
  },
  {
  'patient1' => ["22", "46", "54", "10"],
  'patient2' => ["24", "47", "54", "11"],
  'patient3' => ["25", "51", "56", "13"],
  'patient4' => ["24", "48", "55", "12"]
  }
];
```

This covers all of the data structures possible with Perl—obviously you're not limited to only one level of nesting within hashes and arrays, we just chose not to show more complex examples here. However, the syntax is exactly the same—you just have to remember that you have more than two levels when it comes to dereferencing.

3.3.3   Viewing data structures with `Data::Dumper`

One of the final things that we would like to touch on with respect to references and complex data structures in Perl is how to figure out what is in the data structures without going through complex de-referencing and lots of code. This can be a common task if you inherit poorly documented code from other people or if you're just not sure how things are working. Thankfully Perl has a built in module that can greatly aid in this event: `Data::Dumper`.

`Data::Dumper`, in its most straight forward use, simply allows you to print an entire data structure to the console including its structure and contents, thereby giving you vital clues as to how you can go about manipulating and using your data structure. Here is an example of `Data::Dumper` in use:

```perl
# First we create a data structure...
my $hh_exp_results_ref = {
  'patient1' => {
    'var1' => 24,
    'var2' => 48,
    'var3' => 56,
    'var4' => 12
  },
  'patient2' => {
    'var1' => 25,
    'var2' => 48,
    'var3' => 55,
    'var4' => 12
  },
  'patient3' => {
    'var1' => 23,
    'var2' => 49,
    'var3' => 54,
    'var4' => 11
  },
  'patient4' => {
    'var1' => 24,
    'var2' => 48,
    'var3' => 55,
    'var4' => 12
  }
};
```

```
# Now have a look at it...

use Data::Dumper; # Load the module
print Dumper($hh_exp_results_ref);# Print the structure using
                                  # Dumper()
```

This will produce the following output:

```
$VAR1 = {
  'patient1' => {
    'var3' => 56,
    'var1' => 24,
    'var4' => 12,
    'var2' => 48
    },
  'patient4' => {
    'var3' => 55,
    'var1' => 24,
    'var4' => 12,
    'var2' => 48
    },
  'patient3' => {
    'var3' => 54,
    'var1' => 23,
    'var4' => 11,
    'var2' => 49
    },
  'patient2' => {
    'var3' => 55,
    'var1' => 25,
    'var4' => 12,
    'var2' => 48
    }
  };
```

The above output clearly shows the structure of our data—we can see that it's a hash reference containing other hash references, as denoted by the curly braces. This technique can be applied to any data structure in Perl and is a very useful debugging tool to have around.

3.4 Subroutines and modules

Subroutines are pieces of re-usable code that are often called things like *methods* or *functions* in other programming languages. The typical use for a subroutine is when you have to repeat an operation several times in a program (e.g. to perform the same operation on a series of arrays or hashes). On such occasions you could copy and paste the same section of code several times, with the only difference being the variable names. However, not only does this lead to long programs, it also means that if you want to expand or modify the code you have to edit all of the copied sections. A much better solution is to write just one block of code—a *subroutine*—and call it each time you need to perform that operation. Let's consider the most basic syntax for defining a subroutine:

```
# The line below indicates the start of a subroutine...
sub subroutine_name {
   (input_variables) = @_;      # Optional

   content_of_the_subroutine

   return subroutine_output     # Optional
}
```

Basically, there are four parts that make up a subroutine:

- First is the name of the subroutine—this is the name you are going to use in the body of your program to call your subroutine.

- Second is the list of input variables that you have passed into your subroutine—this can be any Perl variable or data structure, and there may be any number of them. In fact, some subroutines do not need input variables at all—you could just write a subroutine to return a defined output (e.g. displaying instructions on how to use a program is a common application of this feature).

- Third is the content of the subroutine—this is the main body of code that performs the function of the subroutine.

- Finally we have the subroutine output—this is what gets passed back to the main body of your program on completion of the subroutine. Like the input variables, this part of a subroutine is optional, for example, the output from a subroutine could be information printed to the console, and therefore the returning of variables is not required.

As ever, we can better understand subroutines by studying an example:

```
#!/usr/bin/perl

use strict;
use warnings;

my $dna = 'ACTGAAA';
print "My DNA string is " . $dna . "\n";

# Call on our subroutine...
my $revcom_dna = revcom($dna);
print "The reverse compliment is " . $revcom_dna . "\n";

# A subroutine to reverse compliment DNA
sub revcom {
   # Get the DNA to be worked on...
```

```perl
my ($dna) = @_;

# First we reverse the DNA
$dna = reverse $dna;

# Now translate the DNA bases
$dna =~ tr/ACGTacgt/TGCAtgca/;

# Return the output
return $dna;
}
```

The above code forms a complete program that will give us the reverse compliment of a DNA string—something that we have done earlier (a couple of times now!). The main difference in this instance is that producing the reverse compliment is done entirely within a subroutine and all you need to do to use it in your Perl program is to call it. This makes our code very portable—not only can it be called multiple times from within our program, but if we ever need the ability to calculate the reverse compliment DNA of a sequence in another program we can simply copy the subroutine into the new program and use it with no additional work. Better still, if it's something we do regularly, we could save it in a Perl *module* containing some of our most used subroutines so that we can call them as they are needed without physically pasting them into our programs. We will explain how to produce such modules shortly, but first let's look in more detail at the above code as there are some things that need explaining.

First, note the position of the subroutine within the program—we have placed it at the very bottom of the code. This is the normal position for subroutines and is where we would suggest that you place your subroutines in the same position. It is also worth noting that, although subroutines are at the bottom of your code, they will not be executed at the end of your program as the interpreter works its way through the lines of code—they are separate 'sub-programs' that are not run unless they are called within the body of the main program, so it is safe to place them at the bottom of your code, and call them as and when they are needed.

Secondly note the variable declaration within the subroutine. Because we can send more than one input variable to a subroutine the variables are passed in the form of an array (denoted by the @_ symbol). This is why the $dna variable is surrounded by round brackets, to acknowledge that it's an element of the array. If we had more than one input variable, we would simply have more than one variable declared within the brackets.

Thirdly, as we are using the strict pragma we are able to have two variables called $dna (we declare one in the main body of the program, and the other within the subroutine). These two variables are completely separate entities as they were declared within different namespaces, as described when we first introduced strict—the first $dna variable is only usable within the main body of the program, and the second $dna variable is only available and usable within the body of the subroutine in which it was declared. If we were not using the strict pragma (and using my to declare our variables), we would now be coming into problems as our two separate variables would not be separate, they would be the same variable and would be overwriting each other without any warning. This concept is further explained in Fig. 3.3.

Before we move on to looking at Perl modules, let's consider another example of the use of a subroutine:

```perl
#!/usr/bin/perl

use strict;
use warnings;

# Declare some variables
my @array1 = qw(AA BB CC DD EE);
my @array2 = qw(11 22 33 44 55);

# Now print the contents of the arrays
print_array(\@array1);
print_array(\@array2);

# The subroutine we use to print the arrays
sub print_array {
  my ($array_ref) = @_;

  foreach (@{$array_ref}) {
    print $_ . "\n";
  }
}
```

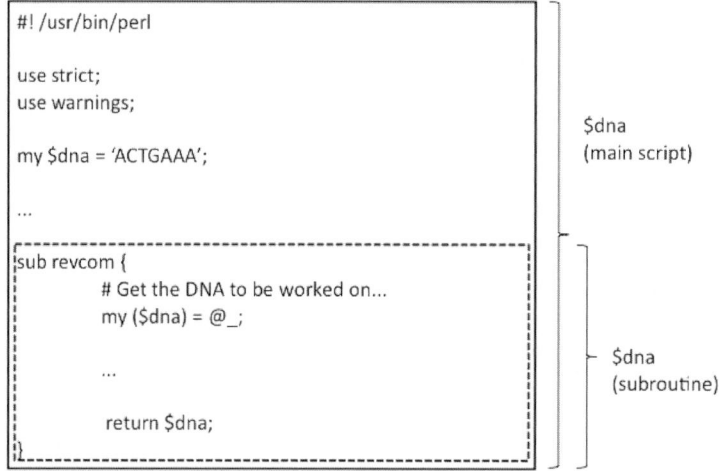

Fig. 3.3 A visual representation of a subroutine, and the concept of namespaces. When Perl's `strict` pragma is in use, any variable defined within a code block such as a subroutine will be a private variable—only be available within that code block. Conversely, variables declared outside of any code block/subroutine will be available throughout the whole program and, indeed, the subroutines if they are not overridden by private variables.

The above demonstrates a short example of the use of a simple subroutine to make the boring task of looping through and printing an array a simple call to the subroutine. We also show the use of references in this example. We could have passed the entire array(s) to the subroutine and this would work; however, as we stated before (when first looking at references), if our arrays are very large, this method will perform much faster and use less memory on your computer as it does not have to copy a large array into the subroutine, as it utilizes a reference to the original array. Such subtleties of coding may seem trivial but ultimately these efficiencies can make the difference between a problem being solved or being totally intractable, particularly in bioinformatics where data sets can be very large.

3.4.1 Making a Perl module

Finally, we shall look at putting the above subroutines together into a Perl module. To put it simply, a Perl module is a text file that contains a collection of subroutines and has the file extension '.pm'—this can then be called from another Perl program allowing use of the contained subroutines as if they were in the present program. Here is an example of the code for a Perl module that contains the two subroutines that we have just looked at:

```perl
# This file will be called 'MySubs.pm' and is
# saved in the same directory as our other Perl programs.
sub revcom {
  # Get the DNA to be worked on...
  my ($dna) = @_;

  # First we reverse the DNA
  my $revcom = reverse $dna;

  # Now translate the DNA bases
  $revcom =~ tr/ACGTacgt/TGCAtgca/;

  # Return the output
  return $revcom;
}

sub print_array {
  my ($array_ref) = @_;

  foreach (@{$array_ref}) {
    print $_ . "\n";
  }
}

# Note: this line below is needed for the
# Perl module to work, and you MUST ALWAYS end
# your Perl modules this way.
1;
```

That is our Perl module written, now here is an example of how we can use these subroutines in another Perl program (note, for simplicity the Perl program must be in the same directory as our Perl module for this to work).

```perl
#!/usr/bin/perl

use strict;
use warnings;

# This is how we call our Perl module
use MySubs;

my $dna = 'ACTGAAA';
print "My DNA string is " . $dna . "\n";

# Call on our subroutine...
my $revcom_dna = revcom($dna);
print "The reverse compliment is " . $revcom_dna . "\n";
```

All you have to add to your program is the line use *name_of_module* and Perl takes care of making the subroutines in that module available to your program. From then you just have to call your methods as if they were at the bottom of your program. This is a great way of re-using code for repetitive and common tasks. Best of all, there are thousands of Perl modules freely available via the web, many of which contain functions relevant to bioinformatics. Provided you can find a module that does what you want (we give you some pointers in section 3.10), you can just call subroutines from it as if they were part of your own program.

This is all there is to cover about subroutines and Perl modules, the only other piece of advice that we can offer is that if you have to type the same piece of code more than twice within the same program, you really should consider moving that bit of code into a subroutine. Like a lot of programming practice, it may take longer in the short term, but could pay dividends later on.

3.5   Regular expressions

We are now going to look at one of the biggest selling points of Perl—the ease with which we can use regular expressions. A regular expression can be defined as a string that is used to describe or match a set of strings—it is a tool that can be used to look for specific pieces of text or patterns in strings. The use of regular expressions in Perl is very straightforward and is one of the reasons that Perl has become the default language for bioinformaticians—as the majority of bioinformatics tasks involve some form of text manipulation.

So how do we get started with regular expressions? Well, we already started back in section 3.2.1 of this chapter, for creating the reverse compliment of a DNA string using the substitution and transliteration operators. The examples so far have been very simple, just looking for and replacing single characters, but regular expressions can be far more powerful than this. Covering everything there is to know about regular expressions is just not possible here, the topic is almost like a programming language of its own and there are whole books dedicated to this subject (e.g. Stubblebine, 2007). What we aim to provide here is an introduction to the concepts of regular expressions and some of their more common uses in bioinformatics.

3.5.1 Defining regular expressions

The best way to get started with regular expressions is to use them in conditional statements—to be more precise, an `if` statement. This allows us to easily tell whether our regular expressions work or not, as when a regular expression gets a match, it returns true, if it does not get a match, it returns false—there is no middle ground here. Consider the example below:

```
#!/usr/bin/perl

use strict;
use warnings;

my $dna = 'ACTGCCGTAAACCCTG';

if ($dna =~/CCG/) {
  print "CCG present in sequence.\n";
} else {
  print "No match found.\n";
}
```

The above example uses a regular expression to test for a pattern of three letters within a string. First we declared our string `$dna`, from here we set up our conditional with the test case `$dna =~/CCG/` – a basic use of a regular expression that needs a little more explanation:

• The first thing to note is the use of the binding operator `=~` that makes our regular expression act on (bind to) whatever variable is to the left of it—in our case `$dna`. It is important to remember this binding operator as without it the regular expressions will not work as intended.

• The second part is the test for the regular expression itself—this is the string housed between two forward slash characters (`/`)—in our example we are looking for the three base sequence 'CCG' within our DNA string.

Metacharacters

In section 3.2.1 we listed special codes for use within double-quoted strings, such as `\n` for newline characters and `\t` for tab characters. These can be used in exactly the same way within regular expressions so that we can look for these special characters if we need to. Indeed, there are further special codes, listed in Table 3.5, which can be included in regular expressions to match certain types of character.

Table 3.5 Codes for use in regular expressions.

Character	Meaning
\w	*Word* characters. Matches any alphanumeric character and '_' (underscore)
\W	Matches any non-word characters
\s	Matches a whitespace character, i.e. space or tab
\S	Matches a non-whitespace character
\d	Matches a digit character
\D	Matches a non-digit character

Another character that is of use within regular expressions is the dot (.) character. This acts as a wildcard character within Perl's regular expressions, matching
any single character except the newline character (\n). Therefore, the pattern
match /CC./ would return a positive match for CCG, CCA, CCT, CCC when used
on a DNA string.

However, what if we would like to search for the dot character? How can we
achieve this without it becoming a wildcard character? This is done by *escaping*
the wildcard action by preceding the dot character with a backslash (i.e. \.), our
regular expression will then look for the dot character. The same is true of the
forward slash character—if we want to match on this we need to escape it with a
backslash character first (\/), otherwise we'll end our regular expression early.

Repeating values

What happens if we want to match more than one wildcard character or any
other character or letter for that matter? We could just repeat the given character (or wildcard) the required number of times, but that is not very flexible as it
requires us to know the exact number of times we would expect our character to
appear. In this instance we should use yet another special operator, the asterisk
(*). This is a *quantifier* that tells the regular expression to match a character *zero
or more* times, and it's placed after the character upon which you wish it to act.
For example, the regular expression /CCGA*/ will match CCG, CCGA, CCGAA,
CCGAAA, etc. You can also use the asterisk symbol in conjunction with the wildcard operator or any other special character, so .* is often used to ignore uninter-
esting pieces of string before or after the patterns that you are looking for.

A related quantifier is the plus symbol (+)—this tells our regular expression
that you would like to match a given character *one* or more times and is used in
exactly the same way as the asterisk character.

Grouping patterns

It's possible to group patterns together within Perl's regular expressions by
enclosing them in brackets. This allows us to look for more intricate patterns,
for example, /CCG+/ would look for CCGGGGG or any other number of trailing

G's, however this might not be the most useful pattern for us. On the other hand, /(CCG)+/ would look for CCGCCGCCG or any number of repetitions of the CCG triplet—most useful if our aim is to seek out CCG repeats.

What happens if we use the asterisk instead? This is something to watch out for as this is a common mistake. The problem is that an expression such as /(CCG)*/ would match anything, not just repetitions of CCG due to the use of the 'zero or more' asterisk character.

Using OR in regular expressions

The logical operator *or* in the form of the vertical bar (|) character can also be used within regular expressions when you want to look for alternatives within your pattern matching. Here are some examples of its use:

- /CCG|GGC/ would match either CCG or GGC.

- /CC(G|C)/ would match CCG or CCC.

- /CC(G+|C+)/ would match CCGGGGGG or CCCCCCCCC or any variation on the number of repeated Gs or Cs following the initial CC.

3.5.2 More advanced regular expressions

Using the concepts and characters introduced in the previous section, it's easy to produce a mind bogglingly large number of fairly complex regular expressions, but Perl allows us to go further still.

Character classes

Character classes are a list of possible characters for use in our pattern match surrounded with square brackets ([]) that would return true if any character within the brackets was found.

For example, a character class [ACTG] would match any of the four nucleic acids. You can also specify ranges within character classes, so [0-9] would match the digits zero to nine, [A-Z] would match any upper case letter of the alphabet. You could use [a-zA-Z] to match both upper and lower case.

Character classes would not typically be used as a regular expression on their own, but would be used as part of a larger regular expression. For example, the program below checks a string to see if it looks like an Ensembl gene ID (i.e. is it a number preceded by the letters ENSG?):

```perl
#!/usr/bin/perl

use strict;
use warnings;

my $gene_id = 'ENSG000041';

if ($gene_id =~/ENSG[0-9]+/) {
  print "Our string is an Ensembl Gene ID.\n";
}
```

More quantifiers

We have already seen that the quantifiers * and + match 'zero or more' or 'one or more' times, respectively. It's possible to be more specific with the number of repeated characters, or sequences of characters if you are using grouping. This is achieved through the use of curly braces ({ }) and a pair of numbers within these braces defining how many repetitions we will accept. Here are a few examples:

- /\w{1,}/ would match one or more 'word' characters.
- /\w{1,10}/ would match anything between one or ten 'word' characters.
- /(CCG){3,}/ would match three or more repetitions of the triplet CCG –e.g. CCGCCGCCG, CCGCCGCCGCCG, etc.

Anchors

Anchors are special characters that allow us to tie our pattern match to certain sections of the test string. The two anchors that we shall discuss here are ^ and $—when used in regular expressions these tie a pattern match to either the start (^) or the end ($) of the test string. For example:

```perl
#!/usr/bin/perl

use strict;
use warnings;

my $id = ' ENSG000041';

if ($id =~/^ENSG[0-9]+/) {
  print "Our string is an Ensembl Gene ID.\n";
}
```

The above test would return false as there is a whitespace character in the first position of our test string. Here is another example:

```perl
#!/usr/bin/perl

use strict;
use warnings;

my $id = 'ENSG000041_A';

if ($id =~/^ENSG[0-9]+$/) {
  print "Our string is an Ensembl Gene ID.\n";
}
```

This test would also return false as we have now tied the numbers at the end of our pattern match to the end of the string—at the end of our string we have a letter (A).

Although both of these examples result in a failure of our regular expression tests, they do show how the two anchors can increase the specificity of regular expressions.

3.5.3   Regular expressions in practice

Now that we have covered the basic syntax of regular expressions, in this final section we can cover some extra pieces of information that are useful in their practical use.

The pattern match operator

So far we have been placing our regular expressions inside two forward-slash characters—this is actually a built-in shortcut for the `m//` pattern match operator. The reason we mention this is not just for completeness, it's useful for cleaning up your regular expressions. Take for example a regular expression that tries to identify a URL:

```
/http:\/\/www.*/
```

This is a pretty straightforward example, but demonstrates how messy something like this can become when you need lots of backslash characters to stop the regular expression ending prematurely. One of the benefits of using the `m` operator is that you do not necessarily have to use the forward-slash characters to delimit your regular expressions—in fact, you can use any set of delimiters: For example, you could use `m( )`, `m{ }`, `m[ ]`, `m< >`, `m! !`, `m% %`, etc.—thus making your original regular expression much easier to read:

```
m(http://www.*)
```

The basic rule is to choose a set of delimiters that make your regular expression as easy to understand as possible.

Modifiers

As described in section 3.2.1 when looking at string substitution, regular expressions allow the use of various modifiers to change the way in which they operate (the substitution operator is one form of regular expression). These come after the closing / character (or whatever character you may be using to delimit your expression), and are single lower case letters. Two important modifiers are `i` and `s`.

- `i`, as described earlier with the substitution operator, makes the pattern match case insensitive.

- `s` modifies the action of the wildcard dot (.) character. Normally the wildcard character matches anything but the newline (\n) character. With the `s` modifier, the dot character will also match the newline character.

As in the substitution example all you need to do is place the modifier(s) required after the closing forward slash of the regular expression and they will modify the regular expression accordingly.

Match variables

Quite often when using regular expressions it is useful to find out the exact snippet of string that is causing the match to occur. This is useful if you are trying

to retrieve something from a string. It can also aid in debugging a rather complicated regular expression.

By default there are three automatic match variables with Perl's regular expressions. When used, these return the section of string before the match, the match
itself, and then the section of string after the match—these can be accessed using
the following special variables: $`, $& , and $' (before, match and after, respec-
tively). Here is an example of their use:

```perl
#!/usr/bin/perl

use strict;
use warnings;

my $string = 'The Human Gene ID is ENSG000041 revision 1';

if ($string =~/ENSG[0-9]+/) {
  print "The gene ID is: '" . $& . "'\n";
  print "The text found before was: '" . $` . "'\n";
  print "The text found after was: '" . $' . "'\n";
}
```

In addition to these automatic match variables it is also possible to define your
own match variables to return specific portions of your pattern matches. To do
this, we make use of pattern grouping, using brackets as described earlier, to
encase the section of the regular expression that you would like to access. To
access these values after the regular expression has been matched we use the special Perl variables $1, $2, $3, etc., where the number refers to the bracket group-
ing when counting from the left. The best way to understand this is by example:

```perl
#!/usr/bin/perl

use strict;
use warnings;

my $string = 'The Human Gene ID is ENSG000041 revision 1';

if ($string =~/^The (.*) Gene.*(ENSG[0-9]+.*$)/) {
  print "Our gene ID is: " . $2 . "\n";
  print "Our species is: " . $1 . "\n";
}
```

It is also worth noting here that even when you are using self defined match
variables (using $1 etc.), Perl's default match variables are still available to you.

Substitutions with s///

We used the substitution operator back in section 3.2.1 to substitute individual
characters, but we can also use this operator on more than one character at
a time. In fact, it's possible to replace large chunks of text and use any of the

regular expression syntax described above. For example:

```perl
#!/usr/bin/perl

use strict;
use warnings;

my $string = 'ACTGCCGTGCCGCCGCCGTTGAC';

$string =~ s/CCG/---/g;

print $string . "\n";

# This would return...
# 'ACTG---TG---------TTGAC'
```

3.6   File handling and directory operations

As we have just discussed, one of the most common tasks performed with Perl is some form of text manipulation using regular expressions. However, what we have not discussed is where this text (e.g. DNA or protein sequence) has come from. So far, we have been typing our text strings directly into our programs, often termed *hard-coding* data into programs. If we want to apply our program to other data, we would have to alter the Perl code itself. In real applications this is not normal practice as it's not practical to type, or cut and paste, large chunks of DNA sequence (or whatever data you're working with) into your programs or onto the command line. An alternative is reading in data from a local text file, while other options would be reading in files from the internet, or taking data directly from a relational database. We shall look at interacting with databases later in the chapter—for now we shall consider using text files with Perl.

3.6.1   Reading text files

First, we will consider opening and reading local files that already exist. Here is the basic syntax for opening a file:

```perl
open(FILEHANDLE,filename);
```

The basic function we call for interacting with files is `open`, to which we pass two arguments; the *file handle* and the *file name*. The file name is simply the name of the file with which you wish to interact with. The file handle is the name used to interact with the file in the rest of our program. Here is a snippet of code to read in a FASTA file containing the genomic sequence for the gene BRCA1 'BRCA1. fasta'—this can be downloaded from our companion website (www.bixsolutions. net/BRCA1.fasta) or you're more than welcome to use a FASTA file of your own if you have one to hand. Copy the file into your current working directory and try this snippet of code in a new program:

```perl
open(FILE,"BRCA1.fasta"); # Open the fasta file
```

```
my @file_text = <FILE>; # Read the entire file into an array
close FILE; # Close the file
print "@file_text \n"; # Print the contents of the file
```

On the first line we open the file—giving it the file handle `FILE`. We then read the entire contents of the file into an array by referring to this file handle. Note the use of an array here—if we had used a scalar variable we would only get the first line of the file. On the next line of the code we close the file, again using the file handle to specify the file to close. On the final line, we print the contents of the array to the console. It is important to always use the `close` function as soon as you have finished with a file as leaving it open longer than necessary can leave the file open to potential damage. In this example the file handle may seem somewhat unnecessary, but these become very important in more complex programs where we have multiple files open simultaneously, as is the case when we are comparing files or moving data from one file to another.

This approach is all you need to read the entire contents of a file entirely into the computer's memory ready for Perl to manipulate. If you're using small files, this works fine, but with larger files like those often found in bioinformatics it may be impractical to load the whole file in memory at once (as some files can be larger than the memory capacity (RAM) of your computer). Instead, you would read them in one line at a time, as opposed to all at once, thus keeping the memory of your computer relatively empty. Consider the following:

```
open(FILE, "whole_human_genome.fasta");
while (<FILE>) {
  print $_;
}
close FILE;
```

In the above code, the opening and closing of the file are the same as shown previously, as is the end result of the program—it prints the contents of the file to the console. The difference here is that instead of reading the file completely into an array (and, therefore, into the computers memory), we keep the file open and read it in one line at a time through the use of a `while` loop. The advantage of this approach is that it allows you to extract data from files of any size without ever exceeding the memory capacity of your computer. As we only read one line of the file into memory at a time, perform whatever operations we would like to perform, and then move onto the next line of the file, this method is suitable no matter what the file size is. The most important thing to consider when using this second approach is that all operations that you would like to carry out on your file must be carried out within the `while` loop, as this is the only section of your code where each line of your file will be available within your program (unless you save portions or the whole file out into a variable).

3.6.2 Writing text files

Just as Perl can read from text files, so we can create and write to text files. This is invaluable for permanently recording the output of our Perl programs. The good news is that there is no need to learn a new function to do this we can write files using the `open()` function that we used previously to read files. The following code shows us how to do just that:

```
open(FILE,">output.txt"); # Open the file "output.txt" for writing
print FILE "Some example text \n"; # Put something in the file
close FILE; # Close the file
```

The above code will create a text file in your current directory called `output.txt`, containing the text 'Some example text'. The differences in this snippet of code that allow us to write, rather than read a file are found within the first two lines: the first change is that we added the > symbol in front of the file name when opening the file. The second difference is the use of the file handle— instead of using it to insert the contents of the file into an array we use the file handle along with the now familiar `print` command to print data into the file, just as if we were printing to the command line. A word of warning when creating and writing to files in this manner: If there is already a file in your working directory with the same name as the file you wish to write to, Perl will overwrite it and you will lose the contents of the original file. There are no warnings or 'are you sure?' questions to make sure you want to overwrite a file, Perl will just go ahead and delete the file before creating its own.

This is not the only way to write to files in Perl. There is a slightly less destructive approach known as appending data to a file. This allows you to add text to the end of a pre-existing file. An example of the code used to achieve this is shown below:

```
open(FILE,">>output.txt"); # Open the file for APPENDING text
print FILE "Yet more example text \n"; # Add something
close FILE; # Close the file again
```

If you create and run the above program, then look in the file `output.txt` you will find the line from the previous program, as well as the new line of text: 'Yet more example text'. This was achieved by using two > symbols in front of the file name—this instructs Perl to add the given text onto the end of an already existing file (although, if no file exists with the specified name, Perl will create a new one). Sometimes you might want to overwrite an existing file, if that is the case use the first approach we showed for writing files (using a single >), otherwise it might be good practice to use the append approach by default as you can always delete text from a file, but you cannot retrieve a file that you have inadvertently overwritten.

3.6.3 Directory operations

Reading and writing files in the current directory is a great way to learn how to handle files in our programs; however, this soon becomes limiting when we start tackling real bioinformatics problems. Thankfully, Perl has many built-in functions for navigating your computer's directory structure.

Creating directories

A typical scenario might be that you are performing operations on a large number of files and the end result of your program is even more files. Doing all this in one directory is feasible, but it could make your life difficult as you have to manually sort out the files afterwards. Another option would be to have your Perl program create a directory in which to store its new results. This can be achieved using the mkdir() function:

```
mkdir('MyResults') # Creates a new directory called MyResults
```

The code above will create a new directory with the name MyResults.

Changing directories

Let's say that we want to interact with some files, but they are not in our current directory. You could move them into your current directory, or even move the Perl program into the same directory as your files and run it from there. Obviously, this is a hassle to do manually, so instead we would use Perl's chdir() function to change the directory:

```
chdir('/home/user') # Moves us to /home/user
chdir('..')         # Moves up one directory
chdir($ENV{HOME})   # Moves into our 'home' directory (unix only)
```

As you can see from the code above—chdir() is quite simple to use, you just put the name of the directory that you want to change to (either the full path or a path relative to your current directory) in the brackets after the command. On Unix systems you can even use the built-in environment variables (such as $HOME) that would immediately get you the full directory path for your home directory.

Getting the contents of a directory (globbing)

Another common task is to retrieve a list of all of the files in a given directory. This can be achieved by using the glob function:

```
my @files = glob "*";   # Gets the entire contents of our current
                        # directory (directories included)
my @html = glob "*.html"  # Only gets the HTML files
my @root = glob "/*"    # Gets the contents of the root directory
my @html2 = <*.html>    # Another way of using glob!
```

The above code shows us the basic syntax for using glob, and the two ways we can go about using it to retrieve a list of files in a given directory. The one thing that you must remember when using glob is that it does not differentiate between directories and files, so you must be careful with what you try to do with the resulting list. For example, if you tried to open a directory for editing as if it were a text file, this would throw an error. When such errors occur, we can handle these as explained in the next section.

3.7   Error handling

If you're new to programming, you might think that a well written program should never throw an error while its running. Surely if the program code has been carefully written, tested and debugged then nothing untoward should ever occur? However, most programs rely on interactions with external resources, such as user input, data files, computer hardware, and network resources. Because these outside factors are beyond the programmer's control, things can sometimes go wrong and Perl will throw an error. In this section, we outline a couple of steps you can take within your programs to watch for, catch, and deal with errors.

The 'or die' approach

One of the simplest ways of dealing with errors in your Perl scripts is to terminate your program in the event of an error—this is done by using the die command that we met earlier. Here are two examples of using this approach:

```
chdir('/home/public') || die "Can't move to/home/public: $! \n";
open(FILE, ">newfile.txt") || die "Can't create file: $! \n";
```

In the above two lines of code, we use the 'or die' approach to error handling twice.[1] In the first line, we try to change our current directory to /home/public. If the move to the directory works, the Perl program continues as normal if, however, something goes wrong (e.g. the directory does not exist or we do not have the correct permissions to view the directory), the chdir() function will return false because as it didn't work and the program will exit via the die command. To make it apparent where and why the program died, it will also print out the message specified after the die statement—the message also includes a message from the Perl interpreter telling us why the error occurred, this is printed using the $! shortcut variable. In the second line of code, we try to open or create a file for writing. In the event of something going wrong (e.g. we do not have write permissions for the file or the directory), the program exits and tells us where it all went wrong and the specific Perl error message again.

The 'or die' approach to error handling is not just used in file operations; you can use it anywhere in your program when you use a function call. This approach to catching errors, whilst useful, is very basic and crucially doesn't allow your program to keep on running. There are, however, more versatile ways of catching an error and letting your program continue to run—we shall look at these next, but if the sole purpose of your program is to create and write files to a certain directory on your system, and if your program cannot access the directory in the first place, the best thing it could do is exit very quickly and tell you why.

---

1 We use the syntax || for consistency with previous examples, but the word or can be used instead.

Catch and deal with errors using 'eval'

If we want our program to do more than just stop when an error occurs, we use `eval` (short for evaluate). Consider the example below:

```
# evaluate this section of code...
eval {
  open (FILE, ">myoutput.txt") || die;
  print FILE "Our output.";
}; # note the ; at the end of the eval block—this is required!

# if an error occurs, do the following...
if ($@) {
  print "Ooops, an error occurred: " . $! . "\n";
}
# the program carries on running from here
```

In the above example we call the function `eval` on a code block that has the potential to throw up errors (in this example, opening/creating and printing to a file). This section of code is run, but if an error occurs, the program does not exit as with `die`, instead it just exits the `eval` block and carries on, but it then sets the value of a special variable `$@` to true to indicate that an error occurred. We then put some fallback code after the eval block to test if an error occurred (using `$@`), so if an error did occur we can do something about it—if not we ignore the fallback code.

Notice in the above code the combination of both `eval` and `die`. This is the most common approach to error trapping and handling in Perl. We still try to catch all of our errors on every line possible via the use of `die`, but we surround blocks of code that we would like to handle more gracefully with `eval`, so in the event of an error the program does not exit, it carries on using a pre-determined back-up plan.

We shall be using error catching for the rest of the chapter in our examples as appropriate, and we will touch more on the uses of `eval` shortly, whilst talking about transaction handling with databases. We just have one final warning about using `eval`. Although it allows a program to continue running, the state of variables, file handles, etc., can be unpredictable after an error's been caught if you're not sure exactly where in the `eval` code block the error occurred. So, the program should continue with caution.

3.8   Retrieving files from the internet

So, we can read data from local files and handle any errors that may occur. In bioinformatics the files we need are often stored remotely, somewhere on the internet, and we needed to write programs to go off and retrieve them. One way to do this is through the use of the built-in Perl module `LWP::Simple` and its function `get()`. This function performs a HTTP request (as a web browser would do) to a given URL and returns the contents of the file that it finds at the given URL as a string.

Below is an example program using LWP::Simple to copy a CSV file from www. bixsolutions.net. The file contains a table of data, which is described in more detail in the next chapter. After acquiring the file, the program performs various manipulations on the data and prints the resulting data object to the screen. Much of this should be familiar—the only new technology is the use of LWP::Simple and get(). You can find the program itself at www.bixsolutions.net—it's called get_example.pl.

```perl
#!/usr/bin/perl

use strict;
use warnings;
use LWP::Simple;
use Data::Dumper;

# This is the URL of the file we wish to fetch, this could
# even just be a webpage - we would then fetch the HTML code.
# (for more information on HTML, see chapter 5)

my $file_data = get('http://www.bixsolutions.net/profiles.csv')
or die "Unable to fetch file! \n";

# Now onto playing with the data, first let's split the lines up...

# NOTE: we use \r\n here to split the file line by line as this is a file
# generated on a Windows machine. If it was a file generated on a Linux/
# Unix/Mac OS machine we would simply use \n

my @data = split("\r\n", $file_data);

# Now remove and process the header line
my $header_line = shift(@data);
my @headings = split(",", $header_line);

# Create an empty array to hold our sample information
my @sample_data;

# Then process the samples
foreach (@data) {
  my @sample = split(",", $_);

  # Now we convert this to a hash using the
  # column headings as the keys and put it into the
  # @sample_data array as a refernce...

  my %sample_hash;

  for (my $i=0; $i<scalar(@sample); $i++) {
    $sample_hash{$headings[$i]} = $sample[$i];
  }

  push(@sample_data, \%sample_hash);
}
```

```
# Now look at the resulting data structure...

print "Here is our data: \n";
print Dumper(@sample_data);

exit;
```

This demonstrates how easy it is to pull data off of the internet. As stated in some of the comments in the program, this can be used for any textual file type or even a web page itself. Other common uses for this technique are retrieving things such as GenBank files of FASTA files containing sequence data needed for analysis. The `get()` function can also be used for a technique called *screen scraping*, where a program is used to extract information directly from web pages by downloading the HTML code that makes up the pages (see Chapter 5) and searching through the code for the information of interest using regular expressions.

3.8.1   Utilizing NCBI's eUtilities

As another example of Perl's ability to retrieve and interpret files off of the internet, we would like to give you a brief introduction to automated querying of the databases available at the NCBI—this is achieved through the use of NCBI's Entrez Programming Utilities (also known as eUtils).

The eUtils are a web-based service that allows efficient searching of the databases through programmatic means, instead of via a web browser. You communicate with eUtils by making a HTTP connection (via `LWP::Simple`) to a given URL that defines our search. The information that is returned is in XML, and is therefore easily readable by machines. There is comprehensive information about eUtils at NCBI (eutils.ncbi.nlm.nih.gov/entrez/query/static/eutils_help. html), so in this chapter we restrict ourselves to demonstrating the capability of eUtils by considering a single case study—retrieving bibliographic information from PubMed. A program to do this is shown below (it's also available on our web site as `eutils_example.pl`).

```
#!/usr/bin/perl

use strict;
use warnings;
use LWP::Simple;

# Set up the query URL
my $utils = 'http://www.ncbi.nlm.nih.gov/entrez/eutils';
my $db = 'Pubmed';
my $query = 'BRCA1';

# Set up a search out to the eSearch program:
# - we set the 'db' param to our database (pubmed)
# - and set the number of results we want as 1 (retmax)
# - leave the search term blank for now (term)
```

```perl
my $esearch = $utils . '/esearch.fcgi?db=' . $db .
'&retmax=1&term=';

# Now submit the search and retrieve the XML based results
my $esearch_result = get( $esearch . $query );

print "----------------------\n";
print "--- eSearch Results ---\n";
print "----------------------\n\n";
print $esearch_result . "\n";

# Get the ID for the paper that we have found
$esearch_result =~ m|.*<Id>(.*)</Id>.*|s;
my $id = $1;

# Now set up a request to the eFetch program to retrieve our paper

my $report = 'abstract'; # we only want to fetch the abstract
my $mode = 'text'; # we want a text output, not XML

my $efetch =
 $utils . '/efetch.fcgi?db=' . $db
 . '&rettype=' . $report . '&retmode=' . $mode
 . '&id=' . $id;

# Get our paper
my $efetch_result = get($efetch);

print "----------------------\n";
print "--- eFetch Results ---\n";
print "----------------------\n\n";
print $efetch_result . "\n";</>
```

This program connects directly to NCBI to search PubMed for a paper about the breast cancer gene BRCA1. This is done using two of the NCBI eUtils programs—eSearch and eFetch:

- We first build up the URL for an eSearch query. This is basically how you use the NCBI's eUtils—you define the program that you wish to use and the parameters that you wish to send in a URL.

- Once we have built up our eSearch query URL, we send a HTTP request (using the get() method), which returns an XML response.

- We then use a regular expression to extract the returned id from eSearch, this is the PubMed ID of the paper that was returned from our search. This takes advantage of the fact that the ID is known to be contained between the <Id> and </Id> XML tags.

- Next we prepare our URL for eFetch—this is used to retrieve more information about the paper of interest. In this URL we define the information that we want to retrieve (the paper's abstract in this case), and how we would like to get it—options are HTML (the default), XML and plain text (in the example, we select the latter). We also add the `id` from the `eSearch` query to denote the paper that we would like to get.

♦ Finally, we send our HTTP request to the `eFetch` URL. This returns the paper's abstract to us in plain text, as requested.

This is the generic approach that you can use to query the NCBI's databases via eUtils. In addition to `eSearch` and `eFetch`, there are several other programs on offer for tasks such as inter-database links. If you're ever likely to need to automatically interrogate the databases at the NCBI, we would most definitely recommend considering the use of the NCBI eUtils. For most other database interactions, we usually connect to the database directly using DBI, which is introduced below.

3.9   Accessing relational databases using Perl DBI

As discussed in the previous chapter, relational databases are the storage method of choice when you have large quantities of data that you need to arrange and query, as is often the case in bioinformatics. So, it is essential that Perl allows us to easily interact with such databases. This provides a platform for automated database manipulation, which forms the basis of many bioinformatics applications, from high throughput data analysis to web-based tools.

The easiest way of dealing with databases in Perl is with the DBI (database interface) module, which comes as standard with Perl installations. Perl DBI works by adding a database interaction layer to Perl. This means that your Perl program interacts with the DBI layer and from there the DBI layer talks to your database by using an appropriate database driver. A graphical overview of how Perl DBI works can be seen in Fig. 3.4. The benefit of this approach is that your Perl code is pretty much database independent and should work no matter what the database server is (MySQL, Oracle, PostgreSQL, etc.), the only thing that you would have to change would be the drivers that you use—these are known as DBD drivers (database dependant drivers).

3.9.1   Installing `DBD::MySQL`

Before we move on to look at an example of connecting Perl to a MySQL database, we must first install the DBD driver (`DBD::MySQL`) on our systems in order for us to be able to use it to connect to our MySQL server.

Windows users

The Windows distribution of Perl (ActiveState Perl) comes with a package manager called the Perl Package Manager or PPM for short. We shall discuss this in more detail later in this chapter, but for now we just need to use PPM to install `DBD::MySQL`. PPM is called and used from the Windows command line. To launch the PPM interface, simply type `ppm` and press Enter—the PPM graphical user interface will then appear and you can search for and install `DBD::MySQL`

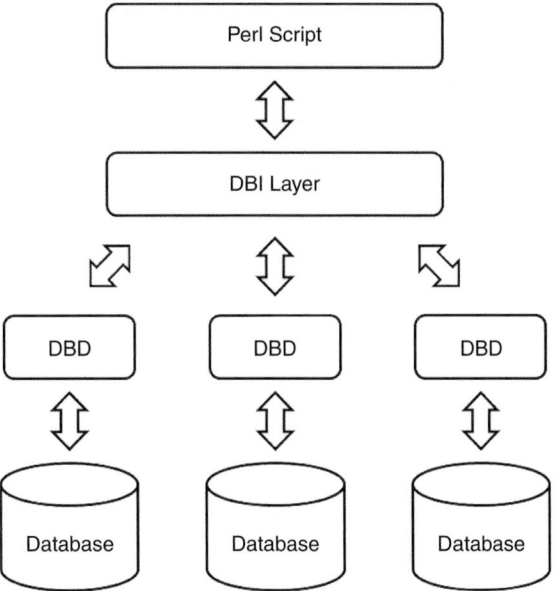

Fig. 3.4 An overview of how Perl DBI works. The DBI layer sits between your Perl code and the database, using a database-specific driver to talk to the database server.

(the interface is simple enough to need no explanation). Alternatively, you can use PPM entirely from the command line by issuing this command to install `DBD::MySQL`.

```
ppm install DBD::MySQL
```

Depending on your specific version of ActiveState Perl, the instructions above may not work because the DBI module may not currently be located in the main ActiveState PPM repository. To install `DBI` you will, therefore, need to add the more comprehensive University of Winnipeg repository (http://theoryx5. uwinnipeg.ca/ppms/) to your PPM setup. You will find the option to add extra repositories in PPM's Preferences menu. Having done this, simply search for and install 'dbd-mysql' within PPM.

Linux

`DBD::MySQL` will be found for install in your distributions package manager. Simply search for 'dbd-mysql' or 'DBD::MySQL' and install the relevant packages and their dependencies.

Mac OS X

Unfortunately, the install of `DBD::MySQL` is not quite as straightforward in Mac OS X. Rather than wasting precious space here explaining how to install it we would direct you to www.bixsolutions.net where you can find a short guide to getting `DBD::MySQL` installed.

3.9.2 Connecting to a database

The first thing that we need to do when working with a database in Perl is to set up the connection details and establish a connection to our database so that the rest of our program knows where to send database requests. The program below uses Perl DBI to connect to the MySQL database created in the previous chapter:

```perl
#!/usr/bin/perl

use strict;
use warnings;

use DBI; # Load in the DBI module
use DBD::MySQL; # Load the MySQL driver

# First, the connection details of the MySQL server

my $ds = "DBI:mysql:PCR_experiment:localhost";
my $user = "user_name"; # Our MySQL username
my $passwd = "pass"; # Our MySQL password

# Now to connect to the database...

my $dbh = DBI->connect($ds,$user,$passwd) || die "Can't Connect!";
```

So, when using DBI in your Perl scripts you need to use two specific modules. The first is DBI itself (the database independent layer that you and your program interact with) and a DBD driver (which is the database specific part that actually talks to our database server). In the example code above, we have loaded in DBI and the DBD::MySQL driver as we are using MySQL databases.

The next section of the above code lays out the connection details for the database that we are using. The first variable that we establish, $ds (short for datasource) is the most detailed and therefore requires some explanation. The datasource is made up of four colon-separated arguments: the first argument is simple—we are stating that we are using DBI; the second argument is the DBD driver that we wish to use (in our case—MySQL); the third argument is the database name; and the final argument is the database server's host name. So the general syntax of the datasource is as follows:

```
DBI:DBD Driver:Database Name:Database Host
```

Following this, we then specified our username and password to be passed onto the database server. The final line of code actually connects to the database:

```perl
my $dbh = DBI->connect($ds,$user,$passwd) || die "Can't Connect!";
```

This tells DBI to create a connection to the specified datasource and store this connection in the variable that we have called $dbh (dbh is short for database handle, and is analogous to the file handles introduced earlier). If there is any sort of error on connection to the server, we catch this using a die statement—there is little point in the program continuing if it cannot access the database. If the connection is successful, all subsequent interaction with the database is done through the database handle variable ($dbh).

3.9.3 Querying the database

Now that we have connected to our database, the next thing we might want to do is get some data out of it. We have seen how to do this with SQL queries in the last chapter. Similar functionality is available in Perl. Querying a database using DBI is a three-step process:

• Prepare an SQL statement.

• Execute the SQL statement.

• Retrieve the results.

The following code snippets demonstrate these three steps. Here is the preparation of the SQL:

```
my $sth = $dbh->prepare("SELECT id, sequence
  FROM Experiment
  WHERE design_software LIKE ?");
```

There are three things to note from the above code. First is that we are creating a new variable ($sth)—known as the *statement handle*, creating this variable enables us to refer to this specific statement when we run queries against the database. The second thing to observe is that we are using our database handle ($dbh) to prepare our SQL statement—this ties the SQL statement to our database handle (this is important to note in case you ever have more than one database connection open at once—you need to specify the database connection that your SQL statement is for). The final thing to note is the SQL statement itself—this is a standard SQL SELECT statement, with the addition of a question mark (?) at the end of the statement. This question mark is essentially a placeholder that allows us to use different arguments as part of our database query when we run the statement against the database, as we will now:

```
my $query_variable = 'Primer3';
$sth->execute($query_variable);
```

The above line of code runs the SQL query against the database. We use the $sth variable to specify the statement, which is run by the execute function. We also pass on an argument to the execute method—a variable called $query_variable—this string variable replaces the ? in the SQL statement. (Alternatively, we could pass a hard-coded string constant to execute.) Using this approach allows us to re-use our prepared SQL statements with different query variables. If we wish to use more than one query variable, we simply put more question marks within our SQL statements and then pass the corresponding number of arguments to the execute method, in the right order, separated by commas.

The third and final step in querying a database with DBI is retrieving the results of our database query. An example of this is shown below:

```
while (my @val = $sth->fetchrow_array()) {
      print "id: $val[0], sequence: $val[1]\n";
}
```

The above section of code uses the method `fetchrow_array()` to get results from the database. This returns us results from the database one row at a time, in this case with each field of the database table that we have selected as an element of an array. So in the case of our SELECT query, we asked to get the `id` and `sequence` fields, so these are returned as the first and second element of the array.

At this point we should issue a warning about the use of SELECT * FROM when accessing a database via Perl—this is a very bad idea. When you use * you have no idea how many fields are going to be returned and in what order, which makes programming for it impossible, so the advice here is to select each field that you want returned from your table explicitly—never use SELECT *.

There are several other methods to retrieve data returned from the database, as alternatives to `fetchrow_array()`. We will not be going through all of them as this is far beyond the scope of this introduction, but it's worth touching on two other popular methods: `fetchrow_arrayref()` and `fetchrow_hashref()`. Here is an example of how we would retrieve our statement using `fetchrow_arrayref()`:

```
while (my $ref = $sth->fetchrow_arrayref()) {
  print "id: $ref->[0], sequence: $ref->[1]\n";
}
```

The difference between `fetchrow_array` and `fetchrow_arrayref` is that `fetchrow_arrayref` returns each result from your query as a reference to an array, instead of a normal array. This method has the benefit of some small improvements in execution speed and memory use on larger queries due to the use of referenced arrays.

The next example uses `fetchrow_hashref` to retrieve the query results:

```
while (my $ref = $sth->fetchrow_hashref()) {
  print "id: $ref->{id}, sequence: $ref->{sequence}\n";
}
```

This returns each row of results as a referenced hash variable. The benefit of this approach is that you can now call each returned field by their actual field names (in this case `id` and `sequence`) instead of using the numbers that you have been using with arrays—thus making your code a little easier to understand. The unfortunate downside of this method is that it is both slower and uses more memory when compared with the previous two methods.

One thing to note if you plan on using either of these other two methods for returning your data is that they return referenced variables; therefore, in order to get at the actual data, we must de-reference the variables. In the above example code this is done using the -> operator, which was introduced back in section 3.3.

Now that we have the results of our database query and have looked at several ways to get this result set, we no longer need our connection to the database so must finish our SQL session, and disconnect cleanly from the database. This is done with the following two lines of code:

```
$sth->finish;
$dbh->disconnect;
```

Please note that you must never forget these lines when working with databases in Perl, as failure to cleanly disconnect and close your session with the database could cause problems with the database and possibly even lead to data loss.

3.9.4 Populating the database

We have looked at getting information out of a database, now let's look at the opposite action—inserting data into and updating a database. This procedure is much the same as selecting data from a database. An example program is shown below.

```perl
#!/usr/bin/perl

use strict;
use warnings;

use DBI;
use DBD::MySQL;

my $ds = "DBI:mysql:PCR_experiment:localhost";
my $user = "user_name";
my $passwd = "pass";

my $dbh = DBI->connect($ds,$user,$passwd) || die "Can't Connect!";

# Prepare our insert statement...
my $sth = $dbh->prepare(
 "INSERT INTO Scientist (email, given_name, family_name) VALUES (?,?,?)"
);

# Perform a couple of inserts...
$sth->execute('b.flemming@bixsolutions.net','Bob','Flemming');
$sth->execute('e.hunt@bixsolutions.net','Ethan','Hunt');

# Finish up
$sth->finish;
$dbh->disconnect;
```

The top portion of the program follows the same pattern as the previous examples in which we selected data. Even the preparation of the SQL is the same, albeit that we use an INSERT SQL statement here because we are inserting data, rather than extracting it. As before, the ? characters get replaced by the specified parameters when we execute the SQL command. The main difference is that we are not retrieving data from the database, so the third step where we get results out is not necessary. To do an UPDATE action on a database table, the process and code is the same, except that we would use an UPDATE SQL statement in the prepare() function.

So that is how you interact with your databases using Perl and DBI. Basically, if you can interact with a database using SQL, you can interact with a database using Perl and DBI. However, now that we are looking at both putting data in, as well as getting it out of our databases, we need to consider the inevitable—something going wrong! We therefore need to prepare for and cope with errors whilst carrying out operations on a database.

3.9.5   Database transactions and error handling

The normal way of handling errors that occur when working with databases is by using the concept of *transactions*, as discussed in the previous chapter. The same approaches can be used in Perl. However, by default, Perl DBI makes permanent changes to the database on the completion of each line of code, so we have to add a small bit of extra code and error handling to ensure that the intended database transactions are carried out correctly and safely. Below is a sample program that shows how to deal with correct transaction handling:

```perl
#!/usr/bin/perl

use strict;
use warnings;

use DBI;
use DBD::MySQL;

my $ds = "DBI:mysql:PCR_experiment:localhost";
my $user = "user_name";
my $passwd = "pass";

my $dbh = DBI->connect($ds,$user,$passwd) || die "Can't Connect!";
$dbh->{'AutoCommit'} = 0; # Turn off AutoCommit

my $sth = $dbh->prepare(
  "INSERT INTO Scientist (email, given_name, family_name) VALUES (?,?,?)"
);

# Now let us check for errors as we insert data
eval {
    $sth->execute('b.flemming@bixsolutions.net','Bob','Flemming');
    $sth->execute('e.hunt@bixsolutions.net','Ethan','Hunt');
};

# Check for any errors in the above
```

```
if ($@) {
  $dbh->rollback;
} else {
  $dbh->commit;
}

# Finish up
$sth->finish;
$dbh->disconnect;
```

This performs the same actions as the previous INSERT example, but now has error and transaction handling added in to ensure that our database activities are carried out cleanly. There are three extra additions to the code, the first is the setting of the AutoCommit option for DBI—basically we are turning it off so that we explicitly have to tell the database server to commit our changes to the database. (By default DBI would commit immediately). The second and third changes are where we use the eval method of error trapping to run our INSERT statements. If the statements are executed without any problems, we then tell the database to commit the changes to storage, but if there are errors we rollback the current session so that everything we have just tried to do does not impact the database, therefore keeping in line with standard transaction handling in databases.

That concludes the basics of using Perl DBI, but there is much more to learn. For more details we would recommend the DBI website (dbi.perl.org) and the Perl DBI CPAN page (search.cpan.org/~timb/DBI/DBI.pm).

3.10   Harnessing existing tools

When creating programs in Perl—or any other language for that matter—there will always be tasks that are common between your scripts. If these are things that are bespoke and only done within your group then you have got some subroutine programming to do, but often, if the activity is quite common to programming or even common in a specific field like bioinformatics, there is a chance that someone will have done this already and possibly released some code on the internet.

This is the great thing about programming within the bioinformatics community—many people like to share their ideas and techniques with each other when they can. If you ever need to do something, but are not quite sure how to get started the answers are probably only a quick web search away. There are many programming blogs and forums on the internet where people dispense advice and give help, tips, and tricks to aid less experienced programmers. In addition to the blogs and forums, there are also code repositories and toolkits that can potentially supply you with ready-made tools to perform your task. In particular, we would draw your attention to two projects that will most definitely help you along your way: CPAN and BioPerl.

3.10.1   CPAN

The Comprehensive Perl Archive Network (CPAN) is a central world-wide repository for Perl code. Within CPAN you will find thousands of Perl modules that you can download and install on your system—it is possibly the richest library of extensions to a programming language available today. CPAN is one of the reasons that Perl is so popular—it can make developing software with Perl quite straightforward.

The basic premise of CPAN is that people supply open source Perl modules to CPAN for anyone to use within their projects. You can simply download and install these on your system, and all of the functionality of the modules you have downloaded will be available to your install of Perl on your system, as discussed back in section 3.4.1. The variety of modules available is far too large to even try to list here, so the best advice we can give is to head over to the CPAN website (www.cpan.org) and read the CPAN FAQ to try get yourself comfortable with how CPAN works and what is available. When you come to install your first CPAN Perl modules, we recommend following these short pieces of advice:

- If you're a Windows user, your distribution of Perl (ActiveState Perl) comes with PPM (Perl Package Manager) as used previously in this chapter. To use this program, simply type `ppm` at the Windows command line and hit Enter—this will launch an easy to use graphical application via which you can install Perl modules on your system. If you cannot find the particular module you are looking for within the lists, look at the install documents for the module on CPAN—there might be a special repository that you need to point PPM to, or some special instructions for Windows users.

- If you're a Linux user, first look through the package management system that came with your distribution—you will more than likely find the vast majority of CPAN modules available, and only a click or two away. If the module you are after cannot be found there, then your next best choice is to look into using the automated command line CPAN module installation program `cpan` (also known as `Cpan.pm`). For information on how to use this either type `man  cpan` at the Linux command line and read the documentation there, or head to `www.cpan.org` and look for some instruction there.

- If you're a Mac user you have several options available for installing modules from CPAN:

  - Cpan.pm—this is the same command-line utility for installing Perl modules as is found on Linux-based systems.

  - MacPorts (www.macports.org)—MacPorts is a framework for easy installation and upgrading of open-source software on your Mac. It's also home of quite a few easy to install Perl modules (among thousands of other programs/libraries).

  - Fink (www.finkproject.org)—Fink is a framework for installing open-source software on your Mac, much in the same vein as MacPorts. We will not go into the differences between the two projects here, but lots of Perl modules can be supplied by this project for your needs. Check out the Fink website for information about the project and how to get started using it.

3.10.2 BioPerl

BioPerl is a set of Perl libraries and subroutines similar to the ones that you would find in CPAN as described above. However, as the 'Bio' in BioPerl might suggest, these libraries are designed specifically for use in bioinformatics tasks. Learning about the functionality of BioPerl and understanding how to harness it will save you massive amounts of work over time. Just take a look at the example code below (adapted from the BioPerl wiki), where we create a DNA sequence object, print some details about it, and then save the DNA sequence in a FASTA format-ted text file:

```perl
#!/usr/bin/perl

use strict;
use warnings;

use Bio::Seq;
use Bio::SeqIO;

# create a sequence object of some DNA
my $seq = Bio::Seq->new(-id => 'testseq', -seq => 'CATGTAGATAG');

# print out some details about it
print "seq is ", $seq->length, " bases long\n";
print "revcom seq is ", $seq->revcom->seq, "\n";

# write it to a file in Fasta format
my $out = Bio::SeqIO->new(-file => '>testseq.fasta', -format => 'Fasta');
$out->write_seq($seq);
```

As you can see, the BioPerl functions `Seq` and `SeqIO` do a lot of the tedious work for you, making your programs easier to read and—most importantly—faster to write. With the basic understanding of Perl provided in this chapter, you should be ready to start exploiting BioPerl in your projects. To get started, visit the website (www.bioperl.org).

3.10.3 System commands

As well as using Perl programming libraries in your programs, it's also possible to integrate entire other programs into your Perl programs. This is done through the use of the `system()` function. With this function we can call any other program or command that it's possible to call from the operating system command line. This function is of great use for pipelining several other programs together—a very common activity in bioinformatics—or for incorporating algorithms that have been tried, tested and optimized for speed (e.g. BLAST). An example of `system()` in use appears in Chapter 5.

3.11 Alternatives to Perl

As stated earlier, Perl is just one of many programming languages that can be used in bioinformatics. Each language has both strengths and weaknesses, and when it comes to deciding which one to use for a given project, you need to carefully consider the requirements of your project and which language is most suited to it. Below, we briefly outline a few of the obvious alternatives to Perl, and give an indication of when and where it might be applicable to consider these languages instead of Perl.

3.11.1   Python, Ruby and other scripting languages

Python and Ruby are scripting languages just like Perl. The big differences between these languages and Perl is the concept of object-orientation—both Python and Ruby are fully object-orientated programming languages, whereas Perl is not. Although Perl can do object-orientated code, it's not as cleanly done as in Python or Ruby, as it has been added into Perl over time, rather than being a founding concept of the language.

   The full benefits of object orientation are well beyond the scope of this book, suffice to say that object oriented code is very good for writing maintainable, well designed, and large applications as you break the tasks of coding down into small, manageable chunks. You can, however, do the same quite easily in Perl, it just takes discipline. In a full object orientated language you are forced to comply with these concepts, which can be challenging for those new to programming and can even slow down experienced coders.

   Python and Ruby are both newer languages than Perl: Perl first appeared in 1987, Python in 1991, and Ruby later still in 1995. Being new is both a blessing and a curse. The blessing is that the newer languages take advantage of more modern programming concepts, such as object orientation, but the curse is that people have been working on and with Perl for much longer so there are more books, modules and other helpful resources available.

   Both Python and Ruby are actively used in bioinformatics circles, and have very similar syntax to Perl, so it might be worth exploring them once you've mastered Perl.

3.11.2   Java, C/C++, and other compiled languages

As we said above Perl, Python, and Ruby are scripting languages (they are also called *interpreted* languages). This essentially means that you can just take a program written in any of the above and just run it, as programs are automatically converted into code that the computer can understand while they run. This makes scripting languages easy to develop programs with as there are few steps needed to get a program going. Java and C/C++, however, are different in the fact that there is an extra step needed to run your programs—you must compile your source code into a binary file before running it. This adds one extra step in the preparation of your programs, but the benefit of this approach is speed—compiled programs run much faster than interpreted programs. This is why these languages are very popular when you have some computationally demanding task that needs to be done. For example, sequence alignment tools, such as BLAST and SSAHA are implemented in C as this makes them as efficient as possible—if they were coded in Perl they would run much more slowly.

We are not really going to say much more than that, as the scope of these other languages is huge. Basically, Java and C++ are object-orientated languages, whereas C is mostly procedural, but like Perl, can be coaxed into some form of object orientation. The great news is that most of the concepts covered in this chapter, such as variables, subroutines, loops and conditionals are common to most programming languages, so if you have grasped these you will find it easy to explore other languages. The biggest irritation will probably be learning the slightly different syntax.

3.11.3 Workflows

Some people will tell you you can automate bioinformatics processes without doing any programming at all, by using the concept of *workflows*. A workflow is a formally defined set of actions designed to achieve a desired goal. As such, a given workflow could be implemented by writing a Perl program, but when referring to workflows in bioinformatics we are usually talking about alternative workflow design processes, such as software that allows you to build a workflow by connecting together visual representations of components. The components might be stand alone programs or resources available on the internet. In our experience, this approach is not as flexible as writing your own programs, but it's a rapidly developing field and certainly worth watching. The best way to find out more about workflows is to experiment with a workflow design system, such as Taverna Workbench (taverna.sourceforge.net).

3.12 Summary

That concludes our introduction to programming in Perl. Clearly, we have not been able to cover every facet of the language, but we covered the fundamentals and those features of Perl that make it such a popular choice for building bioinformatics solutions. As mentioned earlier, a lot of the fundamental concepts in Perl are common to other programming languages, so having worked through this chapter you should feel confident in your ability to master other languages. A good test of this comes in the next chapter, where we introduce the statistical language, R.

References

Stubblebine, T. (2007) *Regular Expression Pocket Reference: Regular Expressions for Perl, Ruby, PHP, Python, C, Java and .NET*. O'Reilly: Sebastapol, California, USA.
Tisdall, J. (2001). *Beginning Perl for Bioinformatics*. O'Reilly: Sebastapol, California, USA.
Tisdall, J. (2003). *Mastering Perl for Bioinformatics*. O'Reilly: Sebastapol, California, USA.
Wall, L., Christiansen, T. & Orwant, J. (2000). *Programming Perl*. O'Reilly: Sebastapol, California, USA.

CHAPTER 4

Numerical data analysis using R

Mathematics and statistical processing of data, and the visualization of the results of such processing are a key part of many bioinformatics applications. The most obvious applications are in domains such as transcriptomics and metabolomics, where there is a wealth of quantitative data, but even when the acquired data is non-numeric, as in sequence analysis, there is a necessity to perform statistical analysis to determine, for example, the significance of the results acquired.

In recent years, the statistical programming language R has become the tool of choice for such analysis. The aim of this chapter is to introduce R, to explain how it can be used to analyse and visualize biological data, and to begin to explain how R functionality can be integrated into bioinformatics solutions. Naturally, in a chapter of this length it is not possible to cover every facet of R. To get some idea of what that might involve, the PDF reference manual provided with R runs to some 1500 pages and that doesn't even cover the many add-on packages available. The intention of this chapter is therefore to introduce the key concepts of R, to provide a starting point, and illustrate the functionality that is most applicable to bioinformatics. We particularly emphasize the use of R as a software development tool as it can be integrated with Perl and MySQL, facilitating the creation of very sophisticated bioinformatics software. Directions to further information, such as R's useful help system, are provided to allow you to then develop your understanding in whatever way your particular applications require.

In terms of the data analysis techniques covered here, this also cannot be exhaustive because the bioinformatics community has spawned hundreds of algorithms for data analysis, and more are being published every month. For this chapter, we have chosen examples of analyses that can be applied to a wide range of datasets, and to which R is particularly well suited. We also emphasize the commonalities between different types of data set; although bioinformaticians often classify themselves according to the type of data they work with, experience shows that many analysis methods can each be applied to data from a range of different analytical platforms. If you do want to find out about a specific algorithm, it should be apparent where to find information about it once you've read this chapter and quite possibly there is an R package out there to do exactly what you want.

One area we have purposefully avoided including in this chapter is univariate statistical methods, such as significance tests and ANOVA. The main reason for this is that such techniques are dealt with at length in most other introductions to R, so we would refer you to those. Furthermore, if you only wanted to do this type of analysis you may choose a less flexible, but more user-friendly software package, such as Microsoft Excel, GenStat, or Statistica. Such packages are very capable tools for numerical data analysis and visualization, but they suffer from three key limitations. First, they are not particularly flexible—adapting or adding a new algorithm or graph type may be possible, but it is not always easy. Secondly, integration with other tools is not straightforward—if we want to incorporate some data analysis functionality into a web-based analysis tool, this is not the way to go. Finally, these packages are designed around the concept of a user sitting down and performing the analysis via a graphical user interface. This is fine for small analyses, but in bioinformatics where data sets can be large and analysis repetitive, there is often a need for automation. Some packages, such as Microsoft Excel, have built-in programming languages for automation and, as we saw in Chapter 3, programming languages such as Perl are ideal for automating repetitive procedures on large amounts of data. Such programming languages are, however, designed to be general purpose, and lack the native data structures, built in functions, and often the performance to tackle mathematical problems efficiently. In a general purpose language like Perl, all but the simplest mathematical procedures have to be implemented from a fairly low level, which can lead to long development times and concerns over the veracity of the implementation, and ultimately programs that are painfully slow when applied to large data sets.

4.1   Introduction to R

Several software packages have been developed to fill the gap between programming languages and point-and-click analysis packages, and R is foremost among these in the bioinformatics community. R is an entirely free open source package, which has at its core an implementation of the statistical programming language S, which is also the basis for the commercial S-Plus software package. R supports the installation of add-ons, called *packages*, to extend its basic functionality into specialist areas, and is available for a range of operating systems, including Windows, Linux, and Mac OS. R has become the data analysis tool of choice in bioinformatics partly due to the open source and platform-independent ethos of bioinformatics, but also because many high quality add-on packages have been produced by the bioinformatics community (for example, the BioConductor packages described in section 4.3.1). The popularity of R in the bioinformatics community is therefore perpetuated, as anyone planning to release data analysis tools to the community will generally want to do this as an R package because there is a large potential audience with R installed, so curious users will not be put off by having to change operating system or buy commercial software in order to try it out.

It is for these reasons that we have chosen R as the platform for the numerical data analysis part of this book. The techniques introduced are, however, reasonably generic and if you're particularly devoted to another package, section 4.4 at the end of this chapter includes information about moving between R and alternatives such as Matlab, Octave, and S-Plus.

4.1.1 Downloading and installing R

The process of getting hold of R may seem a little less slick than you might be used to for other software, but it is, nevertheless, a fairly painless process. R's home on the web is www.r-project.org. Here, you can find some background information about R, links to manuals, and other documentation. The software itself is hosted on the Comprehensive R Archive Network (CRAN)—a worldwide network of servers from which R, R packages, and other related files can be downloaded. Clicking on the CRAN link on the R homepage brings up a list of CRAN servers, from which it makes sense to select the one closest to you. There is a range of different forms in which to download R, but for beginners the pre-compiled binary setup program for the base R system is the file to go for. This is available via the front page of any of the CRAN mirrors simply by clicking on the operating system you're using in the 'Download and Install R' pane.

- For Windows, this file will be called something like R-2.5.1-win32.exe, depending on the version number (in this case version 2.5.1). Executing this file launches a familiar Windows Setup Wizard, which will install R on your computer. The default installation options should be fine for most people, although we recommend that you tick all the boxes relating to installation of PDF documentation as this includes several excellent manuals, which are very useful when learning R. Once installed, you can start R by clicking on the icon on the desktop or in the Start menu, just like any other Windows application.

- If you're running Mac OS X, the file you need will be called something like R-2.5.1.dmg (again this depends on the current R version number). Download and mount this disk image (double-click on it if it doesn't automatically do this), and you will find the R installation package R.mpkg. Double click on the package and it will launch the installation—just accept the defaults and you will be ready to go. Note that the interface through which you can interact with R will be installed into your Applications folder.

- Installing R on Linux is ideally done using the package manager that came with your Linux distribution. Package managers are quite different between the various flavours of Linux, so we won't have the space here to go into how you would install R on each type of Linux. If you have problems using your package manager or R is not available there, pre-built installation files can be downloaded from the R website for some of the more common Linux distributions. These can be found in the same section as the pre-built Windows and Mac OS X files. You will also find some basic install instructions with the files to help you.

In use, R is very similar across all three platforms, so we won't hear much more about specific operating systems in this chapter. However, add-on packages that have been written using features specific to a particular operating system may not work properly on other systems.

4.1.2 Basic R concepts and syntax

The first thing people notice about R is the rather archaic looking user interface, the R *Console*. It is through this console that most interactions with R take place and, as we will see, while it may not look as inviting as commercial software, it is actually the lack of a graphical user interface that gives R a lot of its power. R's user interface is another example of a command line interface—commands are entered into the console at the prompt (in this case a > symbol), and results are returned in the console window, or in a separate window in the case of graphical output. Depending on your operating system and particular installation of R, the console may exist within something called the *RGui*. The Gui part of the name stands for R graphical user interface, which infers some level of sophistication, but at the time of writing RGui only provides very basic features, most of which have command line equivalents.

Because R is essentially a programming language, many of the concepts are the same as in other programming languages such as Perl. So, for example, there are variables and there are functions. One difference with R is that, as well as writing programs, we can work with these variables and execute these functions interactively in real time, right there in the console. This is useful for prototyping or doing a one-off analysis. As an example, let's consider a right-angled triangle, with sides of length x and y, and hypotenuse of length z. We can assign specific values to the variables of x and y by typing the following two commands at the R command line (hit Enter after each command):

```
x <- 3
```

```
y <- 4
```

The backwards arrow formed from the less than character (<) and the minus character (-) indicates the flow of data, i.e. values on the right are being assigned to variables on the left. (Values can also be assigned to variables using the = character, as in Perl, but <- is more commonly seen in R.) We can check the values assigned to these variables simply by typing the variable name at the command line and then pressing Enter. An example of this is action is shown below:

```
> x
[1]  3
```

As expected, the variable x contains the value 3. The [1] part of R's output indicates that 3 is the first element in x. This is not very important in this case as x only has one element, but if the output were to be a list of values spanning more than one line then a number would appear in square brackets at the start of each line to indicate the element number of the first value on that line.

Having assigned values to the x and y variables we can manipulate them using operators and functions, just like in any other programming language. Also like other languages, we can append comments to our commands to make them more easily understandable—in R (like Perl) such comments must be preceded by the # character, which causes R to ignore everything that follows on that line. An example session with R, using the x and y variables defined above, is shown below:

```
> x+y                 # add the two variables together
[1] 7
> x^2                 # the ^ operator raises a number to a power (in
                      # this case the power of two)
[1] 9
> sqrt(y)             # the built-in sqrt function returns the square
                      # root of the number passed to it
[1] 2
> z <- sqrt(x^2+y^2)  # calculate the length, z, of the hypotenuse of a
                      # right angle triangle using Pythagoras' theorm
> z                   # see what value z has been set to
[1] 5
```

An important point to make at this stage is that R, like Perl and other programming languages, is case sensitive, so a variable Y would be distinct from the variable y—each could have a different value. Similarly, typing SQRT instead of sqrt, would cause R to reply with Error: could not find function "SQRT". To avoid this kind of confusion, function names are generally all lower case, as are most variable names, but this custom is not enforced and sometimes there are legitimate reasons for using upper case. To avoid confusion, refer to our general advice in chapter 1 (section 1.6.3).

All the variables (and other objects that we will learn about later) that you define are stored by R in its *workspace*. The content of this workspace can be seen using the objects command:

```
> objects()
[1] "x" "y" "z"
```

If you try to quit R (by typing quit() in the console, or closing the R window), you may (depending on your particular installation of R) be asked if you would like to save the workspace image. If you do, you'll be able to continue where you left off with these variables next time you start R. Conversely, objects can be removed from the workspace using the remove() function:

```
remove(x)                    # remove variable x from the workspace

remove(list = objects())     # remove all objects from the workspace
```

Note that many R functions can be abbreviated, for example, rm can be used in place of remove or q in place of quit. A useful tool for finding out the abbreviated form of a particular function or, indeed, for finding out what a function does, is the built in help() function. This is invoked simply by passing help the name of the function in question, for example, `help(remove)`. This help system is an invaluable aid for learning and using the many functions available in R and it is recommended that you consult the help system on all the functions and operators introduced in this chapter, as space does not permit us to explore each function in detail. Note that if you enter a function name at the command line without the brackets that should follow it, R will not execute the function, but will instead show you the R source code for the function. This is pretty scary for beginners, but can be useful in some circumstances, once you get more familiar with R.

4.1.3   Vectors and data frames

Of course, a major motivation for using R in bioinformatics is that we want to deal with large biological data sets, not simple variables like those in the example above. To get an idea of how R handles larger data sets, let's consider the data shown in Table 4.1. This data is typical of the type of results that would be acquired from measuring the concentration of various compounds in whole blood samples from a number of patients during a clinical study. In reality, we would doubtless have been monitoring more patients and maybe more compounds, but for the purpose of illustrating concepts a small data set is more convenient. Real data sets are introduced later in the chapter.

In R, we can generate a variable for each patient, in which we can store the biochemical profile for that patient, in terms of the concentrations of the compounds from Table 4.1. We do this using the `<-` assignment operator as before, except that this time we combine or *concatenate* a series of numbers into a list using the `c()` function before the assignment takes place:

```
profile <- c(3, 1150,750,310)
```

In mathematical parlance, a list of numbers like this is referred to as a *vector*. In this particular case and, indeed, in many of the applications that we come across in bioinformatics, this is referred to as a *measurement vector* or *sample vector* as it captures the list of measurements acquired from a sample. We can check that

Table 4.1 Concentration of key metabolites in five patients. The urea concentration has not been recorded for patient 3

Patient number	Concentration of compound in whole blood (g/m^3)			
	Bilirubin	Cholesterol	Glucose	Urea
1	3.0	1150	750	310
2	4.5	1650	2200	200
3	5.0	2150	260	–
4	14.0	1200	650	270
5	3.5	2000	700	320

this new vector contains the correct information by typing its name:

```
> profile
[1] 3 1150 750 310
```

This is a bit like a Perl array, but storing data in this way in R is particularly convenient, as we can perform operations on the whole vector in a single command. For example, we can convert this data from the units of g/m³ to the more commonly used g/cm³ but multiplying by a scaling factor of 10^{-6}:

```
> profile * 1e-6
[1] 0.000003 0.001150 0.000750 0.000310
```

Essentially, you should be able to use any relevant R function or operator on a multi-element variable of this type. This is not typically the case in general purpose programming languages such as Perl, and this is one of the features that makes R so well suited to numerical analysis.

What about getting the whole table of results into R? Well, R has a special type of object for representing tabular data, called a *data frame*. The example below shows one way of generating a data frame that captures the first two columns of Table 4.1:

```
> bilirubin <- c(3, 4.5, 5, 14, 3.5)            # bilirubin column values
> cholesterol <- c(1150,1650,2150,1200,2000)    # cholesterol column values

> results <- data.frame(bilirubin,cholesterol)  # combine in data frame

> results                                        # check data frame content
bilirubin cholesterol
1     3.0      1150
2     4.5      1650
3     5.0      2150
4    14.0      1200
5     3.5      2000
```

So now we have half of our table stored in the R workspace, easily accessible under the name `results`. Essentially, a data frame is like a spreadsheet and, indeed, we can view, edit, and add to the contents this data frame in a familiar spreadsheet-like view using R's built-in `edit()` function. Fig. 4.1 shows the data editor, launched by the command below, after the glucose and urea columns have been added:

```
results <- edit(results) # allow editing values in results data frame
```

The `edit()` function does not change the original data frame, but returns a copy of the frame, including any changes made, when the editor window is closed. To update the data frame with the new edits, the output of the `edit()` function must be assigned back to the data frame. No urea value was entered for patient 3 and the editor has placed NA in the empty cell—this is the code that R uses to indicate missing values. Missing values are common in bioinformatics and

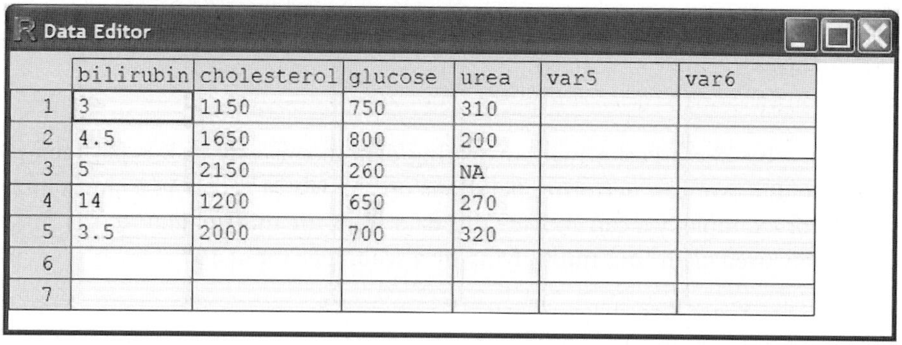

	bilirubin	cholesterol	glucose	urea	var5	var6
1	3	1150	750	310		
2	4.5	1650	800	200		
3	5	2150	260	NA		
4	14	1200	650	270		
5	3.5	2000	700	320		
6						
7						

Fig. 4.1 Editing the content of a data frame in Windows XP.

various methods for dealing with them are described in the literature. Typically, these methods rely on substituting missing values with statistically expected values. For now, it is just good to know that we can flag up such values instead of having to make up a placeholder value such as 0 or −999, which could easily be overlooked and accidentally treated like real data. Before moving on, fill out your `results` data frame with the remaining values.

Just as in the earlier vector example, we can apply most R operators and functions directly to a data frame so, for example, we could multiply the whole frame by a scale factor, just as we did in the previous section. One particularly convenient function is `summary()`, which provides a basic statistical overview of the data contained in a frame. In this case, we can see the range of concentrations of each metabolite across the five patients, as well as mean and median averages:

```
> summary(results)
bilirubin        cholesterol       glucose          urea
Min. 3.0         Min. :1150        Min.: 260        Min. :200.0
1st Qu.: 3.5     1st Qu.: 1200     1st Qu.: 650     1st Qu.: 252.5
Median: 4.5      Median: 1650      Median: 700      Median: 290.0
Mean: 6.0        Mean: 1630        Mean: 632        Mean: 275.0
3rd Qu.: 5.0     3rd Qu: 2000      3rd Qu.: 750     3rd Qu.: 312.5
Max.: 14.0       Max.: 2150        Max.: 800        Max.: 320.0
NA's: 1.0
```

As well as operating on the whole table, it is possible to extract row, columns, or individual elements by specifying specific parts of the table in square brackets (`[]`) immediately after the name of the data frame. Some examples are shown below. There are a couple of counterintuitive things to note in these examples. First, when a single column is extracted the result looks like a row. Secondly, when specifying both a row and column, the row is specified first which seems odd if you're used to working with x, y co-ordinates, where x is the horizontal position and y the vertical:

```
> results[4,] # return just the values in row 4
```

```
        bilirubin      cholesterol      glucose      urea
4       14             1200             650          270

> results[4,1] # return the value at row 4, column 1
[1]     14

> results[,2] # return all values from column 2 (cholesterol)
[1]     1150    1650    2150    1200    2000

> results[1:3,] # return rows 1 to 3
        bilirubin      cholesterol      glucose      urea
1       3.0            1150             750          310
2       4.5            1650             800          200
3       5.0            2150             260          NA

> results[c(2,4),] # return rows 2 and 4
        bilirubin      cholesterol      glucose      urea
2       4.5            1650             800          200
4       14.0           1200             650          270
```

Of course entering data manually as we have done so far is tedious, time consuming, and prone to error. In most real applications data is imported directly from a file or database. This is described later in this chapter. However, the example that we have just worked through gives an indication of how we interact with the R command line. We only used a tiny fraction of R's functionality, but the principle of issuing commands using functions, operators and multi-element variables is really what R is all about, it is just that the functions get more powerful and the variables get larger as you get deeper into R. In the remainder of the chapter, we will look at the general methodology used in biological data analysis, how R can assist us with this, and how we can build programs in R.

4.1.4 The nature of experimental data

A table of numerical data like the `results` data frame used in the previous example is referred to in mathematics as a *matrix* and one of the big breakthroughs in becoming competent in data analysis is realizing that almost all experimental data can be considered in the form of a data matrix. This is because experiments typically entail analysis of more than one sample, and involve the determination of more than one parameter for each sample. We have already seen how a matrix can be used to store metabolic data in the blood analysis example in the previous section. Although that data set was small in terms of the number of metabolites and samples, it would clearly be trivial to extend the number of rows and columns to accommodate the larger data sets that typify metabolomics studies. The general approach is equally applicable to other areas of post genomics, such as transcriptomics and proteomics.

A matrix is a good way of representing experimental data regardless of the type of analytical platform, the number of samples, or the number of measured

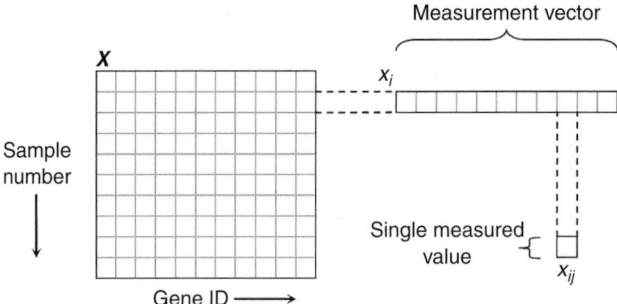

Fig. 4.2 Organization of gene experimental data into a data matrix. For data from a gene expression microarray, the row vector x_i would be the gene expression profile over all genes for a specific sample. Each column of the matrix captures the variation of an individual gene over all samples.

variables. This general way of representing data is shown in Fig. 4.2. Considering the case of a microarray experiment, each variable is a particular gene, and the gene expression levels for each sample can be represented by a vector of expression measurements, denoted mathematically as x_i, where i is the sample number. Within this vector, each element x_{ij} represents the expression level of gene j on the microarray. The expression level of each gene can be considered to be a variable, of which there are many, hence microarray data is referred to as being *multivariate*. Multivariate data analysis techniques, introduced later in section 4.2 , are therefore required to interpret such data.

The vectors representing the gene expression levels from individual samples can be amalgamated into an $I \times J$ data matrix, X, where I is the total number of samples considered and J is the number of genes per microarray. Each row of the X matrix therefore represents an individual microarray, while each column indicates the expression level of each specific gene over all samples. A single data matrix is therefore sufficient to describe all the samples analysed in a given experiment comprising any number of individual arrays.

In transcriptomics more generally, the variables would be the expression level of individual genes, regardless of the analytical platform used. The number of variables considered would be dependent on the platform, ranging from a handful if the data was from traditional PCR, through to many thousands from a microarray experiment. The number of samples would obviously depend on the size of the study being carried out, so may range from a handful through to many hundreds or thousands.

Proteomics data sets can also be considered as a matrix, although exactly what form the data takes depends on the particular proteomics protocol used. If quantitative proteomics has been carried out, then the data will be superficially similar to that seen in transcriptomics except that the value in each element of the matrix will indicate the level of protein expression (either relative or absolute, depending on the protocol) rather than gene expression. However, at the time

Table 4.2 Web server statistics for a very basic web site

	Number of downloads		
	index.html	welcome.png	paper.pdf
Monday	15	13	2
Tuesday	27	26	1
Wednesday	34	30	3
Thursday	10	10	0
Friday	9	7	1

of writing, many proteomics protocols are only capable of indicating whether proteins are present or absent from a sample. For this type of data, we could use some kind of coding scheme, such as 1 for protein present, 0 for protein absent, or R's *factor* data type, which is described later.

There are a lot of different names that can be given to data that is in this form, such as matrix, array, table, or even spreadsheet. As we have seen, R even has its own way of capturing such data—the *data frame*. Exactly which of these classes a dataset belongs to can be technically very important, especially in R, as we will see later, but conceptually they are all the same—they are all matrices. The great benefit of this is that mathematicians have spent many years working with matrices, and developing algorithms for manipulating, analysing, and extracting information from them. The algorithms are there for us to apply to our bioinformatics problems.

To see some matrix mathematics in operation, consider Table 4.2, which summarizes the number of times various files were downloaded from a web server. Each of the files is of a specific size: the front page index.html is just text, taking up 1,624 bytes, welcome.png is a 23,172 byte image on that front page, and paper.pdf is a fairly substantial research paper, taking up 1,234,065 bytes, that can be downloaded via a link in index.html. We can input all this data into R using the commands below. Note that this time, the matrix() function is used to generate a matrix, instead of the data frame used in the previous example (the subtle differences between a matrix and a data frame will be explained soon, in section 4.1.5).

```
> index = c(15, 27, 34, 10, 9)
> welcome = c(13, 26, 30, 10, 7)
> paper = c(2, 1, 3, 0, 1)
> days = c("mon", "tues", "wed", "thurs", "fri")
> filenames = c("index.html", "welcome.png", "paper.pdf")
> downloads = matrix(c(index, welcome, paper), nrow=5,
dimnames=list(days,filenames))

> downloads # check what's in the data frame
```

```
          index.html     welcome.png      paper.pdf
mon       15             13               2
tues      27             26               1
wed       34             30               3
thurs     10             10               0
fri       9              7                1

> filesizes = c(1624, 23172, 1234065)
```

The useful part of this is that R has a built in operator, %*% for multiplying matrices. So, to get the total number of bytes downloaded per day, we can simply multiply the downloads matrix by the filesizes vector:

```
> downloads %*% filesizes
          [,1]
mon       2793726
tues      1880385
wed       4452571
thurs     247960
fri       1410885
```

This is exactly the type of calculation that we do frequently in bioinformatics. For example, we might want to multiply measured values in a matrix by a weighting vector in order to come up with some overall *score* for each sample. R allows us to do this calculation in just one line of code. This is just one example of the matrix functionality built into R—functionality that has great utility in bioinformatics.

Matrices as images—and vice versa

Bitmapped images, such as those coming from microscopes or from scanners of gels or microarrays, are essentially data matrices, in which the value of each element in the matrix represents the colour of the point at that position. Image analysis can therefore be carried out in R by loading images into a data matrix and working with that matrix. This is not as straightforward as it should be, because bitmapped images are not normally stored in a native R format, but in various dedicated image formats (TIF, JPG, PNG, etc.). An appropriate R package or some serious programming is therefore required to convert these files into something that R can handle.

Conversely, experimental matrices can be displayed as images and this is sometimes a useful way of getting a quick overview of a given dataset. Such images are generically referred to as *heatmaps* (although in R a heatmap tends to have additional features). For example, we can generate an image representing the blood analysis results from section 4.1.3 using the image() command below. There is more about heat maps later in this chapter (section 4.3.1):

```
image(as.matrix(results)) # plot results matrix as bitmapped image
```

4.1.5   R modes, objects, lists, classes, and methods

Before going much further it is worth taking time to find out more about how data is stored in the R workspace, and how the various data objects (e.g. vectors, matrices, and data frames) are related.

As we saw in Chapter 2, it is common to consider a particular piece of data as one of several fundamental data types, typically numeric (of which there may be sub-types such as integer and floating point), logical (of which the two-state Boolean type is most common), and character string. R is no exception and every piece of data has to be of one particular basic type: *numeric*, *complex*, *logical*, *character*, or *raw*. In R parlance, these types are sometimes called *modes*. Because some functions can only work with certain data types, R allows conversion from one type to another if necessary. This is done using functions of the form `as.type()`, of which an example is shown below:

```
> x <- 2.17            # assign numeric value 2.17 to x
> y <- as.character(x)  # convert number in x to character string in y
> z <- as.numeric(y)    # convert text in y to number and assign to z
> y                     # show content of y
[1] "2.17"
> z                     # show content of z
[1] 2.17
```

Being limited to these basic data types would be a little restrictive in data analysis applications so R has *objects;* much more complex structures built from these basic data types. Objects are a crucial part of R, and it is impossible to feel comfortable in R without a reasonable understanding of the various classes of object, how to use them, and how they are related. To start with, let's consider the key built-in classes of object in R.

Vectors

We've already come across these, as well as single values (scalars), which are just a special single element type of vector. A key feature of a vector is that every element must be of the same type, e.g. all numbers or all text.

Matrices

Matrices are the next step up from vectors, the only difference being that they can have more than one dimension. As we have seen, two-dimensional matrices are common in bioinformatics and can be considered to be a table of numbers, but a matrix can, in fact, have a third dimension, which transforms it into a cube of numbers. Such a matrix might be used to handle GCMS data, with the three dimensions of the matrix being sample number, elution time, and m/z ratio. Indeed, a matrix may have any number of dimensions if an application requires it, although in most bioinformatics applications two dimensions is enough. As with vectors, it is not possible to mix data of different types (e.g. numbers and text) within a single matrix.

Factors

Factors are R's solution to handling categorical data. A good example of this is capturing qualitative proteomic data, where instead of having a value recorded for each protein in each sample, there is simply an indication of whether the protein is present or not. One solution is to use the Boolean type, with TRUE representing protein presence and FALSE indicating absence of a protein:

```
> proteinpresent <- c(TRUE, TRUE, FALSE, TRUE, FALSE)

> proteinpresent
[1] TRUE TRUE FALSE TRUE FALSE
```

If TRUE and FALSE are not enough we can create our own user-defined discrete states in R by using the factor() function. This can be used to simply represent the data in a more descriptive way, e.g. PRESENT/ABSENT instead of TRUE/FALSE. However, it is most useful when we have more than two states, for example, when we want to flag the level of expression of a protein or gene as one of three states: over-expressed, unchanged, or under-expressed. In the example below an expression vector is created that captures the state of six genes:

```
expression <- factor(c("over","under","over","unchanged",
"under","under"))
```

R functions can be used to manipulate or derive information from such vectors. For example, levels() lists the discrete states present in the data and the behaviour of the summary() function changes to show the occurrence of each level instead of the statistical metrics that would be returned if expression contained quantitative data:

```
> levels(expression)
[1]    "over"     "unchanged"    "under"
> summary(expression)
      over     unchanged     under
       2           1           3
```

Lists

Lists are an extension of the vector concept in which the elements need not be of the same type and may, in fact, be of sophisticated types, such as vectors, matrices, or lists. For example, a list could be used to store information about a protein, specifically the protein name, the PDB accession number, and the formula weight of the protein:

```
protein <- list("glucose oxidase", "1CF3", 63355)
```

This is a bit like a Perl array. Individual elements can be extracted from this list by specifying the number of the element, very much as would be done with a vector, so `protein[2]` would return the accession number 1CF3. Better still, the elements in a list can be named for easy reference and accessed using the `$` symbol. This is similar to a Perl hash:

```
> protein <- list(name="glucose oxidase", accession="1CF3", weight=63355)
> protein$accession # extract the accession number by name
[1] "1CF3"
```

It is also possible to add elements to a list using the `$` symbol. In the example below a vector of Gene Ontology (GO) IDs related to glucose oxidase is created and stored in x. This is added to the `protein` list defined above, and the contents of the list displayed:

```
> x <- c(16614, 50660, 6066, 6118)   # assign list of GO IDs to x
> protein$GOIDs <- x                 # add x to list as new GOIDs field
> protein                            # display content of protein object
$name
[1] "glucose oxidase"

$accession
[1] "1CF3"

$weight
[1] 63355

$GOIDs
[1] 16614 50660 6066 6118
```

Lists are often used in R to pass parameters to a function, such as the parameters required when plotting a graph. Graphing options are necessarily of a heterogeneous type, as they need to include the matrix of data to be plotted, textual labels, and logical settings that specify the plotting style. Similarly, lists are often used to return heterogeneous results from a function in a single object.

Data frames

Technically, a data frame is a specific type of list, but it is more convenient to think of data frames as an extension of the matrix concept. The main benefit over a matrix is that a single data frame can contain columns with different data types. A data frame object is therefore very similar to the spreadsheet object that is common in packages such as Microsoft Excel.

Mixing different data types in a single data frame is particularly useful when dealing with data sets that include DNA or protein sequences, accession numbers, and annotations. Consider the BLAST search results reproduced below:

Accession Number	Description	Score (bits)	E Value
CAA76841.1	albumin [Canis familiaris]	43.1	0.002
P02770	ALBU_RAT Serum albumin precursor	37.1	0.11
AAH85359.1	Albumin [Rattus norvegicus]	37.1	0.11
BAC34360.1	unnamed protein product [Mus musculus]	36.3	0.20
AAA37190.1	alpha-fetoprotein	36.3	0.20

The numerical data can be entered as vectors as in the earlier blood components example. The accession numbers are entered in exactly the same way, we just need to remember to enclose them in quotation marks (") as is common in other programming languages. An example of this in action is shown below:

```
> # concatenate numeric values into vectors as before
> score <- c(43.1,37.1,37.1,36.3,36.3)
> E <- c(0.002, 0.11, 0.11, 0.2, 0.2)

> # list of strings are brought together in the same way
> accn <- c("CAA76841.1","P02770","AAH85359.1","BAC34360.1", "AAA37190.1")

> # now bring the three vectors together to create a data frame
> results <- data.frame(accession=accn, score=score, EValue=E)

> # check contents of the data frame
> results
     accession    score   EValue
1    CAA76841.1   43.1    0.002
2    P02770       37.1    0.110
3    AAH85359.1   37.1    0.110
4    BAC34360.1   36.3    0.200
5    AAA37190.1   36.3    0.200
```

Functions

The objects listed thus far are all designed for holding data. In R, functions are also defined as objects. User-defined functions are therefore stored in the workspace and will be included in the list returned by objects(). Creating functions is explained in section 4.1.8.

Other objects

So, most objects in R fall into one of the above classes. The class of a particular object can be determined using the class() function, so typing class(protein) after the example earlier would reveal that the protein object is a list. In most cases, R functions are written such that they adapt their behaviour to the class of object passed to them—they determine the class of the object before deciding exactly what to do. Other useful functions for finding out about objects are `length()` and `attributes()`, the behaviours of which are demonstrated below:

```
> class(protein)       # get the class of object
[1] "list"
> length(protein)      # get the number of elements in the object
[1] 4
> attributes(protein)  # get other attributes (element names in
                         this case)

$names
[1] "name"      "accession"     "weight"       "GOIDs"
```

It is also possible to define new classes of object, with their own structures. These are sometimes referred to as S3 objects or S4 objects, reflecting which particular version (3 or 4) of the S language definition they relate to, as R supports both versions. This is where R can start getting confusing, but we will see later that this is a very valuable feature, as classes can be created to capture data from complex biological applications. Objects contain individual components called *slots*, which can contain named elements. These slots and elements can then be accessed using the @ and $ operators, respectively, but because the internal structure of objects can be complex and may be subject to change as software develops, the author of a particular class of object will usually produce a series of functions (often called *methods*) that extract data from within the depths of an object. Examples of working with complex objects can be found in section 4.3.1.

4.1.6 Importing data into R

Bioinformatics is characterized by data sets that are usually large and often heterogeneous. Standard formats to capture much of this data are gradually emerging, but even so a lot of time is spent converting between file formats and getting data in and out of different software packages. R offers a great deal of functionality for importing data from a range of sources.

The built-in R function `read.table()` makes importing tabular data very simple, provided the data is available as delimited text file (i.e. a text file containing one or more rows of data, each of which contains values separated by a specific character such as comma). The example below loads data from the file "blood. csv" into the data frame `loadedresults`. The `sep` parameter is set to indicate the character used to separate columns—in this case a comma (,) and the `header=TRUE` option tells the function the first row of the file contains column headings:

```
loadedresults <- read.table("blood.csv", sep=",", header=TRUE)
```

For this to work, the file "blood.csv" will need to be in R's current working directory, because this is where R looks for files if a full path is not specified with the file name. Some people create a directory called work within the R program directory—a more resilient approach would be to work from a directory in your particular user area on a networked drive that is regularly backed up. You can find out the current working directory by using the getwd() function, set it using setwd(), and see which files are in that directory using the dir() function:

```
> getwd()                                # get working directory
[1] "C:/Program Files/R/R-2.5.1"

> setwd("C:/Program Files/R/R-2.5.1/work")   # set working directory

> dir()                                  # list files in directory
[1] "blood.csv"
```

There is a range of optional arguments that can be used with read.table(), to cope with the many different ways in which tabular data can be represented in text files. These are thoroughly documented in the R help system (type help(read.table)). It is also possible to import data that has been stored in binary format, although this is never easy due to the many different ways in which binary files can be constructed. It is even possible to load files directly from remote servers on a network, or on the internet, simply by specifying a full URL instead of just a file name, as in the example below which loads a file from our web site:

```
filename <- "http://www.bixsolutions.net/blood.csv"

loadedresults <- read.table(filename, sep=",", header=TRUE)
```

It is also possible to import data directly from a relational database by issuing queries to a database server such as MySQL, which is clearly of great value in bioinformatics applications. This functionality is covered later in this chapter, in section 4.3.2.

4.1.7   Data visualization in R

Visualizing data is useful in many bioinformatics applications and R provides a number of built-in functions for graphing data, with many more elaborate graphing functions contributed by users. This is a distinct advantage of R over general purpose programming languages, as they don't have such native functionality. To illustrate R's visualization capabilities we will use as an example a collection of protein fractionation profiles. These were constructed by determining the abundance of several individual proteins in different fractions taken from a sample. The aim of the experiment was to determine which of the 12 proteins studied has the most similar properties to a particular protein of interest (we'll call it protein x) by comparing the fractionation profiles. Such studies are often carried out to determine previously unknown characteristics of proteins, for example to infer their sub-cellular location by association with proteins of known sub-cellular location (as in Sadowski *et al.*, 2006). The data in our example comprises protein abundance data from six fractions for each of the proteins, and our basic aim is to find which protein has the most similar fractionation profile to the protein of interest over these six fractions. The data can be loaded in directly from a CSV file at www.bixsolutions.net:

```
X <- read.table("http://www.bixsolutions.net/profiles.csv",
sep=",", header=TRUE)
```

Looking at the data, we see that each column represents a protein (labelled p1 to p12), or the protein of interest (labelled x), and reading down a column gives us the abundance profile with respect to the six fractions. The magnitude of the values are clearly different for the different proteins, but this is of little importance as we are only interested in identifying profiles of similar shape:

```
> X
    x    p1   p2   p3   p4    p5   p6   p7    p8   p9   p10  p11  p12
1   0   148  6    5    197   1    12   9     0    4    0    11   0
2   4   185  5    9    180   73   6    5     1    5    12   15   3
3   11  149  177  282  446   400  7    7     3    0    8    223  2
4   29  103  210  299  1264  912  3    599   2    2    6    865  387
5   7   72   131  197  520   171  181  301   411  864  561  266  763
6   1   75   7    11   125   34   241  1222  611  1175 216  133  511
```

The `matplot()` function is a powerful R function for plotting data contained in matrices and data frames. Using this, we can very quickly produce a graph of all the profiles together:

```
matplot(X,type="l") # type="l" specifies a line plot
```

This will produce a basic plot, but to create a more professional and useful graph, it is necessary to utilize more of `matplot`'s many arguments—use `help(matplot)` to find out more about these. The example below uses the `col` argument to specify that R should cycle through six colours while plotting the lines, the `lty` argument to cycle through five different line types (solid, dotted, dashed, etc.), the `lwd` argument is used to boost the line width to 2, and axis labels are added to the plot using `xlab` and `ylab`. This results in the graph shown in Fig. 4.3.

```
matplot(X,type="l",xlab="fraction",ylab="quantity",col=1:6,lty=1:5,lwd=2)
```

It is not really possible to see what we are looking for here because the profile of interest is too low. One way to resolve this is to scale each profile so that it has a maximum value of 1. We can do this by dividing each column of the matrix by the maximum value in that column. To calculate the vector of these maximum values, we use the `apply()` function. Normally, functions such as `max` return a single value, but by using `apply()` we can apply such functions in a column-wise or row-wise manner. In this case, we apply the `max()` function to the columns of

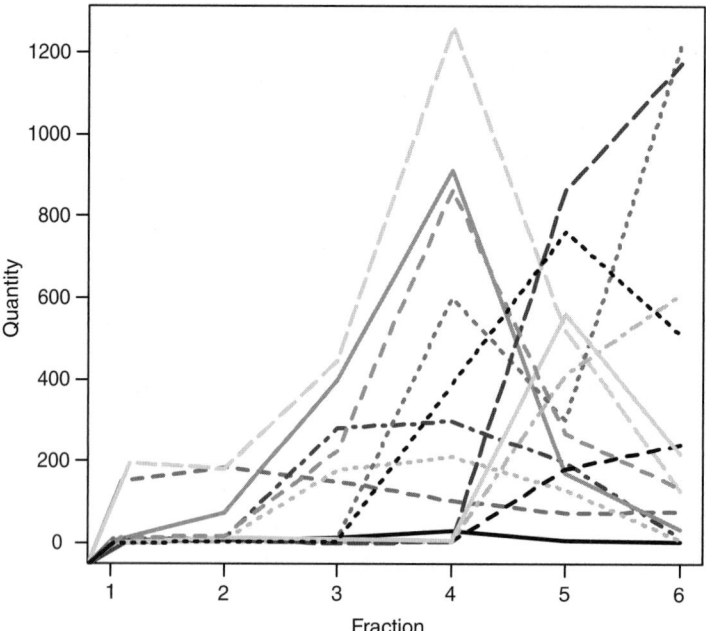

Fig. 4.3 The 13 individual protein profiles plotted together using the matplot function.

the X matrix. Setting the second argument to 2 indicates that we want to work on columns—if we wanted to work on rows this would be set to 1:

```
Xmax <- apply(X, 2, max)    # returns a vector containing the
                            # maximum value of each column
```

Another built-in function, `scale()`, can then be invoked in such a way that it divides each column by the maximum value of that column. By default, `scale()` also adds an offset to each column to centre the data, but in this case zero values have an important significance as these are the baselines of the profiles, so we switch centring off using `center=FALSE`:

```
Xscaled <- scale(X, scale=Xmax, center=FALSE)
```

The scaled version can be plotted using the `matplot()` function exactly as before—just replace X with `Xscaled`. However, the similarity between protein x and the rest of the proteins is still impossible to see because there is no indication of which line relates to which column. We can solve this problem by adding a legend using the `legend()` function. The key arguments here are x, which sets the horizontal position of the legend box in the graph's axes, and legend, which specifies the labels to apply to each line. In this case, we just take the names direct from the data frame by using `names(X)` as the legend text. The plotting arguments `col`, `lty`, `lwd` must be set to match the arguments passed to `matplot()` if the legend and plot are to match up. Note that a background colour has been

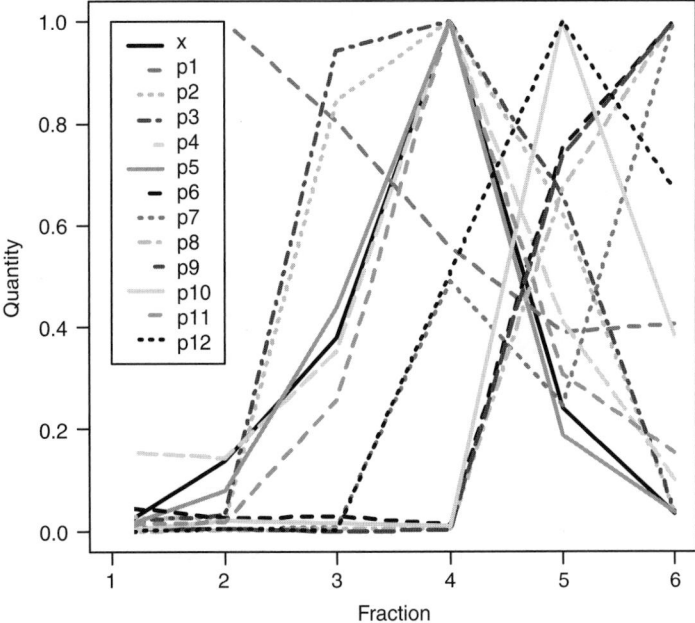

Fig. 4.4 The same data as in Fig. 4.3, after range scaling and addition of a legend. Looking at the legend box, we can see the effect of the col=1:6 and lty=1:5 plotting arguments. As we look down the box, we can see six colours (black, red, green, blue, cyan, and magenta) repeating every six lines and different line styles repeating every five lines, ultimately combining to produce a set of uniquely identifiable lines.

specified for the legend box by setting the `bg` argument to "`snow`"—this is the name of one of many pre-defined colours in R, for a full list type `colours()` at the R prompt. So the legend command is:

```
legend(x=1,legend=names(X),col=1:6,lty=1:5,lwd=2,bg="snow")
```

We can now see from the resulting plot (Fig. 4.4) that the protein with the most similar profile to the protein of interest (labelled x) is p5. Reading off a graph like this is always going to be somewhat subjective, so we will look at more rigorous ways of quantifying these similarities later in the chapter, but for the moment this is a promising result, and a good indication of how graphs can be generated with just a few lines of R code.

The graphing capabilities we have seen so far are provided by R's built-in `graphics` package, which contains a range of other high level graphics functions for visualizing data. These include `barplot()` for plotting bar charts, `boxplot()` for producing *box and whisker* plots, `contour()` for contour plots and `pie()` for pie charts. Each of these functions can be called using basic syntax as in the examples below, which generate graphs from the protein profile data. Alternatively, these functions can be embellished by passing various other parameters, which you can learn about using the `help()` function:

```
barplot(Xmax)        # bar chart showing max quantity of each protein
boxplot(X)           # distribution of quantities for each protein
pie(apply(X,2,sum))  # comparison of total quantity of each
                     # protein across all fractions
```

Lower level graphics functions

The above example shows how easy it is to generate graphs in R compared with using other programming languages such as Perl. The `legend` function is the epitome of this simplicity, in that it creates a complete legend box in a single line of code. Of course, other packages can produce similar graphs, via a much more intuitive point and click interface, but what sets R apart is the ease with which these powerful commands can be combined with low level graphics functions to produce complex bespoke visualizations. This is crucial in bioinformatics because we often need to generate complicated visualizations such as linkage maps, or unusual combinations of different graph types. R's `graphics` package facilitates such visualizations by supplementing its many high level graphic functions with a suite of more primitive functions for plotting basic shapes. For example, we can add a rectangle around the central part of the plot in Fig. 4.4 using the following call to R's `rect()` function. The minimum set of values passed to the function specifies respectively the left, bottom, right, and top bounds of the rectangle:

```
rect(3,-0.01,5,1.01)
```

Other parameters can be passed to specify other features of the rectangle such as the fill colour and outline style. Similar functions include `arrows()`, `lines()`, `polygon()`, `points()`, `segments()`, and `symbols()`, all of which are reasonably self-explanatory. Information about these functions and all the parameters that can be passed to them can be found using the `help()` function. Textual annotations can be added at a specified point in a plot by using the `text` function, for example:

```
text(3.0,0.6,"similar \nprofiles")
```

These low level graphics commands can be typed at the command line, but are more normally combined together in R programs to automatically generate bespoke plots (there is an example of this later, in section 4.1.8). This functionality can be used directly within R or can be used to generate graphical output as part of another tool, such as a web-based application (see Chapter 5). R uses vector graphics rather than the bitmapped graphics of tools like GD (also in Chapter 5) so plots generated by R can be easily scaled up without loss of quality, which is ideal in situations where you might want to zoom in to a complex plot, or prepare figures for publication.

Creating interactive graphics

In some applications, it can be useful to interact with visualizations, to enable zooming in to regions or retrieval of annotations or data from another dimension.

R has built-in functions that make this possible. For example, the locator() function allows the user to select a specific position within a graph by clicking on it with the mouse. To see this in action, type locator(n=1) at the R command line while the graph in Fig. 4.4 is open. Then click somewhere in the graph. You will hear a sound (depending on how your computer is configured) and the *x* and *y* co-ordinates of the position you clicked will be returned in the R console. In an R program, this information could be used as the starting point for adding annotations to the plot or to retrieve some additional information about whatever is displayed at that point.

Devices

In the examples so far we have issued plotting commands and graphs have appeared in a window. Working like this means that each new graph causes the old one to be lost, which is not helpful if we want to look at multiple graphs simultaneously, to compare results for example. To accommodate this, R allows multiple windows to be open simultaneously. There are different functions for opening a new window, depending on which operating system you're using. These are shown below, but in practice we have found that x11() works in all three operating systems, so would recommend using that in your R programs to ensure that they are cross-platform:

```
x11()        # open a new window for plotting (in Linux)

windows()    # open a new window for plotting (in Windows)

quartz()     # open a new window for plotting (in Mac OS)
```

In R, a window is one particular instance of a *device* on which graphics can be displayed. Windows are therefore manipulated using a suite of device handling functions, whose names begin with dev.. Some examples are shown below:

```
> dev.list()       # list open devices
windows       windows       windows       windows
2             3             4             5

> dev.set (3)      # make window 3 the active device
```

The active device is where any graphics commands will be sent. If a window is currently the active device, the word ACTIVE will be shown in brackets in the title bar of that window. Windows are not the only type of R device. Another useful device is PDF, which can be created using the pdf() function. This creates a PDF (portable document format) file with the specified name, in the current working directory. For example:

```
pdf("figure1.pdf")  # create a PDF device called figure1.pdf
```

All graphical output will now be sent to that file, as long as it is the active device. This is very useful for capturing the output of an automated data analysis program, or for printing figures or sharing them with colleagues. A PDF reader such as Adobe Acrobat Reader is required to view the PDF, and you will probably need to close the device by issuing the command `dev.off(which = dev.cur())` before being able to access the file without throwing a sharing violation error. The functions `bmp()`, `jpeg()`, and `png()` are similar to `pdf()`, except that they create bitmapped image files (in BMP, JPEG, and PNG formats, respectively), instead of PDFs. Again, these devices need to be closed before the file can be viewed.

Summary

This section has given an indication as to how R's built-in data visualization capabilities are used and, although this is just the tip of the iceberg in terms of what's possible, the general approaches hold regardless of the type of graph being drawn. There are more examples later in this chapter, but to see the full extent of the graphics functionality available in R's base graphics package, type `help(graphics)` at the R prompt.

4.1.8 Writing programs in R

At this point, you have probably realized that everything covered so far could have been done just as effectively, and probably much more quickly, in a spreadsheet application such as Microsoft Excel. You would be right, of course, and there is no doubt that Excel is a fine tool for simple one-off manipulation of small data sets. However, bioinformatics is typified by large data sets, complex analysis algorithms, and the need for repetitive analysis. This is where R really comes into its own, as its command line ethos is ideal for writing programs that automate data processing workflows. For example, producing an R program to automate the generation of the fractionation profile plots in the previous example is as easy as pasting all the relevant commands together in the correct order in a text file— the result of this is shown below. Any text editor can be used to do this and the choice of editor to use with R is really down to personal preference. We would refer you to the survey of editors provided at the beginning of the previous chapter (section 3.1.2), as the basic process of writing an R program is similar to writing Perl code. If you find a particular editor convenient for programming in Perl, they you may as well use the same editor with R.

Depending on your operating system, R may have some kind of internal text editor for writing programs or will know about an editor installed on your computer. If so, you can initiate editing of a file either by opening a file using the RGui's File menu, or by using the `edit()` function in the R Console:

```
edit(file="profiles.r")
```

If you feel uncomfortable with whatever editor R is presenting you with, you can tell it to use any other editor installed on your system by using the `options()` function. In the example below (for Windows), R is told to fire up Komodo Edit whenever we call the `edit()` function to edit a program:

```
options(editor = "komodo.exe")
```

Note that it is customary, but not compulsory to give R programs file names with the extension .r. Hence, the example below, which captures the sequence of commands issued in the graphing example from the previous section, should be saved in the working directory as profiles.r:

```
# PROFILES.R
#
# Simple R program to load a data matrix, scale it and plot the result.

# clear out the workspace first
rm(list = ls())

# load data frame from web site
X <- read.table("http://www.bixsolutions.net/profiles.csv", sep=",",
header=TRUE)

# rangescale data by dividing by the maximum value in each column
Xmax <- apply(X, 2, max)
Xscaled <- scale(X, scale=Xmax, center=FALSE)

# plot columns in matrix as lines on a single graph
matplot(Xscaled,type="l",xlab="fraction",ylab="quantity",col=1:6,
lty=1:5,lwd=2)

# add legend to graph
legend(x=1,legend=names(X),col=1:6,lty=1:5,lwd=2,bg="snow")
```

To execute a program we use the source() function. For this to work, the program file must be in the current working directory. We can then issue the command below:

```
source("profiles.r")
```

Alternatively, it is possible to run this program directly from www.bixsolutions. net by specifying the full URL. The command is:

```
source("http://www.bixsolutions.net/profiles.r")
```

So, now we have our program and we know how to execute it. If a laboratory colleague sends us a new data set, we can just change the filename in the read. table line and run the program on that new data, automatically generating the required graph in a matter of seconds. This type of scripting is a great time saver, and clearly very useful in its own right. However, R goes beyond simple scripting by allowing the creation of new functions, and fully fledged programs with structures similar to those covered in the Perl chapter.

Beyond scripting: loops and conditionals

To avoid repetition, we refer you to Chapter 3 for more detailed descriptions of control structures and their uses. In this section we just cover the basic syntax needed to define these structures in R. The syntax is, in fact, very similar to Perl.

Conditional statements are constructed using the `if` statement, a simple example of which is shown below:

```
> value <- -1
> if (value < 0) print("value is negative")
[1] "value is negative"
```

In this example, the less than (<) operator is used to check whether the number stored in `value` is less than zero (i.e. is it negative). Other comparison operators include greater than (>), equal to (==), combinations of these (<= and >=), and not equal to (!=). Multiple conditions can be combined using the and (&&) and or (||) operators, just like in Perl. If multiple commands need to be executed when the condition is met, it is necessary to group the commands into a code block defined by enclosing the commands between curly braces ({ }). Again, this is just like Perl and an example is given below. It makes little sense to enter such complicated constructs at the command line, so such things are usually only used as part of programs.

```
if ((residue == "D") || (residue == "E")) {
  print("negatively charged amino acid")
  negativeresiduecount = negativeresiduecount + 1
}
```

R provides three statements for creating different types of loop: `for`, `repeat`, and `while`. A loop can be constructed using the `for` statement in very much the same way as it would be in Perl. The generic format of the `for` statement is for (*i* in *range*), where *i* is the loop variable, and *range* is the list of values that will be attributed to it on each pass through the loop. Typically, *range* is a series of integers, which in R is defined using the colon operator, e.g. `1:10` returns the integers from 1 to 10. However, `range` can, in fact, be any numerical R vector. As with `if` statements, multiple commands may be grouped together using curly braces such that they all execute on each cycle of the loop. The statements `next` and `break` may be used to exit the current cycle, or the whole loop, respectively.

The program below shows an example of a typical program combining a `for` loop and conditional statements with some of the low level graphics functions introduced earlier to produce a view of a protein sequence annotated with its secondary structure. A vector called `struct` is used to define the structure at each amino acid position, with 1 indicating that a residue is part of an alpha helix, 2 denoting a beta sheet, and 0 for other features such as turns and loops. The output of this program is shown in Fig. 4.5.

```
SSSEQ.R
#
# Simple R program to display a sequence with structural
annotation
```

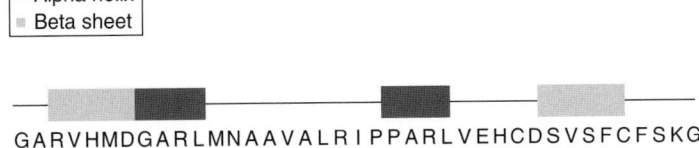

Fig. 4.5 Annotated protein sequence produced using low level R graphics functions.

```
# define sequence and secondary structure
seq <- "GARVHMDGARLMNAAVALRIPPARLVEHCDSVSFCFSKG"
struct <- c(0,0,2,2,2,2,2,1,1,1,1,0,0,0,0,0,0,0,0,0,0,
  1,1,1,1,0,0,0,0,0,2,2,2,2,2,0,0,0,0)
residuecount <- 39;

# set up the window for plotting
x11() # may need quartz() for Mac or windows() for PC
plot.new()
plot.window(c(0,40),c(-20,20))

# plot a line representing the length of the sequence
segments(0.5,0,39.5,0)

# plot the sequence and features
for (i in 1:residuecount) {
  text(i,-2,substr(seq,i,i))      # write residue letter
  if (struct[i] != 0) {
    if (struct[i] == 1) boxcolour <- "firebrick"# alpha helix
    if (struct[i] == 2) boxcolour <- "yellow3"# beta sheet
    rect(i-0.5,-1,i+0.5,1,col = boxcolour, border = NA)
  }
}

# plot a legend
legend(x=0,y=8,legend=(c("alpha helix","beta sheet")),
  pch=15,col=c("firebrick","yellow3"),bg="snow")
```

Writing functions

Functions are essentially R programs that can be called just like the built-in functions we have been using so far in this chapter. They are analogous to functions/subroutines in Perl, and as in Perl the benefit of an R function is that if we need to perform something often, we can wrap the relevant code up into a function that can then be called with just one line of code, either in a program or (in the case of R) from the command line. This type of program code reuse increases efficiency of program development, not just by reducing the need to re-type things, but also by reducing debugging time.

R functions are defined using `function()`. Consider the example program below, which defines a function called `rangescale`. This function scales all columns in a matrix such that their maximum value is 1 by dividing by the maximum value of each column, just as we did in section 4.1.7. The R commands that make up the function are grouped together in the curly braces ({ }). This group of commands is assigned to a function called `rangescale`, with the first line statement `rangescale <- function(X)`. Variables named between the `function` brackets indicate that objects must be passed into the function, and the variables listed in the brackets following the `return` command indicate variables that are passed out of the function on completion. In this case, the function expects to see an object coming in, which is assigned to `X`, and returns the range-scaled matrix, `Xscaled`. Note that any other variables used in the function, (in this case just `Xmax`), are internal to the function and therefore don't appear in the R workspace after the function is called. This concept of the *scope* of variables is exactly the same as when the `strict` pragma is used in Perl (see section 3.2.6).

```
# RANGESCALE.R
#
# R program to define a function to rangescale columns of a matrix

rangescale <- function(X) {

  Xmax <- apply(X, 2, max)
  Xscaled <- scale(X, scale=Xmax, center=FALSE)

  return(Xscaled)

}
```

Before we can use a function, we first have to save the program that defines it (let's save the above program as `rangescale.r`), and then run that program using `source()`. The newly defined function is treated by R just like any other object, so once defined it is visible in the workspace. It can then be called just like any other function.

```
source("rangescale.r")    # run the program to define the function

N <- rangescale(M)        # call the function to rangescale
                          # matrix M and place the result in N
```

4.2 Multivariate data analysis

Much has been made of the relatively large size of datasets emanating from modern bioanalytical techniques, such as high throughput sequencing and gene expression analysis. As mentioned previously, another key characteristic of such data is that it is multivariate, by which we mean that multiple values are acquired from each sample or time point we analyse. These values might be gene expression ratios, protein quantities, or metabolite concentrations. Multivariate analysis techniques have been developed specifically for the investigation of this type of data. Typical tasks include exploratory analysis, where we simply want to visualize a dataset in some meaningful way, through to classification, where we seek to assign each sample to a defined class according to the characteristic pattern of the measured variables. In rare cases, we may seek to perform multivariate calibration, where multiple measured variables are reduced to a continuous value relating to something of interest. The built-in support for matrix mathematics makes R an ideal platform for multivariate data analysis.

4.2.1   Exploratory data analysis

The aim of data exploration techniques is to provide a way of visualizing variation within large multivariate data sets. This is sometimes an end in itself, but it is also a useful way of evaluating whether the data is of sufficient quality or sufficient information content to warrant further study. For example, there is clearly no point in expending effort attempting to classify samples into different groups according their gene expression profiles if initial exploration of the data shows that there is no sign of correlation between the data acquired and the sample types analysed.

4.2.2   Scatter plots

One of the simplest, yet most effective, forms of exploratory analysis is the construction of scatter plots. A typical application of this in bioinformatics is the identification of differentially expressed genes from microarray data. By plotting, for each gene, a point on a graph at co-ordinates (a_j, b_j), where a_j is the expression level of gene j in sample A and b_j is the expression level in sample B, genes which show substantially different expression levels between the two samples can be clearly seen. Typically, the expression values are plotted on log scales to provide more clarity to the figure. Genes with similar expression levels fall along a diagonal line across the plot. Genes that fall more than a specified distance from this line can be considered to exhibit a significant difference in expression between the two samples. The definition of a significant difference varies depending on the application, and according to the general level of noise in the data, but typically a two-fold change in expression would be considered significant. Lines marked on the scatter plot representing a two-fold change can be superimposed so that the genes of interest can be clearly seen.

4.2.3   Principal components analysis

A significant limitation of the scatter plot approach is that it is limited to pairwise comparisons, with just two samples in any one plot. If we want to compare the data from more than two samples or compare the actual expression profiles of multiple genes, then more advanced techniques are required. One such technique is principal components analysis (PCA).

  PCA is a way of reducing a large multivariate data matrix into a matrix with a much smaller number of variables (called principal components, or PCs), without losing important information within the data. In mathematical terms, PCA is the reduction of the original data matrix, X, into two smaller matrices, the scores, T, and loadings, P. The product of the scores and the transposed loadings, P', plus a residual matrix, E, gives the original data matrix (Equation 1):

$$X = T.P' + E \tag{1}$$

There are a number of algorithms for calculating T and P, the most common being singular value decomposition (SVD)—one of the standard matrix manipulations alluded to in section 4.1.4. We will not delve further into the maths here, suffice to say that the way that the PCs are calculated means that they are delivered in the order of largest variance first, hence the first PC (PC1) captures the most information in the data, PC2 the second most information, and so on. The scores matrix T is determined by multiplying X by the matrix of loadings, P, as shown in Fig. 4.6. In simple terms, this means that the scores for a particular sample are weighted sums of the original variables. For example, the first PC score for the third sample in the data matrix shown in Fig. 4.6 would be calculated as:

$$t_{3,1} = x_{3,1}p_{1,1} + x_{3,2}p_{2,1} + x_{3,3}p_{3,1} + x_{3,4}p_{4,1} + x_{3,5}p_{5,1} + x_{3,6}p_{6,1} + x_{3,7}p_{7,1} \tag{2}$$

In many cases just the first two or three components are sufficient to capture the bulk of the variance (hence, the bulk of the information) in a given data set. Each sample can then be plotted on a simple two or three dimensional graph at the position dictated by its first two or three PCA scores. The relative positions of the samples in this plot indicate the relative similarities between samples, with similar samples appearing at similar positions within the graph. Variance in the higher PCs is often due to experimental noise, so plotting only the first two or three PCs not only simplifies interpretation of the data, it also reduces the noise.

To do PCA in R, we can use the `prcomp()` function, which is part of the `stats` package included in the basic installation of R. A program to perform PCA on the protein profiles data from section 4.1.7 is shown below. Much of this

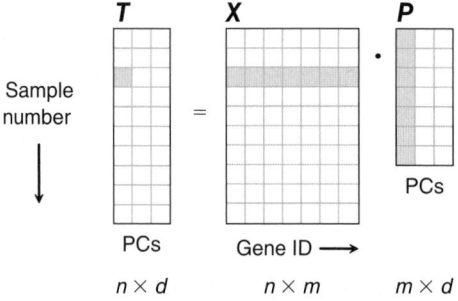

Fig. 4.6 Relationship between the data matrix (X), scores matrix (T) and loadings matrix (P) in principal components analysis. In this simple example, the number of samples, n, is 10, the number of measured variables (e.g. genes), m, is 7, and the number, d, of PCs considered is 3. The highlighted row in X and column in P show what is required to generate the first PC score for sample 3.

program will be familiar from the previous examples, indeed it makes use of the `rangescale()` function defined previously. (So, for the program to work, `rangescale.r` should be available in the working directory.) The new material is in the latter part of the program, which performs PCA and then generates a labelled scatter plot in which the position of the point representing each profile is defined by its PCA scores.

```
# PCA_EXAMPLE.R
#
# Program to load in data matrix, calculate principal
# components and plot resulting scores.

rm(list=ls())              # clear workspace

source("rangescale.r")     # define our rangescale function

# load data matrix from file
X <- read.table("http://www.bixsolutions.net/profiles.csv",
sep=",", header=TRUE)

Xscaled = rangescale(X)    #scale the profiles

result = prcomp(Xscaled, center=FALSE)  # perform PCA

# extract the scores matrix from the result
scores=result$rotation

# plot PC1 against PC2
plot(scores[,1], scores[,2], xlab="PC1",ylab="PC2")

# add labels to point (note 0.005,0.003 offset to avoid
obscuring points)
text(scores[,1]+0.005, scores[,2]+0.003, names(X))
```

Note that `prcomp()` returns the results in an object of the specially defined class `prcomp`. The PCA scores are contained in the `rotation` component of this object and are extracted using the $ operator. The result of running this program is shown in Fig. 4.7.

4.2.4 Hierarchical cluster analysis

Hierarchical cluster analysis (HCA) is another exploratory data analysis technique that, like PCA, is designed to reveal relationships between samples or between the molecular entities (e.g. genes) being studied. The result of HCA is a tree diagram or dendrogram in which each sample is represented by a branch, and the distance between branch tips indicates the level of similarity between samples. Such diagrams are used in many areas of bioinformatics, due to their ability to represent large multivariate data sets in a reasonably intuitive way.

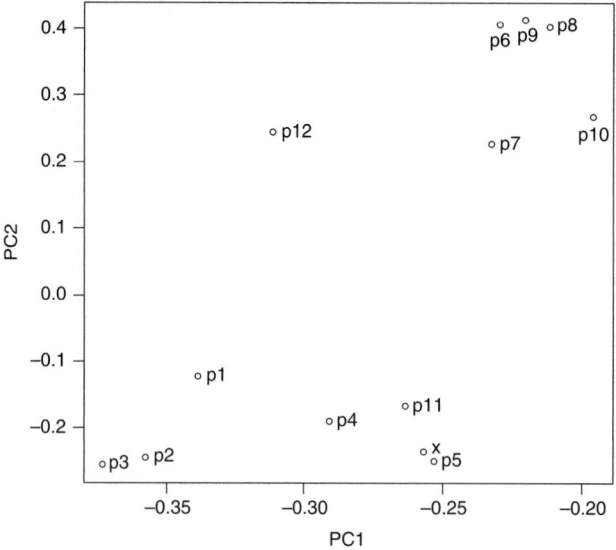

Fig. 4.7 PCA scores plot generated from the profiles data set. The protein of interest (x) and protein p5 appear very close in the plot, indicating that their profiles are similar, suggesting that the two have similar properties. Other groupings, such as p6, p8 and p9 are also eminently sensible if we refer back to the profiles in Fig. 4.4.

The dendrograms are created by a recursive process in which the pairwise similarity between every sample and every other sample is calculated. The samples representing the two most similar samples are then joined using branches whose length is related to the level of similarity between the samples. The process is then repeated, with the two samples already accounted for being agglomerated in such a way that they can be considered as a single sample. This process is repeated until all samples have been joined together. This method is capable of displaying the relationship between entities in a data set and, unlike PCA, it is easily extended to very large data sets without cluttering the plot or loosing information.

All hierarchical clustering follows the general approach set out above, but there are a lot of variations in how the similarity between samples is calculated and how samples are joined together. The primary method of determining the level of similarity between two samples is by calculating the distance between them in the multidimensional space of the measured variables (e.g. the quantity of protein measured in the fractionation example). The process is easy to understand for two measured variables, as shown in Fig. 4.8, but is equally applicable to any number of variables. Taking the two-dimensional case in the figure as an example, the most intuitive distance measure is the Euclidean distance—the shortest distance between the two points. This distance, d, is trivially calculated using Pythagoras' theorem:

$$d_{A,B} = \sqrt{\left(A_1 - B_1\right)^2 + \left(A_2 - B_2\right)^2}$$

(3)

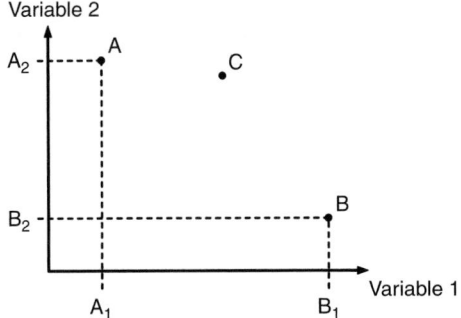

Fig. 4.8 Illustration of distance between samples in variable space. In this case, we consider two samples, A and B, with two measured variables. There are many ways in which the distance between the samples can be calculated.

Extending this to further variables simply involves adding the squared differences for the other variables within the square root. For the case of N variables, the calculation for each sample would be:

$$d_{A,B} = \sqrt{\sum_{n=1}^{N}\left(A_n - B_n\right)^2} \qquad (4)$$

However, the Euclidean distance is not the only measure. If we want to particularly emphasize samples that are markedly different from others, we can amplify the distance by squaring it. For the two-dimensional example, the squared Euclidean distance is simply Equation 3 with the square root removed.

If we want to emphasize the difference between samples according to the value of the largest difference between values of a single variable, regardless of what that variable is, we can use the maximum distance (sometimes called the Chebychev distance):

$$d_{A,B} = \max\left|A_n - B_n\right| \qquad (5)$$

R has a built-in function, dist(), for calculating the distance between objects described in a multivariate data matrix. The distance measure used is selected by setting the method parameter to one of the following methods: "euclidean", "maximum", "manhattan", "canberra", "binary", or "minkowski". The command for calculating the Euclidean distance matrix is shown below. Note that the data frame, Xscaled, is transposed, using the t() function, because the distance function expects each row of data to represent an object:

```
d <- dist(t(Xscaled), method = "euclidean")
```

A dendrogram object can then be created from this distance matrix using R's hclust() function. This object can then be plotted using the plot() function, resulting in the dendrogram shown in Fig. 4.9. The commands to do this are

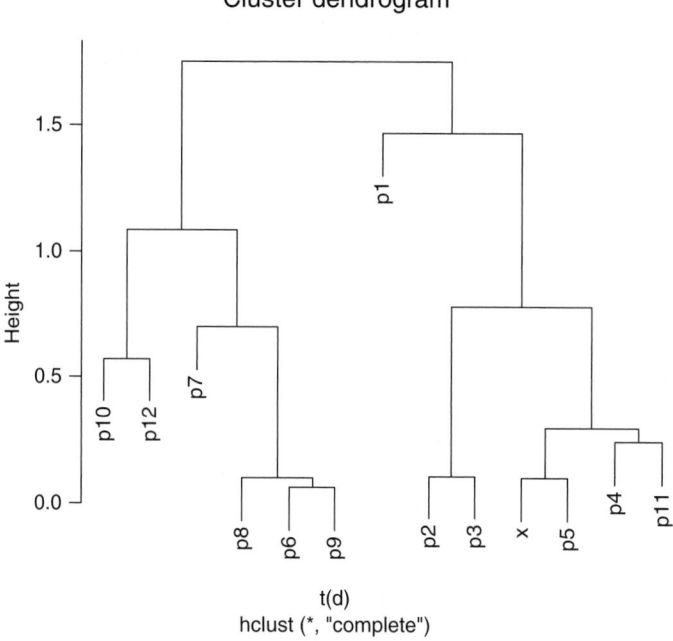

Cluster dendrogram

Fig. 4.9 Dendrogram generated from the protein profiles dataset. Note that the profile of protein p1 is shown as very different to the other profiles. Looking at Fig. 4.4, this is not surprising as the profile of p1 is clearly different from the others, effectively peaking much earlier. In the PCA plot in Fig. 4.6, p1 did not appear as such an outlier because, taking a global view of the dataset across all samples, the variance associated with the first few points in the profile was not particularly significant, so p1 would only appear as a outlier if less significant PCs were plotted (i.e. PCs other than 1 and 2).

shown below. Note that the `plot()` function detects that an `hclust()` dendrogram object has been set to it and deals with it accordingly:

```
dendrogram <- hclust(t(d), method = "complete", members = NULL)

plot(dendrogram)
```

Just as there is a choice of method for calculating the distance or similarity between two samples, so there is a range of linkage algorithms for joining clusters together as the clustering process progresses. Essentially, a linkage algorithm defines which point in a cluster is used to represent that cluster when the distances are calculated. The most obvious approach is the weighted average, where each cluster is represented by the average position in the variable space of the samples that make up the cluster—this essentially represents the centre of gravity of the cluster. Other popular methods include complete and single linkage. Using complete linkage the distance between two clusters is calculated using the largest distance between individual points in those clusters—this promotes tight clusters over those with more variance. Single linkage is the opposite, where the distance is measured according to the closest two points in the two clusters—this allows clusters to be joined on the basis of just two similar samples, regardless of the spread across the variable space that each cluster exhibits.

A more advanced linkage algorithm, called Ward's method, moves away from simple geometric solutions and joins clusters not just on simple distance measures, but according to which of the agglomerated clusters will have the least variance. This approach has the benefit of promoting tight clusters, but doesn't suffer the sensitivity to outliers found in complete linkage. For this reason, it is often used as the linkage algorithm of choice. The `hclust()` function supports all the above linkage methods, and these can be selected by setting the `method` parameter to `"average"`, `"complete"`, `"single"`, or `"ward"`.

Clearly there is a wide range of possible combinations of parameters for performing HCA, and experience shows that these can result in markedly different dendrograms, leading to potentially different interpretations of the data set. It is, therefore, very important to ensure that the particular distance measures and linkage algorithms used are appropriate, either by considering in detail how each approach works and how this relates to the particular data set being analysed, or by following best practice described in the literature for similar data sets. It is also important to consider the *robustness* of the results obtained—if a particular clustering behaviour is observed only in the dendrogram created by a very specific set of HCA parameters then it may not be wise to assume that the clusters genuinely represent the relationships between the samples.

In most applications, the purpose of hierarchical clustering is to reveal relationships between samples according the multiple measured variables for each sample. Sometimes, however, we may instead (or also) want to reveal the relationships between the measured variables. A good example of this is gene expression data, where instead of clustering the samples, we often want to cluster the genes according to the similarity of their behaviour across those samples. Doing this in R is simply a matter of using the `t()` function to transpose the data prior to the process of creating a dendrogram, so that the samples become variables and *vice versa*.

In situations where it is beneficial to get an indication of the detailed content of the data matrix, as well as both the relationship between the samples and between the variables, R has an excellent built-in function called `heatmap()`, which uses `dist()` and `hclust()` to perform hierarchical clustering on the data matrix and its transpose, and then appends dendrograms generated from this to the two sides of a square image representing the original data matrix. The rows and columns of the data matrix are rearranged such that they line up with their respective dendrogram branches. The results of using this function with microarray data are shown in a later example.

4.2.5 Classification

In many applications, we are particularly interested in being able to classify samples according to their analytical response. For example, many papers have been published showing how genomic, metabolomic, or proteomic profiles can be used to classify biological samples into *healthy* and *diseased* states for particular diseases.

This is important because it raises the possibility of detecting diseases according to the behaviour of multiple biomarkers, rather than a single biomarker as has traditionally been the case. This has the potential to improve accuracy of diagnosis, simply because it takes into account more biological factors. Indeed, it is also the first step towards discovering diagnostic biomarkers, which is a valuable activity in its own right. Such classification could be done by looking at the output of an exploratory technique such as HCA or PCA, but we really want an automated computational method if we are to ensure objectivity and high data throughput.

Multivariate classification is the name given to the data analysis approach used to achieve this. It involves building a classification model from a data matrix acquired from samples of known class. The model is effectively a mathematical transformation relating the measured variables to a number indicating the class of sample (e.g. 0 for healthy, 1 for diseased). Crucially, a separate matrix of data from samples of known class is collected and used to test the resulting classification model. The performance of the classification model can therefore be quoted using easily understood quantitative measures, such as the proportion of test samples that are correctly identified by the model. Alternatively, the performance can be specified in terms of the specificity and sensitivity of the model, which are derived individually from the proportion of correctly identified positive samples and correctly identified negative samples. Some pointers for starting to build classification models in R are provided in section 4.3.3.

4.3 R packages

So far in this chapter, we have limited ourselves to using the basic installation of R. This is useful in its own right, thanks to a number of powerful built-in packages, including `graphics` and `stats`, functions from both of which we have already used in this chapter. It is possible to find out which packages are present in your particular installation of R by typing `library()` at the command prompt. Although R clearly has a lot of functionality with just the basic packages, what makes R particularly popular among the bioinformatics community is the vast number of high quality user-contributed packages that are available. The number of packages available is already impressive and more are being released all the time. Indeed, for many bioinformatics applications, there is probably an R package out there that does at least part of what you want—it is just a case of finding it. This clearly saves a lot of coding effort, but you need to be prepared to spend a substantial amount of time searching for packages, finding out how to use them, and incorporating them into your own analysis pipeline. At the time of writing there is no easy way to find the right package for a specific task, other than browsing through the CRAN archive or searching the web with relevant queries, e.g. 'R SVM package' for a package that implements support vector machines.

If you know the name of the package you want, the process of downloading and integrating it into R is actually very straightforward. You simply select a package from the CRAN archive and install it from within R, either via the Packages menu in the R GUI if that is available in your operating system (Windows or Mac OS), through the Linux package manager if you're using Linux (like Perl modules, R packages are often available through the regular Linux package managers), or by typing the following at the command line and following the on-screen instructions:

```
install.packages()
```

Alternatively, packages can be added from local archive files (.zip or .tar.gz), which you might have acquired from the web, from a colleague, or perhaps even written yourself (see section 4.3.4). As with the CRAN packages, this can be done via the R GUI in Windows and Mac OS, or under Linux with a command issued from the Linux command line (not the R console):

```
R CMD INSTALL name_of_package
```

Some of the best known, and most useful, are part of the Bioconductor Project (www.bioconductor.org). The Bioconductor packages fall roughly into two groups. Packages in the first group are designed to provide basic infrastructure support for doing routine tasks, such as fetching data from repositories and manipulating data for later analysis—these can save a huge amount of development time as you don't need to reinvent the wheel when it comes to tedious things like parsing specific data formats. The second type of Bioconductor package provides R implementations of innovative techniques for the analysis of biological data. It is gradually becoming the norm that someone publishing a new data processing algorithm will make the algorithm available as an R package for the benefit of the community, possibly as part of Bioconductor. For historical reasons, many of the Bioconductor packages are orientated around microarray data analysis, particularly using the Affymetrix platform, but lately packages have been generalized or expanded to cover other data types, as bioinformatics has matured.

4.3.1 Installing and using Bioconductor packages

Bioconductor packages can be installed like any other R packages, for example, Bioconductor's popular `limma` package for microarray analysis can be seen in the list of CRAN packages shown by `install.packages()`. However, as Bioconductor is made up of a number of individual packages, many of which are dependent on one another, it is recommended that newcomers start by installing the core packages using the `biocLite.R` script provided at www.bioconductor.org. This can be done by typing the following at the command line:

```
source("http://www.bioconductor.org/biocLite.R")
```

```
biocLite()
```

This can take a few minutes as the packages are downloaded, unpacked, and installed. Typing `library()` will confirm that R now has a number of additional libraries installed, with names like `affy` and `Biobase`. Note that, although the installation of the package copies the relevant files and makes the package available to R, to actually use the functions within that package it is necessary to load the package into the current R session using the `library()` function. Once a package has been loaded in that way, it is possible to find descriptions of the functions within that package using the `help()` function as described earlier. This obviously requires you to know the names of functions in the packages. Larger packages often have general information about the package, which can be accessed by passing the name of the package to the `help()` function. For example, to get started with Bioconductor's Biobase package, we would type:

```
library(Biobase)      # load package

help(Biobase)         # tell us something about the package
```

After loading Bioconductor packages, PDF documentation covering key topics can be accessed from within R by typing `openVignette()` at the R prompt, and selecting from the list of options that appear. You can also access the PDF documentation directly via the web, which is useful for researching which packages to use without having to install them.

Getting data from GEO using the GEOquery package

Other elements of Bioconductor can be added at any time, simply by passing the name of the desired package to the `biocLite()` function. In the example that follows, we are going to see how a Bioconductor package called `GEOquery` can be used to load data from the NCBI's Gene Expression Omnibus (GEO) into R. The `GEOquery` package can be added to R using the command below:

```
biocLite("GEOquery")      # add GEOquery package to R
```

To make the functions from the package available for use in the current R session, we must load it using the `library()` function:

```
library(GEOquery)        # load package
```

The `GEOquery` package contains a function called `getGEO()`, which provides an excellent example of the powerful capabilities of Bioconductor packages. `getGEO()` provides a one line solution to loading data from GEO straight into R. For example, to load the dataset with accession number GDS2577 into an object called `dset`, the command is:

```
dset <- getGEO("GDS2577")
```

The GDS2577 dataset was collected as part of a study into tissue repair mechanisms (Otu *et al.*, 2007). The dataset contains gene expression data collected from two very different mouse tissue types: developing embryonic liver and regenerating liver. Furthermore, each tissue type was analysed at different time points.

It can take several minutes for `getGEO()` to download and parse the data, due to the amount of data involved, and during the parsing stage R may become unresponsive. Patience is a virtue here—eventually control will be passed back to the R command line. The whole data set is now stored in the object `dset`.

To avoid having to go through the download and parsing process again, you might want to save this object locally using R's `save()` function. This function saves the specified object, or list of objects, in a file with the specified name. In the example below, we save the `dset` object in the file `"GDS2577"`.

```
save(dset, file="GDS2577")  # save dataset to the file "GDS2577"
```

The object can then be quickly loaded back into workspace in a future session using the load function:

```
load("GDS2577")  # load dataset from file "GDS2577"
```

The `dset` object created by `getGEO()` is an instance of a fairly complex data class, the structure of which mirrors that of the GEO database (specifically GEO's GDS class in this case). It is possible to extract information from the GDS object using the operators discussed towards the end of section 4.1.5. For example, typing `dset@header$description` at the R prompt will return the description of the dataset from the header slot in the GDS object, which contains metadata from the GEO record. However, this approach is not recommended as it depends on the internal structure of the object, which may be different in future versions of `GEOquery`. Instead, you are encouraged to use *methods* included in the `GEOquery` package that extract information from the data structure for you. One such method is `Meta()`, which is used to return metadata associated with the dataset, including the description of the study, which would be retrieved by typing `Meta(dset)$description`. The `Columns()` method returns a data frame containing information about the individual samples. The first three columns returned from the GDS2577 dataset are shown below (a fourth column called *description* has been omitted as the entries within it are rather detailed descriptions of each sample that would not fit on the page).

```
> Columns(dset)
         sample       specimen              time
1        GSM161128    developing liver      10.5 dpc
2        GSM161129    developing liver      10.5 dpc
3        GSM161130    developing liver      11.5 dpc
4        GSM161131    developing liver      11.5 dpc
5        GSM161132    developing liver      12.5 dpc
6        GSM161133    developing liver      12.5 dpc
7        GSM161134    developing liver      13.5 dpc
8        GSM161135    developing liver      13.5 dpc
9        GSM161136    developing liver      14.5 dpc
10       GSM161137    developing liver      14.5 dpc
11       GSM161138    developing liver      16.5 dpc
12       GSM161139    developing liver      16.5 dpc
13       GSM161108    regenerating liver    0 h
14       GSM161109    regenerating liver    0 h
15       GSM161110    regenerating liver    1 h
```

16	GSM161111	regenerating liver	1 h
17	GSM161112	regenerating liver	2 h
18	GSM161113	regenerating liver	2 h
19	GSM161114	regenerating liver	6 h
20	GSM161115	regenerating liver	6 h
21	GSM161116	regenerating liver	12 h
22	GSM161117	regenerating liver	12 h
23	GSM161118	regenerating liver	18 h
24	GSM161119	regenerating liver	18 h
25	GSM161120	regenerating liver	24 h
26	GSM161121	regenerating liver	24 h
27	GSM161122	regenerating liver	30 h
28	GSM161123	regenerating liver	30 h
29	GSM161124	regenerating liver	48 h
30	GSM161125	regenerating liver	48 h
31	GSM161126	regenerating liver	72 h
32	GSM161127	regenerating liver	72 h

This output shows the two types of sample in the dataset, regenerating liver, and developing liver, and shows which sample is which. For each liver type, samples were taken for analysis in duplicate at different time points. A data frame containing the actual expression data from these samples can be extracted from the `dset` dataset object using `GEOquery`'s `Table()` method. One way to inspect the data is by assigning it to another object and then using the `edit()` function on that object.

```
X <- Table(dset)

X <- edit(X)
```

Looking at the table in the data editor provides a detailed view of the whole dataset. Each row is associated with a particular gene, which is identified by the spot ID_REF (e.g. 1415672_at) and the gene name (e.g Golga7). Each column is associated with a particular sample, identified by its unique GEO ID, e.g. GSM161129. The data clearly takes the form of a matrix, which means it is suited to many different types of analysis, as explained earlier in this chapter (section 4.1.4). Indeed, since the object returned by `Table(X)` is a data frame, we can deal with it exactly as we dealt with date frames earlier. However, to make full use of the many functions that Bioconductor provides for microarray analysis, it is necessary to convert the dataset object from the GEO-specific GDS class into a more generic object based on the Biobase *ExpressionSet* class. `GEOquery` provides a function, `GDS2Set()`, which does this conversion for us. If the `do.log2` parameter is set to TRUE, the expression values are transformed by taking logs to base two during the conversion process, something that is commonly done in microarray data analysis.

```
eset <- GDS2eSet(dset, do.log2 = TRUE)  # covert data to experiment set
```

Again, this may take some time to complete, due to the size of the data set, but now that we have the data in this generic Bioconductor format we can analyse it using a wide range of functions from different Bioconductor packages. For example, we can extract a matrix containing the actual expression data from the data set using Bioconductor's `exprs()` method, and use the familiar `summary()` function to get some headline statistics on the gene expression for example.

```
X <- exprs(eset)    # extract the expression values

summary(X)          # show some statistics for each sample
```

Among other things, this reveals that there is a large number of missing values associated with each sample, as evidenced by the number of NA entries. About 3% of 45,101 values are missing from most of these samples, which is not uncommon in such data. We can also have a cursory look at the relationship between the samples by using R's `heatmap()` function to plot a heatmap and associated dendrograms for a subset of the data (just the first 50 genes in this case).

```
heatmap(X[1:50,])
```

The result is shown in Fig. 4.10. A difference between the sample types can clearly been seen, even with this very small arbitrary selection of genes. This is not unexpected given the very different biology of regenerating and developing tissue, and the clustering is very similar to that seen in the heatmap for this experiment at the GEO web site, which takes into account data from all the spots. This kind of quick and dirty analysis of data is not recommended! Normally, we would use proper gene selection criteria and take into account factors such as data scaling, but the aim of this example is simply to give a taste of how—with very little code—data can be imported into R and visualized. Indeed, the danger of using powerful tools such as R and Bioconductor is that complex functions can be used without any knowledge of their underlying statistical algorithms, potentially leading to bogus results. We therefore recommend that you always gain a good understanding of algorithms that you're using by reading relevant background material, or by consulting experts in the subject.

Getting data from GEO is quite handy for a tutorial like this, because the pre-processing has already been done before the data is deposited in GEO. In many applications, the starting point is raw data from an instrument (e.g. `.CEL` files from Affymetrix microarray analysis) and pre-processing is required before any meaningful analysis can be done, but Bioconductor includes a number of packages that include functions to make the transformation from raw data to *ExpressionSet* object fairly painless. These packages tend to be platform dependent, and include `affy`, `arrayMagic` and `oligo`.

Bioconductor is a truly massive resource and is one of the reasons for the popularity of R among bioinformaticians, particularly those dealing with microarray data. In this section, we have only scratched the surface of its functionality. The main reason for not going further is the fact that the particular Bioconductor functionality of interest is naturally application dependent. Indeed, if you're

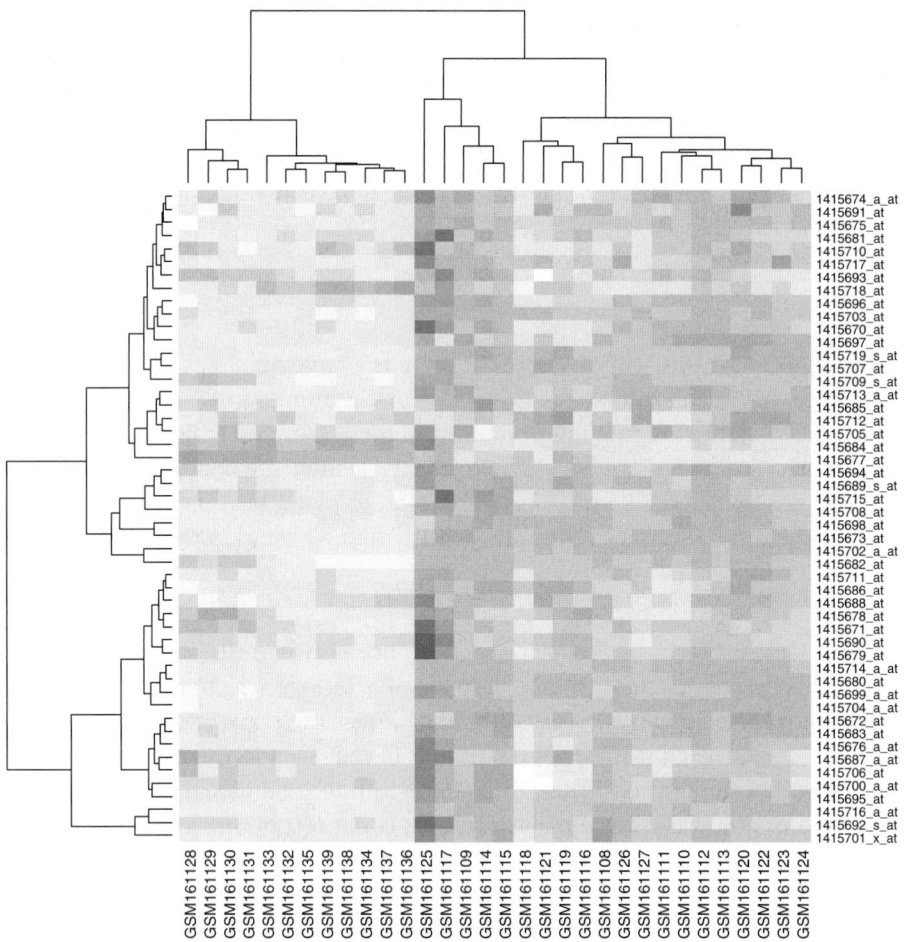

Fig. 4.10 Heatmap and associated dendrograms generated from the first 50 genes from GEO dataset GDS2577. The expression of individual genes is clearly different between the two sample types (developing and regenerating liver).

working on something other than microarray data you may well have to look elsewhere to find useful packages. To learn more about Bioconductor we thoroughly recommend the book *Bioinformatics and Computational Biology Solutions Using R and Bioconductor* (Gentleman *et al.*, 2005). Such books should be quite accessible now that this chapter has helped you overcome the hurdle of getting started with R.

4.3.2   The RMySQL package for database connectivity

In the previous chapter we saw how easy it is to access MySQL databases in Perl programs using the Perl DBI modules. Similar connectivity is provided in R by a package called RMySQL, and the DBI package on which it is built. All we need do to enable this functionality is to install the RMySQL package from CRAN and load it into R. The associated DBI package will be installed and loaded automatically.

(If you're using Linux, it may be more straightforward to search your package manager first as this can solve problems with unmet dependencies). Together, these packages allow us to connect to a MySQL database, find out information about it, input data, extract data directly into R objects, and even issue standard SQL queries like those described Chapter 2. Similar packages are available for other RDBMSs, but we focus on MySQL here, since it is the RDBMS of choice in this book. After downloading from CRAN, to load the RMySQL packages into R ready for use, we must not forget the command:

```
library(RMySQL)
```

The examples below show how the available functions can be used to interact with the example database from Chapter 2.[1] If you have that database to hand, you can issue these commands (inserting the correct username and password) and you will get results back from the database. The process is very similar to using Perl DBI, in that the first step is to establish a connection to the database. This is done with the command below (entered on one line):

```
dbh <- dbConnect(dbDriver("MySQL"), dbname = "PCR_experiment",
user="conrad", password="donuts")
```

If the connection is successful, a database connection handle is returned (in this case into dbh) and this is then used to refer to the database in subsequent commands. For example, we can get a list of tables in the database by passing the handle to the dbListTables() function. This is very similar to the MySQL SHOW tables command, except that the tables are returned as a list within R instead of just being printed to the screen.

```
> dbListTables(dbh)
[1] "experiment" "kit" "kit_order" "scientist" "supplier"
```

Where this functionality gets really useful is when we use much more powerful functions, such as dbReadTable(), which allows us to read data directly into a data frame and dbWriteTable() is used to populate a table with data from R. An example of an R session in which the contents of a whole table is extracted from the PCR_experiment database (previously opened with handle in dbh) is shown below:

```
> orders <- dbReadTable(dbh,"Kit_order")    # copy data to data frame
> orders                                     # display content of data frame
    order_number   manufacturer             kit_name           supplier
1   1              The Epsilon Kit Company   Basic PCR Kit 1    Epsilon Chemicals
2   115            The Epsilon Kit Company   Basic PCR Kit 2    Epsilon Chemicals
3   121            The Epsilon Kit Company   Basic PCR Kit 1    Epsilon Chemicals
4   380            Simply Solutions          PCR Visual Dye Kit Experiments_R_US
```

---

1 If you don't already have it, you can create and populate this database using the PCR_database_create.txt and PCR_database_populate.txt source files available at www.bixsolutions.net.

Reading whole tables into R somewhat defeats the purpose of having the data in a database—normally it is desirable to only copy out the data you need, to minimize memory usage and maximize performance. This can be achieved by issuing queries using dbGetQuery(). In the example below, this function is used to import just the costs of PCR kits from the Kit table of the example database:

```
> dbGetQuery(dbh,"SELECT kit_cost FROM Kit")
     kit_cost
1     49.99
2     19.99
3     29.99
```

Indeed, any valid SELECT query can be executed in this way and the results will be returned to a data frame in R, allowing you to process those results using all the power of R and its associated packages. This ability to harness the complementary strengths of R and MySQL makes for a very powerful combination. In the example interaction below, one of the more complex queries from Chapter 2 is issued and the output placed in a data frame called result.

```
> result = dbGetQuery(dbh,"SELECT scientist_email,
COUNT(scientist_email) FROM Experiment GROUP BY scientist_
email;")
> result # check the results
  scientist_email COUNT(scientist_email)
1   c.bessant@bixsolutions.net        1
2   d.oakley@bixsolutions.net         2
3   i.shadforth@bixsolutions.net      2
```

Even SQL commands that make major changes to the database, such as CREATE and DROP statements can be issued by calling dbGetQuery().

Finally, as with Perl, it is good practice to disconnect from the database once you have finished with it, by calling the dbDisconnect() function:

```
dbDisconnect(dbh)
```

4.3.3 Packages for multivariate classification

There exists a plethora of methods for constructing a classification model—far more than can be dealt with in detail here, but the details can be found in chemometrics textbooks (Brereton 2007; Otto 2007). Provided that samples from similar classes cluster well in a PC scores plot, one of the easiest solutions is to divide up the scores plot into sections using a collection of linear boundaries. New samples are then identified according to which side of the boundaries they fall on. This approach is referred to as linear discriminant analysis (LDA). LDA is capable of automatically generating the boundaries using fairly simple mathematics, and the technique can be extended to multiple dimensions—in three dimensions the boundary becomes a two-dimensional plane and in higher dimensions it is a hyper plane. This means that LDA can be used on the original data matrix, as well as on PCA scores, regardless of the number of variables measured. An R implementation of LDA is provided as the function `lda()` in the MASS package included in the basic R installation.

In more complex data sets, where there are many classes of sample or classes of sample that cluster in an unusual shape or with a lot of variance, it is not always possible to separate classes using simple linear features defined by LDA. There are various approaches that can be tried for these tougher problems, including support vector machines (of which there is an implementation in a CRAN package cryptically called `e1071`) and neural networks (see the CRAN `nnet` package). There are many good books on neural networks (e.g. Demuth *et al.*, 1995).

4.3.4   Writing your own R packages

In the future, after acquiring a wealth of R experience, you might end up producing some really useful functions that you would like to share with the community. The best way to do this is by making these functions available as a package. Anyone can create a package, using commands available within R and anyone may submit a package for inclusion in CRAN.

An R package is not just a collection of functions—it must also include documentation and various other bits of information about the package. A package may also include data, demos, and examples. When putting a package together, these different components need to be placed in specifically named files and subdirectories so that R knows where to find the relevant information when someone installs your package on their computer. If you explore the directory into which you have installed packages (typically the `library` subdirectory of wherever you installed R) you will see that each package has its own directory, each containing files and directories with standard names, e.g. `CONTENTS`, `help`, and so on. The whole process of creating a package is necessarily prescriptive, with a particular data format being required for the documentation and special attention being paid to filenames to ensure that the package functions on all the operating systems that R supports. Perhaps most importantly, you also need to make sure your package is thoroughly tested, and is optimized for speed and memory usage. For these reasons, production of an R package is really only a task for a very experienced R programmer, so it is therefore not sensible to go into details in this introductory chapter. Suffice to say, producing your own packages is possible, and if you want to know more you should check out the *Writing R Extensions* PDF manual that comes with R.

4.3.5   Integrating Perl and R

As we have emphasized throughout this book, increasingly few bioinformatics tasks can be solved efficiently using a single tool. Integration of tools is therefore crucial. We have already seen above how easy it is to hook up R to MySQL to enable R's sophisticated analysis and visualization capabilities to be applied to data stored in a relational database. What about integrating Perl with R? One of the great benefits of R's command line interface is that it is very easy to construct commands outside of R and pass them to R for processing. This means that we are able to make use of the visualization capabilities of R, and the analysis capabilities provided by R and the plethora of available packages, from within Perl programs. Furthermore, the fact that R is open source means that such hybrid software solutions can be distributed without concerns about licensing. Integrating Perl and R is discussed further in the next chapter.

4.4   Alternatives to R

There are many software packages available for the analysis of biological data. Such software may be freely available via the web, it may come bundled with an instrument (for example microarray scanners are likely to ship with image processing software) or the software may be sold commercially (for example, for protein identification from mass spectrometry data). Almost without exception, these packages feature graphical user interfaces to make their full range of functionality available to the average biologist. As mentioned earlier, such user interfaces actually make it more difficult to build bioinformatics solutions, particularly where there is a need to integrate with other tools. In considering genuine alternatives to R, we therefore restrict ourselves to packages that are primarily command line-based, and which have native support for storage and manipulation of matrices, something that we have seen is key in many bioinformatics applications. It should be noted that this section is not exhaustive, but it captures the main packages that we have seen in use across the bioinformatics community.

4.4.1   S-Plus

S-Plus is a commercial statistics package from Insightful software (www.insightful.com). In many ways, it is the obvious alternative to R, as both R and S-Plus are based on the same underlying statistical language—S. Most code is therefore interchangeable between the two packages and some R packages can be used with S-Plus. Insightful also offer their own S-Plus specific add-ons, called *modules*. Having said that, although R and S-Plus share the same core language, there are differences in the S-Plus implementations of additional features such as devices, certain graphics functions, and internet connectivity. So, for example, the main example programs in this chapter will not work in S-Plus without modification.

The main benefits that S-Plus offers are a more developed graphical user interface and more consistent documentation. This makes the learning curve of S a little less challenging than that of R, but the downside is there are fewer S users than R users, so free help and code are harder to find on the web. Due to the similarity with R, there is little to add about S-Plus, except to say that Insightful tend to offer free trials of the software and that is, by far, the best way to find out whether it is the tool for you.

4.4.2   Matlab

Matlab from Mathworks (www.mathworks.com) is another commercial alternative to R, currently available for a range of operating systems including Windows,

Mac OS, and Linux. It has a strong pedigree in numerical data analysis in the engineering sector, and its use has more recently spread to the analysis of chemical and biological data. Being a commercial package, it has many of the same benefits as S-Plus, particularly excellent and consistent documentation. There is a lot of common functionality between Matlab and R, but the syntax is different. A sample Matlab session is shown below. The double arrow (>>) is the Matlab command prompt, and the % symbol is used to denote the start of a comment:

```
>> x = [2.0, 2.8, 3.9, 4.0, 4.8, 6.5] % assign vector to x

x =

    2.0000    2.8000    3.9000    4.0000    4.8000    6.5000

>> y = round(x.^2) % square elements of x and round to
nearest integer

y =

    4         8        15        16        23        42

>> plot(x, y, 'b:') % plot y as a function of x with dotted
blue line
```

If you're moving from Matlab to R, or *vice versa*, there is a very useful document on CRAN called *R for Octave Users* (cran.r-project.org/doc/contrib/R-and-octave.txt), which catalogues direct relationships between Matlab syntax and the R equivalent. Alternatively, if you're moving from Matlab to R, there is an R package called matlab available via CRAN, which provides a subset of popular Matlab functions for use in R, such as imagesc(), ones(), and reshape().

Matlab offers similar programming capabilities to R—programs can be written in text based .M files, and can include loops, conditional statements, and user defined functions. Matlab also has a reasonable object-oriented programming model, which can be easier to get to grips with than R objects. A major benefit of Matlab over R is the user interface, which includes a fully integrated development environment (IDE), allowing programs to be written and debugged in relative comfort. The IDE includes a graphical user interface designer called GUIDE, which allows for the creation of sophisticated front ends for Matlab code, such as the one shown in Fig. 4.11.

Visualization is another area where Matlab challenges R. Matlab's graphs are somewhat slicker, and as well as being able to manipulate the figures using low level graphics functions like those in R, all figures are interactive and their detailed appearance can be tweaked via the graphical user interface. This is particularly useful when preparing figures for publication.

Toolboxes are the Matlab equivalent of R packages. Many toolboxes are sold by Mathworks themselves, but there are several third party commercial toolboxes on the market, and even more freely available efforts. There is a dedicated

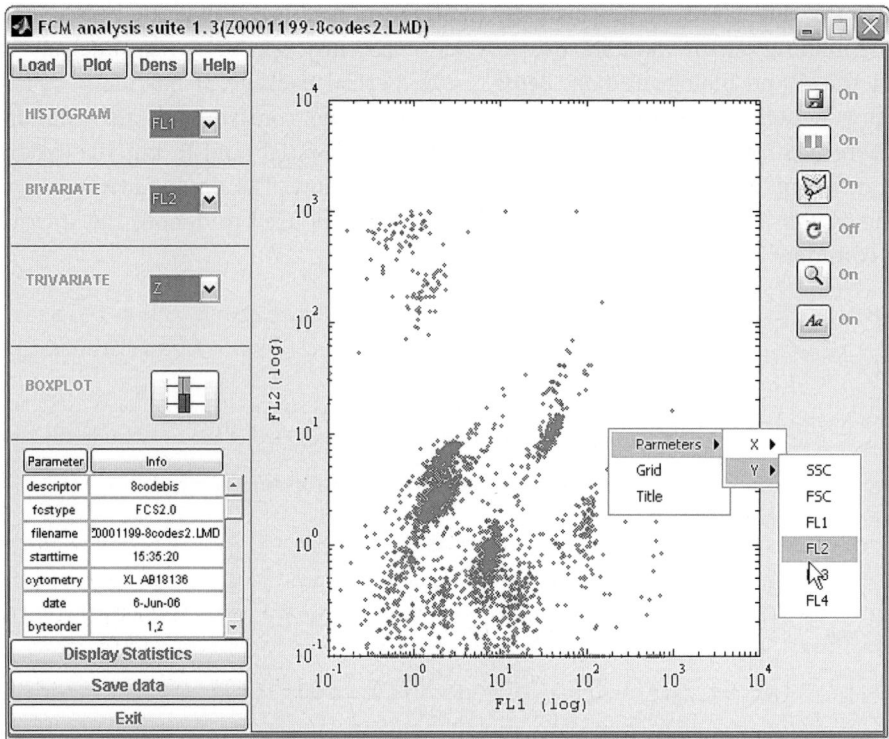

Fig. 4.11 A graphical front end for a flow cytometry data analysis application, created by Colin Clarke while at Cranfield University, using GUIDE in Matlab.

bioinformatics toolbox, which provides a reasonable core of functionality, but does not have the breadth of coverage provided by Bioconductor.

The great disadvantage of Matlab is that it costs money and people with whom you may want to share your programs may not have access to it. Mathworks do sell a compiler that allows Matlab programs to be made available as stand-alone entities that don't require the user to have a Matlab license, but this is not quite the same as being able to pass someone your source code.

4.4.3 Octave

Octave, also referred to as GNU Octave, is to Matlab was R is to S-Plus. It is a free package that has very similar syntax to Matlab. Indeed, with sufficient care, programs can be written that run on both Matlab and Octave without modification. Octave's web site is www.octave.org and the software can be freely downloaded from there. Like R and Matlab, Octave is compatible with a range of operating systems, including Windows, Linux, and Mac OS. Interactions with Octave are via a command line interface very similar to R and Matlab. The similarity with Matlab means that Matlab syntax can be typed in right away, with familiar results. For example, the interaction below mimics the Matlab example given previously:

```
octave:1> x = [2.0, 2.8, 3.9, 4.0 4.8 6.5] % assign vector to x
x =

  2.0000   2.8000   3.9000   4.0000   4.8000   6.5000

octave:2> y = round(x.^2) % square elements of x and round
y =

  4       8       15      16      23      42

octave:3> plot(x, y, 'b:')
```

Like R and Matlab, Octave offers various visualization capabilities. Visual results are actually rendered by a separate program, Gnuplot, to which Octave sends commands to produce the required graphics. In general, the visual output is inferior to both R and Matlab.

Programming in Octave is very similar to programming in Matlab, thanks to the similarity of syntax between the two. Like R and Matlab, Octave's functionality can be increased through the addition of packages, many of which can be found on Octave-Forge (octave.sourceforge.net). Generally, the Octave community tends to be focused more on engineering than biology, so there are slim pickings for the bioinformatician in the packages available.

4.5 Summary

The ability to reliably perform advanced data analysis using the latest algorithms is a key requirement in many bioinformatics applications and R allows us to fulfil this requirement in most cases. R's key features are the inherent support for importing and manipulating data matrices, the ease with which graphs can be constructed, and the plethora of packages that have already been written to do the majority of bioinformatics tasks. We have seen in this chapter how R can provide a wide range of analyses, ranging from simple statistical analyses through to microarray pre-processing and sophisticated data visualization and analysis, all with very little actual coding. In the next chapter we see how this power can be harnessed for use in web-based tools through integration with Perl and MySQL.

References

Brereton, R. G. (2007). *Applied Chemometrics for Scientists*.Chichester: Wiley.

Demuth, H. B., Beale, M. H., & Hagan, M. T. (1995) *Neural Network Design*. PWS: Boston (USA).

Gentleman, R., Carey, V. P., Huber, W., & Irizarry, R. A. (2005). *Bioinformatics and Computational Biology Solutions Using R and Bioconductor*. Berlin: Springer-Verlag.

Otto, M. (2007). *Chemometrics: Statistics and Computer Application in Analytical Chemistry*. Chichester: Wiley.

Otu, H. H., Naxerova, K., Ho, K., Can, H., Nesbitt, N., Libermann, T. A., & Karp, S. J. (2007) Restoration of liver mass after injury requires proliferative and not embryonic transcriptional patterns. *Journal of Biological Chemistry*, **282**: 11197–11204.

Sadowski, P., Dunkley, T. P. J., Shadforth, I. P., Dupree, P., Bessant, C., Griffin, J. L., & Lilley, K. S. (2006) Quantitative proteomic approach to study subcellular localization of membrane proteins. *Nature Protocols*, **1**: 1778–1789.

CHAPTER 5

Programming for the Web

In this chapter we show how to bring together the skills covered in the previous three chapters to make data and analysis tools available via the web. This moves us into the subjects of web servers and web development, skills that are frequently required in the field of bioinformatics. It is no coincidence that all the major biology databases, and many of the key bioinformatics tools, are accessed via the web. The reason is that everyone has a web browser, regardless of their operating system, and there are plenty of helpful tools available for developing web interfaces to Perl programs and MySQL databases. You might think that web interfaces are only important in situations where we want to make our work accessible via the internet, but even for local applications used by a single organization or group, a web interface accessible over a local network is often the most painless way to interface users with your software.

5.1   Introduction to web servers and Apache

Before we get onto the task of web development, we first need a basic understanding of the tools responsible for serving content to web users—*web servers*. A web server is a software package that runs on a computer (typically also called a server when used for this, although it may be just a humble PC), and serves web pages and related files to other users over a network. Apache is the most popular web server used in the world today and is the web server solution that we recommend. It is the server of choice in bioinformatics due to being free, open source, fast, highly configurable, and available on most operating systems.

To follow the examples in this chapter, you will need access to a functioning web server on which you can put and modify files. There are several ways you can do this:

◆ *Use a server provided by your organization.* If you are working for a company, or in an educational establishment, your organization may have server hardware on which web server software such as Apache is already installed. The administrator of this server would have to give you a user account with permission to upload files to this server. You can then copy files and programs over to the server, and access them by pointing your web browser to that server.

◆ *Buy a hosting package.* There are many companies around the world offering space on their servers for hosting web sites, often at very competitive prices.

However, it is important to realize that not all web hosting is equal. In particular, to get a server capable of running programs that you have written yourself, particularly incorporating database functionality, can be expensive.

• *Use a second computer.* If you own more than one computer, you can install web server software such as Apache on one computer and use that as a web server. You can then use a second computer to develop your web pages and programs, before copying them to the server. You would test your material by connecting to the server using your web browser. One benefit of this approach is that the operating system on the server (Linux would be a good choice) can be independent of the operating system on the other computer (e.g. a Windows laptop or desktop PC).

• *Use your own computer.* This is the cheapest and simplest option, and the one that we assume most people will adopt for this chapter. We explain how to install Apache on your computer—this referred to as running the server *locally* (as opposed to over a network). You can then connect to the Apache server from a browser on that same computer, just as if you were accessing it over the internet. This is not a very practical way of hosting a real web site, as it requires your computer to be permanently on and accessible via the internet, and you will be sharing your computer's processor and memory with visitors to your web site. However, it is a perfect approach for learning about developing web resources.

5.1.1   Using the Apache web server

A detailed guide to installing and configuring an Apache web server is beyond the remit of this book, but this section points you to the information needed to get Apache up and running, and details how you would load your web-based documents and programs into a pre-configured default install of the Apache web server so that they can be accessed through a web browser.

The process for installing and configuring your own instance of Apache depends on your operating system[1]. We recommend making sure that all network related programs (e.g. browsers, email, Skype, and any other chat software) are closed prior to installing Apache, as these can interfere with the installation process. Also, we don't recommend installing more than one web server on a single computer!

• Windows users will find all the necessary instructions within the Apache documentation (httpd.apache.org/docs). Click on the documentation for the latest version of Apache and then you will find specific instructions for Windows installation in the *Platform Specific Notes* section. As with software downloaded in other chapters, it is best to look for the MSI file for easy installation (this can be found from httpd.apache.org/download.cgi). During installation, you will be prompted to enter a domain name, sever name, and email address. Depending

---

1 At the time of writing, there is a choice of Apache installations—one with additional security (SSL) and one without. For simplicity, we recommend using the version without SSL while you are learning, but suggest investigating SSL in future if you need secure connections to your web pages.

on how your computer is set up, these fields may already be filled in, but if not you can enter `localhost` for both domain and server, and your normal email address.

- If you are a Linux user, consult the documentation specific to your distribution—Apache is a central part of the success of the Linux operating system and is easy to install on all distributions.

- Macintosh users already have Apache installed as part of the operating system, all web documents (HTML files) and CGI programs (we'll introduce these soon) are stored in the `Documents` and `CGI-Executables` directories found in `/Library/WebServer/`. All you need to do to start Apache is to activate 'web sharing' in the system preferences.

The way to test an Apache installation is to point your browser to your server—the URL will be `http://localhost` if you are running Apache locally. If the installation is successful you should see a simple 'It works!' message. At this point, you might begin to wonder who else can see this page and which of your other files they can see. The answer is that only files placed in a specific location on your computer can be accessed via Apache (see the next section), and these can only be seen from remote computers if you do not have a firewall (or it is turned off), or you have allowed incoming access to port 80 through your firewall. If you do not want your web server accessible from other machines, make sure that your firewall is turned on and is blocking incoming connections. If you do want to allow access to your web server, consult the documentation for your firewall (most likely found with the documentation for your operating system) and look for information on how you can open up connections on specific ports to outside machines.

Once Apache is installed, using it to serve up your documents is quite simple. The only things that you need to know are where Apache expects certain types of documents to be stored and the permissions that need to be applied to these documents.

5.1.2   Apache fundamentals

Before we get into the details, we'll just take a moment for a brief overview of the most important concepts when developing material for a web server.

HTML documents

HTML documents are text-based files that get served up as static web pages by your web servers. In order for these to be served by Apache, they must be stored in a specific directory on the server—this is often known as the DocumentRoot or `htdocs`, and its location should be detailed within the server installation documentation. Basically, if you store all of your HTML files here (or in subdirectories within this directory), you will then be able to access these files via a web browser by pointing your web browser at the server. On Windows, your DocumentRoot will be something like `C:\Program Files\Apache Software Foundation\Apache2.2\htdocs`, depending on where you installed Apache and which version you have (in this case 2.2), on Linux it is usually located at `/var/www/`, on Mac OS it is located at `/Library/WebServer/Documents`.

CGI programs

CGI programs are programs that dynamically generate web pages. Like HTML files, Apache expects CGI programs to be stored in a specific directory before it will serve them to incoming connections; this is usually called the *cgi-bin* directory. On Windows the cgi-bin directory will be something like `C:\Program Files\Apache Software Foundation\Apache2.2\htdocs\cgi-bin`, on Linux it is usually located at `/usr/lib/cgi-bin`, and on Mac OS it is located at `/Library/WebServer/CGI-Executables`.

Unix file ownership and permissions

Understanding the basics of file ownership and permissions is critical to working successfully with the Apache web server on Linux and Mac OS, as such we provide here an overview of the key concepts. Windows users need not read this section as in Windows file permissions are much less strict, so there is no need to consider permissions and ownership.

All files and directories on a Unix-based system are owned by a user and a group, and the user, group, and everyone else can be given specific privileges to use, or indeed, not use a file or directory. To find out what user and group a file belongs to, open up a terminal and run the following command in a directory of your choice: `ls -l`. You will get an output similar to that shown below:

```
-rw-rw-r-- 1 daz staff 4.5K 2007-02-28 14:40 image.gif
drwxr-xr-x 11 daz staff 374 2007-09-10 11:13 directory1/
drwxr-xr-x 8 daz staff 272 2007-12-01 15:31 directory2/
drwxr-xr-x 16 daz staff 544 2007-03-29 21:48 directory3/
-rw-rw-r-- 1 daz staff 3.9K 2007-02-28 14:40 index.html
```

In this example, all the files here belong to the user `daz` and the group `staff`, indicated by the names to the left of the file listing. We also need to take note of the permissions granted to the files and directories—this is the matrix of d, r, x, and w symbols on the left. This basically tells us if the line refers to a directory (signified by a d), and then which users can read (r)/write (w)/execute (x) a file. The layout of this matrix is shown below:

```
        d    rwx    rwx    rwx
       /    /         \        \
     dir  user      group  everyone
```

It is basically three groups of the letters r, w, and x for each possible type of user that could access a file. If a letter is present, it means that the appropriate permission is granted to that type of user.

The reason that we need to have an understanding of this is that the Apache web server runs as if it were being run from a user account—not from the root account (which is used for most other server processes)—in order to protect the server from being compromised should a security flaw be found in Apache. Therefore, any document that you create for the Apache web server to use must have the appropriate permissions set so that Apache can both access and handle the file accordingly. As such, from here we shall assume that all documents and programs that you create and place in your `DocumentRoot` or `cgi-bin` directories will be owned by the `root` user and also belong to the `root` user group (as if they were created by the administrator of your system). If you decide to create files in your own directories and then move/copy them into the Apache served directories, you can change the ownership of the files (over to the root user) using the `chown` command, for which the generic syntax is:

```
chown new_owner:new_group file_name
```

An example of this would be:

```
chown root:root index.html
```

Then finally you will need to ensure the following rules for the permissions of your files:

• If your file is a text file (i.e. HTML, CSS, JavaScript, etc.), it only needs to be readable by the server, so we should ensure that the files are readable by all users, but not writable or executable.

• If your file is a program that needs to be run by the server (i.e. a Perl program), it not only needs to be readable by the server, it also needs to have executable permissions.

These permissions can be altered using the `chmod` command, the syntax for which is:

```
chmod modification_code file_name
```

The modification code refers to a code that defines the permissions that will be applied to the file after using this command. The way these codes are constructed is complicated, but there are only really two that you are likely to need whilst working with Apache, 744, and 755. For example:

```
chmod 744 index.html
chmod 755 my_program.pl
```

Code 744 sets the permissions of a file to be readable/writable/executable by its owner, but only readable by everyone else, (`rwxr--r--` if viewed via `ls -l`) this is suitable for text documents. Code 755 sets the permissions of a file to once again be readable/writable/executable by its owner, but this time the file is readable and executable by everyone (`rwxr-xr-x` if viewed via `ls -l`), so this is used for programs that we wish Apache to execute at the request of people using the server.

5.2   Introduction to HTML

HTML (short for HyperText Mark-up Language) is the text-based data format that is the basic building block of the web that we know and love today. It is a mark-up language based on the concepts of *tags* and content—very similar to the XML described in Chapter 2. Since it is a text-based format, it is possible to generate and edit HTML documents in a standard text editor, such as those reviewed at the start of Chapter 3. Just be sure to save the file with the extension `.html`. One main difference between HTML and XML is that in XML the tags are freeform—you get to decide what they are, as the tags are directly relevant to the data that they contain. In HTML, the tags are already defined in a vocabulary. The reason for this is that XML is a data storage/description language, so it needs to be very flexible, HTML on the other hand is more concerned with data presentation, therefore most of the tags used in HTML dictate how your data is presented in a web page, so the definitions and syntax of these tags needs to be established up front. Here are some simple examples of HTML tags:

```
<p>This is a paragraph</p>
<p>This is a paragraph with some <b>bold</b> text</p>
```

As you can see, this is very similar to XML. Textual data is simply surrounded by tags that indicate how the text will be formatted on the final web page. You may also remember *attributes* in XML, these are options that can be added to a tag—these are also present in HTML. For example:

```
<table border="1" cellpadding="5" cellspacing="5">
  <tr>
    <td>Column 1</td>
    <td>Column 2</td>
  </tr>
</table>
```

As with XML, the attributes infer extra properties on the data that the tags encase—in the above example we are dictating the size of the border, and the spacing between the cells and text of a table of data.

Before we move on to explaining how we can structure and build our first web pages, we need to look at the syntax that we are going to use in this section.

5.2.1   HTML versus XHTML

HTML has been around since the beginning of the web. XHTML on the other hand is a slightly more recent take on the standard and is based on the concept of making HTML XML compliant—giving you XHTML, a slightly more strict form of HTML mark-up. The basic differences between the two are as follows:

- In HTML, single (often known as *empty*) tags such as `<br>`, which produces a line break, do not require a closing tag; in XHTML, they need to be self-closing: i.e. `<br>` would become `<br/>`, where the forward slash before the greater than symbol indicates that the tag is self-closing.

- Nested tags, i.e. tags opened inside another set of tags, must be closed within the first set of tags, as tags are not allowed to overlap in XHTML. Here is an example: `<strong><em>Hello</em></strong>` is allowed, while `<strong><em>Hello</strong></em>` is not allowed as the tags overlap.

♦ Another difference is case-sensitivity. In XHTML, you must use lowercase letters for all tags and attributes. In addition to this, attributes must be surrounded by quotes.

Although HTML still works fine in browsers, it is generally considered good practice to use XHTML, so all the examples of code we give you from here on in will be XHTML. It is the more recent standard and is fully supported in the vast majority of web browsers. For more information on XHTML we recommend the official documentation (www.w3.org/TR/xhtml1).

5.2.2   Creating and editing HTML/XHTML documents

Before we move on to discussing the details of XHTML, we need to decide on a tool to use to create our web pages. As with Perl and R programming, the writing of HTML and XHTML documents (as well as CSS and JavaScript which we'll cover later) can be greatly aided by the use of a good text editor in which to write your code. There are many editors available that are suitable for the job, in fact most of the tools listed in Chapter 3 can also be used as editors for HTML/XHTML, CSS, and JavaScript. As such, if we had to give a recommendation, we would recommend the continued use of Komodo Edit.

5.2.3   The structure of a web page

The basic structure of a web page is shown below:

```
<doctype/>
<html>
  <head>

  </head>
  <body>

  </body>
</html>
```

The entire page is surrounded in <html> tags—note that the <html> tag is used even though we are writing XHTML (similarly, we tend to always save files with the extension .html). Within the page there are two main sections—the <head> and <body> tags. In the head section we place metadata about our web page, such as title, author, any copyright messages, keywords, and we also place links to external resources that can be used in our web page such as CSS style sheets or JavaScript files, which we introduce later. The body section of the web page is home to all of the actual content of the web page.

However, before we move on, we should briefly explain the doctype entry at the top of the page. This declaration is your way of telling a web browser how your web page is formatted (be it either HTML or XHTML, and a specific version of the latter), so it knows how to interpret your mark-up. Without this declaration at the top of the page, the browser would have to guess which form of mark-up you are using, or would just default to standard HTML. This is not normally a problem, but for the sake of completeness including the `doctype` on a web page is a good thing.

Here is an example of a doctype declaration for standard HTML (version 4.01 Transitional):

```
<!DOCTYPE HTML PUBLIC "-//W3C//DTD HTML 4.01 Transitional//EN"
 "http://www.w3.org/TR/html4/loose.dtd">
```

Here is an example for XHTML (version 1.0 Transitional):

```
<!DOCTYPE html PUBLIC "-//W3C//DTD XHTML 1.0 Transitional//EN"
 "http://www.w3.org/TR/xhtml1/DTD/xhtml1-transitional.dtd">
```

These are not things that you need to commit to memory. If you are using a decent text or HTML editor, they will have shortcuts to write these `doctype` declarations for you. Observant readers will also note that the `doctype` tag is not self-closing, even for XHTML. This is the only exception to the rule in XHTML.

Finally, you will notice that there are two types of `doctype`—*strict* and *transitional*. The basic differences between the two are the rules that are applied to the mark-up. As the name would suggest, *strict* is exactly that—only the most strictly correct mark-up will do and even the slightest error will be found upon validation (a topic we will touch on a little later)—this will teach you how to code very good HTML/XHTML, but can be a pain for beginners, who may write code that although technically wrong does not impact on the appearance of the web page. This is where the *transitional* scheme applies—it is slightly more relaxed, but still ensures good clean coding standards. As such, all of our examples in this chapter should be considered to be 'XHTML 1.0 Transitional' to give us a good grounding in standards-based web programming.

5.2.4   XHTML tags and general formatting

Tables 5.1 and 5.2 list some of the most common XHTML tags available for use within web pages. For completeness, we also provide the commonly taught HTML equivalents to the XHTML tags. We say commonly *taught* HTML tags here for a reason. All of the tags presented here as XHTML are also part of the HTML specification—they are just not the commonly taught tags when learning HTML. Modern web programmers prefer the default tags taught with XHTML, i.e. `<strong>` instead of `<b>`.

For more information on the tags available in HTML and XHTML we strongly recommend visiting the W3Schools website (www.w3schools.com)—there you will find more complete descriptions of the tags above, as well as more examples, and the full list of available tags.

5.2.5   An example web page

Now that we have given you an overview of some of the more basic XHTML tags, we can put that all together to create an example web page that we can view in a web browser. Create a file called `test1.html` with your text editor

Table 5.1 Tags commonly used in the `<head>` section of web pages

HTML	XHTML	Description
`<title>`	`<title>`	This defines the title of the webpage
`<meta>`	`<meta>`	This is used for metadata such as author or keywords. i.e.:
		`<meta name="keywords" content="genes, genome" />`
		`<meta name="description" content="..." />`
		`<meta name="author" content="name or email" />`
`<style>`	`<style>`	Used for in-line CSS style declarations (discussed later)
`<link>`	`<link>`	Used to link an external file into our webpage i.e. a CSS stylesheet file
		`<link rel="stylesheet" href="style.css" type="text/css" />`:
`<script>`	`<script>`	Used to add in-line JavaScript code to your webpages or link out to an external JavaScript file:
		`<script src="code.js" type="text/JavaScript" />`
		`<script type="text/JavaScript"> code... </script>`

and enter the code below (alternatively, you can download the code from www.
bixsolutions.net):

```
<!DOCTYPE html PUBLIC "-//W3C//DTD XHTML 1.0 Transitional//EN"
  "http://www.w3.org/TR/xhtml1/DTD/xhtml1-transitional.dtd">
<html xmlns="http://www.w3.org/1999/xhtml">
  <!--
    NOTE: The above xmlns attribute is also required in
    your <html> tag for XHTML...Again, this is something
    your editor normally does for you.
  -->
  <head>
    <title>An Example Web page</title>
    <meta name="author" content="Joe Bloggs" />
    <meta name="description" content="My First Web page!" />
  </head>
  <body>
    <h1>My First Web page</h1>
    <p>This is a quick test of the tags from the book...</p>
    <p>This is a <a href="http://www.bixsolutions.net">link to
    the book's web site</a>.</p>
    <p>This is an unordered list:</p>
    <ul>
      <li>unordered element 1</li>
      <li>unordered element 2</li>
    </ul>
```

Table 5.2 Tags commonly used in the `<body>` section of web pages

HTML	XHTML	Description
`<p>`	`<p>`	A paragraph tag—used to denote a paragraph of text `<p>This is a paragraph of text.</p>`.
` `	` `	A line break (note that this is self-closing in XHTML).
`<b>`	`<strong>`	Used to make your text bold. `<p>This is some <strong>bold</strong> text.</p>`
`<i>`	`<em>`	Used to write text in italics `<p>This is text in <em>italics</em>.</p>`.

`<h1>,`
`<h2>,`
`...,`
`<hx>`
	`<h1>,`
	`<h2>,`
	`...,`
	`<hx>`
		Headings—the numbers indicate the level of heading.
		`<h1>Page Title</h1>`
		`<h2>Sub-Title</h2>`
		`<h3>3rd Level Title</h3>`

`<a>`	`<a>`	Links—these are used to create links between different pages within a website, and also to link out to other websites.
		`<a href="/about">internal link</a>`
		`<a href="http://www.google.co.uk">external link</a>`
		`<a href="mailto:help@bixsolutions.net">email link</a>`

`<ul>,`
`<ol>`
	`<ul>,`
	`<ol>`
		Unordered (bulleted) and ordered (numbered) lists. These tags work in the same way and share the same tag to define a 'list item': `<li>`
		`<ul>`
		`  <li>First on list</li>`
		`  <li>Next on list</li>`
		`</ul>`

`<table>`	`<table>`	These are used to make up tables and require the use of the extra tags `<tr>` for a table row, `<th>` for a table heading column, and `<td>` for a normal table column.
		`<table>`
		`  <tr>`
		`    <th>Heading 1</th>`
		`    <th>Heading 2</th>`
		`  </tr>`
		`  <tr>`
		`    <td>Content 1</td>`
		`    <td>Content 2</td>`
		`  </tr>`
		`</table>`

`<img>`	`<img />`	Used to insert images into your web pages. The `src` attribute indicates the image filename and its position in the file system relative to the XHTML file. The `alt` attribute is a given name for your image that may be displayed under certain circumstances. `<img src="/images/image1.png" alt="Image 1" />`

HTML	XHTML	Description

`<code>`	`<code>`	This is used to indicate computer code and will be printed to the screen exactly as it is typed in the document.
		
		`<code>`
		`  #! /usr/bin/perl`
		`  print "Hello World!\n";`
		`  exit;`
		`</code>`

`<!-- -->`	`<!-- -->`	This is how we put comments in our document. These comments will not be shown when the page is viewed in a browser. `<!-- This will not be printed to screen -->`
`<form>`	`<form>`	This creates a form for user input. A form can contain numerous other elements such as text fields, check boxes, radio-buttons and more. We shall go into forms and the elements that they contain in more detail shortly.

```
<p>This is an ordered list:</p>
<ol>
  <li>element 1</li>
  <li>element 2</li>
</ol>
<h2>More Stuff</h2>
<p>This is an image:</p>
<!-- We're using an external image here for convenience -->
<!-- Oh, by the way - this is a comment! -->
<img src="http://www.rcsb.org/pdb/images/1cf3_bio_r_250.
jpg" alt="Glucose Oxidase" />
<p>This is a table:<p>
<table border="1" cellspacing="5" cellpadding="5">
  <tr>
    <th>Header 1</th>
    <th>Header 2</th>
  </tr>
  <tr>
    <td>Data 1</td>
    <td>Data 2</td>
  </tr>
</table>
<p>Finally, this is a code example:</p>
<code>
  #! /usr/bin/perl<br />
  print "Hello World!\n";<br />
  exit;
</code>
  </body>
</html>
```

Save this file and then open it up in a web browser (there is no need to use Apache at this point). If all was entered correctly you should now have a simple web page in front of you, demonstrating some of the structures and tags that we have just described. If things do not look quite right, recheck your code or, alternatively, read the next section about page validation and use this as a way of finding the faults in the page.

This is all we are going to cover on basic XHTML. A good way to get more comfortable with it is to try to modify `test1.html` and see the results of your changes. If you want to go further, we recommend reading through the tutorials on the W3Schools website and making a few more web pages that link together to form a mini website—one good challenge would be to put your CV in the form of three separate web pages, (one for contact details, one for education, and one for work experience) and then link the pages together using hyper-links (the `<a>` tag).

Finally if you wish to make your documents available on your web server, simply copy the HTML files to your DocumentRoot directory (not forgetting to set the correct permissions on the files with `chmod` if you are using Linux or Mac OS) and the Apache web server will be able to access them and serve them to incoming requests. For example, the simple page above would be accessible via the URL http://localhost/test1.html. If you would like one of your pages to become the *home* page for your server—i.e. the page that is shown by default when someone browses to your server—simply name your file `index.html`.

5.2.6   Web standards and browser compatibility

Thus far in this chapter, you may have noticed a recurring theme in our descriptions of HTML and XHTML, and that is one of *standards*—what we are trying to get across is the importance of *standards based* web programming. As with all of the other subjects in this book, HTML/XHTML are forms of programming languages, and as such they can be programmed correctly or incorrectly—the main difference here is that when you make a mistake in your HTML/XHTML code, nothing tells you that you have made a mistake. In Perl, the program would refuse to run if there was a mistake in the code, a web browser, on the other hand, will try to render a web page with many errors in its code, and often does quite a good job at covering up the mistakes.

The ability of web browsers to deal with poorly formatted HTML/XHTML code is both a blessing and a curse. It is a blessing in the fact that you can get away with small mistakes without ever realizing that you made them, and it is also a curse when something very subtle goes wrong with your web page on a certain web browser and you have to then spend hours trying to find what is casing the mistake. This is where following and adhering to the standards in the first place can help because if you have standards compliant mark-up (HTML/XHTML), all browsers should render it nearly identically. We say *nearly* for a reason—unfortunately, the rendering engines used in the different web browsers available today are quite different to each other in the way that they handle fonts and spacing, and even their default behaviour. This is why you should always test your web pages on different web browsers, even when your site has perfectly valid HTML, just to make sure the page renders as you want it to.

To ensure that we are following the standards correctly we can check the code using a validation tool. There are numerous different validation tools available on the internet either in the form of web-based services or plug-ins for certain web browsers. The one we recommend is the W3C validation service found at validator. w3.org. This is built and run by the World Wide Web Consortium (W3C), the people who write the specifications for HTML and XHTML, so it is safe to say that if your page passes as valid here, it really is valid. To use the validation service you can simply give the tool a URL to check, upload a HTML file or cut and paste in some HTML code; it will then check your code for correctness.

That covers the basics of creating *static* web pages—pages that always display the same information. If we want to use the web as an interface for users to interact with databases and analysis tools that we have written, then we need to combine HTML with a programming language such as Perl. A great way to do this is with CGI.

5.3   CGI programming using Perl

CGI (Common Gateway Interface) is a way for programming languages to interact with web servers. It allows us to write a program in a given programming language that results in the construction of a web page with its contents defined by our program—this is commonly termed as producing a *dynamic* web page. Many languages can be used with CGI, but given the importance of Perl in bioinformatics, we concentrate here on how you can create interactive web pages using Perl and CGI.

Like a lot of things in Perl, CGI operations are handled by a built-in Perl module, in this case the CGI.pm module that comes with a default Perl installation. Here is a short test program to get started with the concepts of Perl CGI. Remember, the first line is the *shebang*. This is essential, regardless of operating system, as it tells Apache where to find Perl. The line shown in the example is typical for Linux and Mac OS. If you are using Windows, you will need to change it to something like #! c:/Perl/bin/perl.exe, depending where you installed Perl.

```
#! /usr/bin/perl

use strict;
use warnings;

use CGI qw(:standard);

my $cgi = new CGI;

print
  $cgi->header,
  $cgi->start_html('Hello World'),
  $cgi->h1('Hello World!'),
  $cgi->end_html;

exit;
```

Copy this code into a file called `hello_world.pl` and store this in your Apache web server's `cgi-bin` directory. Then, if you are on a Linux or Mac OS X system, make sure that the file is executable by all—as was described earlier, this can be done from the terminal by navigating to the cgi-bin directory and then running the following command:

```
chmod 755 hello_world.pl
```

Then you can open up a web browser and visit your web page at http://localhost/cgi-bin/hello_world.pl (assuming you are running Apache locally). Instead of just displaying the content of the `hello_world.pl` file, Apache will execute it, generating a new web page on the fly. The result will be something like Fig. 5.1.

Once you have this displayed in your web browser, view the HTML source code generated by our program (by choosing Source or Page Source from the browser's View menu). You will find that this source is completely valid XHTML 1.0 Transitional syntax that has been produced by the Perl program.

If you have problems with any of the above, first ensure that your Apache web server is set up correctly, is running, and that you know where your cgi-bin directory is; then follow these steps:

• If you have trouble writing a file into the `cgi-bin` directory on Linux or Mac OS, make sure you have administrator permissions and create these files using the administrator user account.

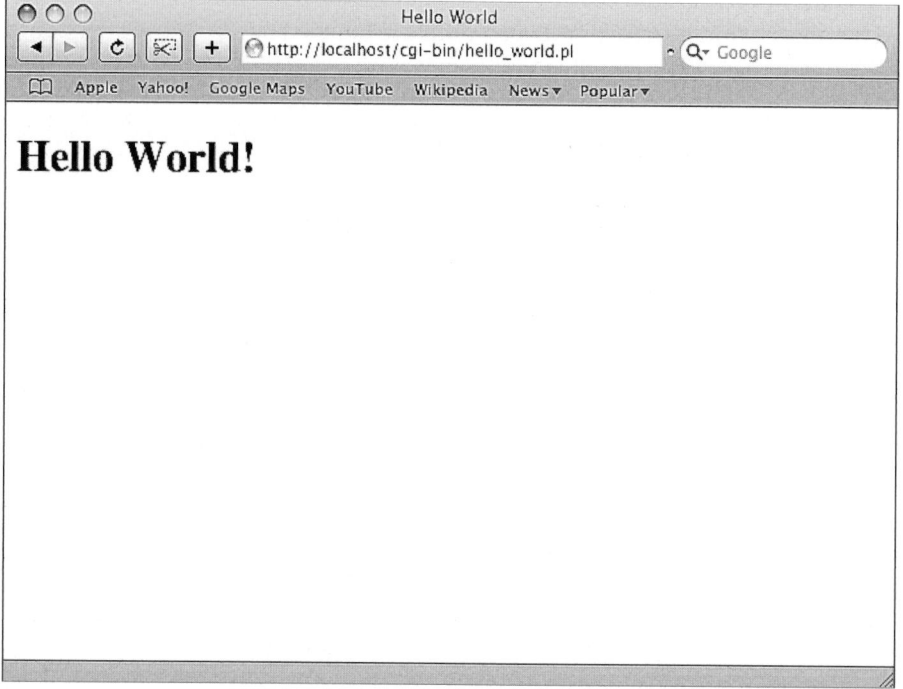

Fig. 5.1 The output of our first Perl CGI program, as seen in the Safari browser.

- If you get an error on the web page saying something like 'Permission Denied', you have not configured the files permissions correctly. Go back and check that the file is executable by all.

- If you get a 'Internal Server Error' message, this means that there is an error in your Perl code—go back and check that, then try again.

If you are still having problems getting your first CGI program to run at this point, see the notes on debugging below (section 5.3.1), and if that doesn't help head over to www.bixsolutions.net and ask for help.

Now let's move on and look at what the code we have written actually does. As you can see, `hello_world.pl` is just a normal Perl program, the only thing that is different is that, instead of you running your program from a terminal window, the Apache web server runs the program, presenting the results via a web browser.

As we said previously, Perl's ability to perform CGI operations is done through the use of a built-in Perl module; as such we invoke this by the use of the `use` command. Following this we create a CGI 'object' variable—this is then used for all of our CGI interaction throughout the rest of our program. The final part of the program is simply using the built in CGI functionality to create the 'Hello World!' page. This is a laborious way of making a one line web page, but the benefit of using CGI is that we can now tap into all the power of Perl discussed in Chapter 3 to create web pages on the fly in response to user input, database queries, the results of data analysis, or whatever we want.

5.3.1   Debugging CGI programs

Now if you are still stuck staring at the 'Internal Server Error' message, fear not, help is at hand. The ability to debug Perl CGI programs is provided through the use of another Perl module, `CGI::Carp`. This allows us to detect errors in our code and print the errors to an error log, or even more usefully whilst we are developing—to the browser window. To use this functionality, all you have to do is add the following line to your Perl code beneath the `use` CGI line:

```
use CGI::Carp qw(fatalsToBrowser);
```

Now any errors that cause a program to fail will be displayed within the browser window, rather than a less than useful 'Internal Sever Error' message. If you do still see 'Internal Server Error', the most likely cause is a missing or incorrect shebang preventing Apache from finding your computer's installation of Perl, so check that first.

In addition to the basic functionality described above (program stopping errors shown to the screen), you can also use the normal `warn()` and `die()` functions within your program as you would to debug your programs normally. If a `die()` statement occurs, you will see output within your browser, but warn statements will not normally be seen. Instead, you will find these within Apache's error logs. These logs are usually stored in the `logs` subdirectory of DocumentRoot, but if you are unable to find them consult the documentation for your Apache installation.

5.3.2   Adding dynamic content to web pages

Let's move things up a gear and look at a more useful example of CGI—displaying information from a database within a web page. This is a common use of CGI in bioinformatics and is a good way to combine the techniques of Perl DBI covered in Chapter 3 with the power of CGI.

In the following example program we connect to the public Ensembl database (www.ensembl.org), query the database for a short list of genes and other information, and then print these to a web page. Here is the code:

```perl
#! /usr/bin/perl

use strict;
use warnings;

use CGI qw( :standard );
use CGI::Carp qw( fatalsToBrowser );
use CGI::Pretty; # This is used to make our HTML code look
                 # nicer...
use DBI;
use DBD::MySQL;

# First we connect to the database
my $dbh = DBI->connect(
  'DBI:mysql:homo_sapiens_core_47_36i:ensembldb.sanger.ac.uk',
  'anonymous'
) or die "Cannot connect to database $!\n";

# Prepare our query
# NOTE: q() is the same as surrounding our text in single
quotes.
my $query = q(
  SELECT es.synonym, sr.name, g.seq_region_start, g.seq_region_end
  FROM seq_region sr, gene g, external_synonym es
  WHERE es.xref_id = g.display_xref_id
  AND sr.seq_region_id = g.seq_region_id
  AND es.synonym IS NOT NULL
  ORDER BY g.seq_region_start ASC
  LIMIT 500
);
my $sth = $dbh->prepare($query);

# Before we run our query and handle the results,
# start the creation of our web page
my $cgi = new CGI;
print
  $cgi->header,
```

```
$cgi->start_html('Example Database Query'),
$cgi->h1('Example Database Query'),
$cgi->p(
  'The table below was created by running this query on the ',
  '\'homo_sapiens_core\' database at',
  a({href=>"http://www.ensembl.org"},'Ensembl'),':'),
$cgi->pre($query),
$cgi->p('Here are the results:');

# Now to run the query and handle our results
$sth->execute();
my @query_results;
while ( my $results = $sth->fetchrow_arrayref() ) {
  push( @query_results, $cgi->Tr($cgi->td($results)) );
}

# And print the results
print $cgi->table(
  { -border => '1', cellpadding => '3', cellspacing => '3' },
  $cgi->Tr([
    $cgi->th([
      'External Synonym', 'Seq Region Name',
      'Seq Region Start', 'Seq Region End'
    ])
  ]),
  @query_results
);

# Clean up
$sth->finish;
$dbh->disconnect;
print $cgi->end_html;
exit;
```

The above program is quite large, but when we break it down into smaller sections, very little of the program is new to us—it is just a combination of the techniques of CGI and DBI. All of the code up until we run the SQL query against the Ensembl database should be familiar:

♦ We declare the modules we are going to use.

♦ We connect to the database.

♦ We prepare an SQL query. Note that this SQL query is not as straight forward as some of the examples that you have seen thus far. Unfortunately, this is the reality of us using the Ensembl database for our query—the Ensembl database has a large and complicated schema. That said it is only a combination of three table joins to gain access to the information that we need—given time working with databases, queries such as this will become second nature.

• Prior to running the SQL query, we set up the beginning of our web page and print the SQL code we are using in <pre> tags as it is pre-formatted text.

Following this we execute the SQL statement against the Ensembl database, retrieve our results and format these in a HTML table. This is the only section of code that should be slightly unfamiliar, so let's look at this section of code in more detail:

```
# Now to run the query and handle our results
$sth->execute();
my @query_results;
while ( my $results = $sth->fetchrow_arrayref() ) {
  push( @query_results, $cgi->Tr($cgi->td($results)) );
}

# And print the results
print $cgi->table(
  { -border => '1', cellpadding => '3', cellspacing => '3' },
  $cgi->Tr([
    $cgi->th([
      'External Synonym', 'Seq Region Name',
      'Seq Region Start', 'Seq Region End'
    ])
  ]),
  @query_results
);
```

The top section of the above code should be familiar from Chapter 3, we simply execute the SQL query and fetch each row of results as an array reference within a `while` loop—however, it is what we do within the `while` loop that is interesting: within this loop we use the CGI object to create a table row entry for our current set of results, which is made up using the following tag syntax:

```
<tr>
  <td>Table column</td>
  <td>Table column</td>
</tr>
```

What you will notice is that the CGI object is clever enough to produce multiple <td> tag sets for all of the results in our array reference, so we do not have to do any special handling of the data. Once we have created our table row of data, we then push it onto the end of an array. Note that we have not printed anything to our page at this point—we are just preparing data.

We then start to create our results table (once again using the CGI object). In the first line we pass a series of attributes to the table to dictate how it will look; following that we add the table headings. This is once again done with the CGI object and uses the <tr> and <th> tags—note how we populate each of these using array references (signified by the use of square brackets around the lists).

Finally, we add on the @query_results array that we prepared previously as this houses a series of table rows containing our results. This then allows us to form a complete HTML table.

The final section of the program (the sections that follows the 'clean up' comment) should be familiar too—we are simply disconnecting from the database cleanly and then adding the closing tags to the HTML.

You can download this program from www.bixsolutions.net (we've called it simple_gene_query.pl). We suggest you copy it onto your web server (into the cgi-bin directory) and have a play with it. Experiment with altering the way in which you represent the data, for example can you figure out a way to put a counter (indicating the number of genes we have returned) at the beginning of each table row?

So, we have dynamically generated content in our web pages using Perl CGI, but what if we want to let users interact with our web pages? We need to add some more skills to our armoury.

5.3.3   Getting user input via forms

The most common way of getting information from users on the internet is via forms. They can be found on almost any web site that allows user interaction, and should be instantly familiar to you and your users. Forms are a standard part of HTML and are therefore very easy to implement. Here is the basic structure of a HTML form:

```
<form action="URL for form handling" method="get/post">
  contents of our form – standard HTML and form elements allowed
</form>
```

Basically it is a `<form>` tag, with two attributes. The two attributes dictate how the form, and the information contained within it, are handled:

- The first attribute `action` details where the information entered into the form should be sent to be processed when it is submitted via the user clicking a *submit* button. You set this attribute to a URL that points to a CGI program to handle the input from the form.

- The second attribute is the method that the web browser is to use to pass these details onto our program. This is explained in more detail later.

The actual content and appearance of the form is defined by elements that are placed between the two `<form>` tags. Table 5.3 lists the various input elements available, but take note of the fact that most use the same tag (`<input>`), it is only the `type` attribute that is used to differentiate them.

You will notice that there are three common attributes shared between the form elements described. These are `type`, `name`, and `value`. Here is a brief description of their uses:

- `type`—this attribute defines the type of input element that you would like to use.

Table 5.3 Commonly used HTML form elements

Input type	Description
Text fields	Text fields are used wherever you want your users to type letters or numbers into a form. `First name: <input type="text" name="firstname" /> ` `Last name: <input type="text" name="lastname" />`
Password fields	Password fields are used whenever you want a user to input sensitive information such as a password. They are basically text fields, but the text in the box is only visible as a series of asterisks. `Username: <input type="text" name="user" /> ` `Password: <input type="password" name="password" />`

Text areas	Text areas are used when you want your users to enter a large chunk of text (that could not reasonably be entered into a text field). Note that you must define the size of the text area that is to be displayed with the `rows` and `cols` attributes.
	
	`<textarea rows="10" cols="30">`
	`  Please enter your text here.`
	`</textarea>`

Radio buttons	Radio buttons are used when you want your users to select exactly one item from a number of choices that you offer them. `<input type="radio" name="sex" value="male">male</input>` ` ` `<input type="radio" name="sex" value="female">female</input>`
Checkboxes	Checkboxes are used when you want users to select zero or more options from a number of choices. `I have a bike:` `<input type="checkbox" name="vehicle" value="Bike" />` ` ` `I have a car:` `<input type="checkbox" name="vehicle" value="Car" />` ` ` `I have an airplane:` `<input type="checkbox" name="vehicle" value="Airplane" />`

Drop down boxes	Drop down boxes are used as alternatives to radio buttons or check boxes. In their default mode (shown below), the user can only select one option from a defined list.
	
	`<select name="go_ontologies">`
	`  <option value="BP">Biological Process</option>`
	`  <option value="MC">Cellular Component</option>`
	`  <option value="MF">Molecular Function</option>`
	`</select>`

Buttons	Buttons are used to submit or reset forms. Reset buttons clear all user entered information from a form, whereas a submit button will pass all of the information held within the form to the handling code that is defined in the form's `action` attribute. Note, unlike other form elements, the value attribute on submit and reset buttons simply defines the text that is shown on the button.
	
	`<input type="submit" value="Submit" />`
	`<input type="reset" value="Reset" />`

♦ `name`—this is used as an identifier for the information that a user enters into a given form element. When we describe passing data from the form on to a program to process the data, the information that is entered into each form element will be accessed via the `name` attribute. A good way to think of this would be that you are passing a data structure similar to a Perl hash, so the information contained within the form can be accessed via the name values of each element. Note that things such as checkboxes and radio buttons should share the same name attribute when they are together in a group (for a single question in your form). If they all have different names, the form would treat them as if you were asking a separate question with each button/box.

♦ `value`—in the case of check boxes, radio buttons and selection drop downs, (where we have pre-defined content) the content of the value attribute is what is passed on to your form parsing program (via the `name` attributes). Note that the value attributes of buttons (`submit` and `reset`) are not passed onto our form handling programs—these are used purely to tell the browser what text to place on the buttons.

Now what happens once a form has been filled out by a user and they hit the submit button? The information contained within the form is passed onto a handling program, but before we show an example form and its related handling program we need to first describe the two methods of form submission.

Submitting forms via POST and GET

With HTML forms there are two ways to submit data, these are via POST and GET. These two methods are introduced below:

♦ *GET.* This method of form submission is used whenever your users are not submitting sensitive data (i.e. a search form). It is not normally used when data from a form is to be used to submit data to a database linked to a website (as this can inadvertently reveal too much about the underlying structure of your site and database, and potentially leave you open to security breaches), and it is most definitely NOT used for submissions that involve things like passwords. The reason for this is that the information contained within your form becomes part of the URL that the form gets submitted to, i.e. if you had a text box with the name `search_query`, the URL the form would be sent to would be something like `/cgi-bin/form_handling.pl?search_query=user_entered_string`, where every entry in the form would follow the question mark (?) and multiple name/value pairs would be linked with an ampersand (&).

♦ *POST.* The POST method of form submission is used whenever you would like to keep the information that your user has submitted in the background, so it is not so clear for anyone to see once the form has been submitted. Post is suitable for forms that are used to enter information into a database and password entries. The information submitted from a form using POST is not appended onto the end of the processing URL.

So the basic rule of thumb is for simple things such as searches, use GET. One of the benefits of this is that it allows people to link to predefined searches, as the search parameter forms part of the URL and would save them submitting a form each time they wanted to repeat an old search. One example of this is YouTube links, e.g. http://www.youtube.com/watch?v=MkxvpAsMxrA. For anything that involves entry to a database or things such as password handling use POST.

Now that we have covered this, let's look at an example of a form. The example web page below defines a form for submitting a gene name to a program for processing (we will put this program together in the next section). Copy this code into a HTML file called gene_query.html, or download it from www.bixsolutions. net and save it in your Apache DocumentRoot directory.

```
<!DOCTYPE html PUBLIC "-//W3C//DTD XHTML 1.0 Transitional//EN"
  "http://www.w3.org/TR/xhtml1/DTD/xhtml1-transitional.dtd">
<html xmlns="http://www.w3.org/1999/xhtml">
  <head>
    <title>Basic Web Form</title>
  </head>
  <body>
    <h1>Basic Web Form Example</h1>
    <p>
      Please enter a gene name and click 'Search' to get a
      report of information for a gene.
    </p>
    <p>
      (If you are at loss for a something to search for,
      try <strong>p53</strong> or <strong>ATP%</strong>).
    </p>
    <form action="/cgi-bin/form_gene_query.pl" method="get">
      <p>
        Gene:
        <input type="text" name="gene" size="15" />
        <input type="submit" value="Search" />
        <input type="reset" value="Clear" />
      </p>
    </form>
  </body>
</html>
```

Here we have a form that is made up of one text field, and has submit and reset buttons. We have also defined an action and a submission method for the information contained within our form—the form is to be processed using a CGI program called form_gene_query.pl and the data within the form will be passed using the GET method. Note that if we were to want to use the POST method of data submission, the only edit that we would have to make to all of our code is to the method attribute—to change it to method="post"—everything else stays exactly the same from a code perspective (both in the XHTML and the Perl program that follows).

Processing form data with Perl CGI

Now we need to write the program that will be used to handle the data submitted via the form. This needs to be saved in an executable file called `form_gene_query.pl` in your cgi-bin directory.

```perl
#! /usr/bin/perl

use strict;
use warnings;

use CGI qw( :standard );
use CGI::Carp qw( fatalsToBrowser );
use CGI::Pretty;
use DBI;
use DBD::MySQL;

# First we connect to the database
my $dbh = DBI->connect(
  'DBI:mysql:homo_sapiens_core_47_36i:ensembldb.sanger.ac.uk',
  'anonymous'
) or die "Cannot connect to database $!\n";

# Then create our CGI object
my $cgi = new CGI;

# Prepare our query
my $query = q(
  SELECT es.synonym, sr.name, g.seq_region_start, g.seq_region_end
  FROM seq_region sr, gene g, external_synonym es
  WHERE es.xref_id = g.display_xref_id
  AND sr.seq_region_id = g.seq_region_id
  AND es.synonym LIKE ?
  ORDER BY g.seq_region_start ASC
  LIMIT 500
);
my $sth = $dbh->prepare($query);

# Before we run our query and handle the results, start the
creation of our web page
print
  $cgi->header,
  $cgi->start_html('Example Database Query'),
  $cgi->h1('Example Database Query'),
  $cgi->p(
    'The table below was created by running this query on the ',
    '\'homo_sapiens_core\' database at ',
```

```perl
      a( { href => "http://www.ensembl.org" }, 'Ensembl' ),
      ':'
   ),
   $cgi->pre($query),
   $cgi->p('Here are the results:');

# Now to run the query and handle our results
# NOTE: The line below is the ONLY completely new thing here...
$sth->execute( $cgi->param('gene') );

my @query_results;
while ( my $results = $sth->fetchrow_arrayref() ) {
  push( @query_results, $cgi->Tr( $cgi->td($results) ) );
}

# Now print the results
print $cgi->table(
  { -border => '1', cellpadding => '3', cellspacing => '3' },
  $cgi->Tr([
    $cgi->th([
      'External Synonym',
      'Seq Region Name',
      'Seq Region Start',
      'Seq Region End'
    ])
  ]),
  @query_results
);

# Another search?
print $cgi->p(
  'Click ',
  a({ href => '/gene_query.html' },'here'),
  ' to submit another search.'
);

# Clean up
$sth->finish;
$dbh->disconnect;
print $cgi->end_html;

exit;
```

The vast majority of the above program should already be familiar. It is essentially the same as the `simple_gene_query.pl` CGI program from earlier in this section. The only addition here is that it is no longer a static query—we are now accepting input from the user via a form (or via adding parameters to the URL). The way that we accept input parameters within a CGI program is through the use of the `$cgi->param` function, which is used in the above program as follows:

```
$sth->execute( $cgi->param('gene') );
```

This returns the content of the element with the name `gene` on the form that we set to forward to this program and we use it as the argument in our query to the database defined earlier in the program. This query is then run against the Ensembl database, and we return the results as a web page exactly as before.

This is the way we pass parameters from a web form to a program for processing, something that is widely used in on-line bioinformatics tools. As long as you construct your web forms correctly—taking care that each element has a different name—and you remember the security/usability issues related to POST and GET, you will have no problem constructing these types of basic forms.

This brings us to the end of our introduction to Perl CGI, although we will return to CGI shortly to look at dynamically generating graphics for our web pages, but first we'll look at some of the more advanced technologies that are required to produce web sites with a more modern look and feel.

5.4 Advanced web techniques and languages

The basics of HTML and CGI described so far are ideal for developing basic in-house bioinformatics tools, but if your aim is to become an accomplished bioinformatics web developer you will need to understand the more advanced technologies that build on this basic foundation. In particular, we would like to mention cascading style sheets (CSS) and JavaScript.

5.4.1 Cascading style sheets

Cascading style sheets (CSS) help make our web applications look nicer—taking us beyond plain white backgrounds and standard black text. This is done by defining a standard *style* for how the various different aspects of your HTML pages are displayed—you can change almost anything; the font, colour, and size of your text, as well as where different sections of your content are positioned. The things that you can do purely with a good understanding of CSS are vast. Unfortunately, we do not have space to provide a thorough and detailed introduction to using CSS, but we will arm you with some basic understanding and direct you to further learning resources.

As we said beforehand, CSS is used entirely to dictate how a web page looks, as such the syntax of CSS is quite simple—it is just a list of style declarations that can be stored in a separate file (known as a CSS stylesheet) or placed at the top (within the `<head>` section) of a HTML page. A web browser will use these styles when rendering the page. Here, we concentrate on the latter (embedded within a HTML page) use of CSS.

Open up an HTML file that you have created (for example, `test1.html`, which we used to show off our knowledge of HTML tags) and add this segment of code somewhere between the `<head>` tags (i.e. just below the last `<meta>` tag) and see how this affects the visual appearance of your web page:

```css
<style type="text/css">
  body {
    font-family: 'Lucida Grande', Verdana, Arial, Sans-Serif;
    color: #444;
  }

  code {
    color: blue;
  }

  table th {
    background-color: black;
    color: white;
  }

  a:hover {
    text-decoration: underline;
    color: red;
  }
</style>
```

This example of code demonstrates the use of CSS within a HTML document. The CSS itself is the code enclosed within the two `<style>` tags, these are used to inform the web browser that the code within is CSS and should be treated appropriately. The CSS is made up of a list of declarations; these start with the name of the element that the declarations are to be applied to (e.g. the first declaration here is `body`) then all styles that are to be applied to that element are enclosed within curly braces.

In the example above we apply two style declarations to the contents of the `<body>` tag within the HTML (everything that we see on our web page is housed within the body tag so this is a good place to set default styles for the entire page to follow)—these declarations are `font-family` and `color`. These two declarations affect the font that is used to display all text within our web page and the colour that is used for the text. The font colour is defined by a hexadecimal code `#444`—this translates to a light grey colour text; all colours in web pages can be defined in this notation—for further information, consult the Wikipedia entry on web colours (en.wikipedia.org/wiki/Web_colors).

In the next declaration we alter the way in which code blocks appear in our web page—we have changed the font colour to blue (notice how we can also use the word `blue` to define the colour we wish to use—for simple colours we can use the names, for more exotic shades we would have to revert to using the hexadecimal codes).

The third declaration defines new rules for table heading cells (`<th>` tags). We colour the text white and make the background colour of the cell black.

Finally, we demonstrate one last concept of CSS—states. In this last declaration we define what happens to links when they are *hovered* over (when a user puts their mouse pointer over a hyperlink)—this is known as the `hover` state. In this instance we define that the text that makes up the link should become underlined and red in colour—this is an effect that you would have no doubt noticed in use all over the internet to signify links. Other available states for use with links and CSS are as follows:

- `link`—this is a link that has not been used, nor is a mouse pointer hovering over it.

- `visited`—this is a link that has been used before, but has no mouse on it.

- `active`—this is a link that is in the process of being clicked.

- `hover`—this is a link that currently has a mouse pointer hovering over it/on it (as used above).

As you can see from viewing your altered web page in a browser, just a small amount of CSS can considerably alter the appearance of a web page. (The modified `test1.html` example is available at www.bixsolutions.net/test1css.html.) To find out more about CSS, we recommend looking at the W3Schools website again– the section covering CSS techniques (www.w3schools.com/css) is very clear and concise. If you prefer a book, *CSS: The Definitive Guide* (Meyer, 2006) is a very good text to introduce you to the subject and will help you progress into more advanced aspects of CSS quickly.

5.4.2 JavaScript, JavaScript libraries, and Ajax

We could not write a book chapter on putting content on the internet at the moment without discussing one of the most important technologies for the web over recent years—JavaScript. What we have looked at so far with Perl and CGI are server-side technologies—all of the data processing happens on the web server and only HTML is sent out to the user's browser. JavaScript, on the other hand, is a client-side programming language—it runs within the browser of the person viewing your web page and can only act on the content of the web page that the user is viewing at the time. This sounds a lot more restrictive than Perl CGI, but the great benefit of JavaScript is the immediacy of feedback, which can make web pages seem much more dynamic and interactive. Some common uses are:

- *Validation*—you can write JavaScript functions to check the content of web forms, for example, when you ask a user for an email address you can immediately check that they have actually entered something that looks like a valid email address.

- *Dynamically changing the content of a web page*—you can write JavaScript functions that adapt the content of your web page based on a user's actions. Examples include multi-part forms where the latter parts of the forms are dependant on what was entered/selected in the earlier part of the form, and collapsible lists.

◆ *Animation*—recent advances in JavaScript techniques make it possible to produce detailed and very slick animations on almost any element of your HTML pages. It is possible to hide a section of content, and upon the click of a button (or even just hovering over a defined section/link/button on your page), have another section slide, fade, or just come into view, ready for the user to use.

◆ *Ajax*—Ajax (Asynchronous JavaScript and XML) is a term used to describe one of the more complex uses of JavaScript. The traditional method of sending data to and from the server in web technologies is before and after each page refresh (i.e. when you submit a form, data is sent to the server, and the web page does a complete refresh whilst the form data is processed). Ajax changes this concept slightly in that it allows communication of data in small pieces between the web page and server without page refreshes so you can submit forms or perform searches on databases without having to do a full page refresh to get your desired results to the screen. This allows web developers to produce a much *richer* experience for their users and can make web-based applications behave much more like desktop applications. Many books and web resources introducing Ajax are available. The *Getting Started* guide at the Mozilla Development Centre (developer.mozilla.org/en/docs/AJAX:Getting_Started) is as good a starting point as any, complete with example code.

As we have already covered several languages in this book, we won't go into detail about JavaScript here. However, there are many good resources for learning about JavaScript and Ajax, and we dedicate the remainder of this section to helping you find them. If you're a book person, we recommend *Learning JavaScript* (Powers, 2006), as this covers the basics of the language and goes all the way up to more advanced techniques such as Ajax.

If you would prefer to get started with a web-based resource, as we recommended with CSS, the W3 Schools site is a great place to get started (www. w3schools.com/js).

Having already got to grips with Perl, JavaScript should not be too much of a challenge, but there is one important caveat—JavaScript can behave differently in different web browsers. This is why you need to test your code on the browsers that you think your users are likely to be using. However, there is help at hand—there are numerous JavaScript library projects (essentially collections of pre-written JavaScript functions and code) that are now helping to make cross-browser JavaScript much less of a problem. Here is a short run down of some of the more recent popular libraries:

◆ *Prototype* (www.prototypejs.org)—This is one of the more popular JavaScript libraries on the internet. It is very easy to learn once you have grasped the basics of JavaScript, and provides numerous helpers and shortcuts to JavaScript coding that make cross-browser JavaScript code and Ajax very simple to generate.

◆ *Yahoo! User Interface Library* (developer.yahoo.com/yui)—This is a set of utilities and controls (sometimes called *widgets*), written in JavaScript, for building richly interactive web applications. YUI is not as straightforward to learn and start working with as Prototype, but many web developers prefer the approach that YUI adopts.

- *jQuery* (jquery.com)—This is another of the more popular JavaScript libraries. jQuery aims to be 'a fast, concise, JavaScript Library that simplifies how you traverse HTML documents, handle events, perform animations, and add Ajax interactions to your web pages'.

Once you have learnt the basic syntax of JavaScript, it would be wise to look into using one of the libraries listed above (or one of the many others that can be found on the internet) when creating your own JavaScript code, as they help by creating a standard platform for you to program with that is more likely to work in all web browsers, so you spend more time working on what you want to do—rather than figuring out why your functions are not working in a particular browser.

5.5 Data visualization with Perl and CGI

One of the more challenging tasks that you might need to perform in bioinformatics is that of producing a graphical output or display for a given data set. We saw in Chapter 4 that R is a very powerful tool to use for this, but what if you want to make such figures available to people dynamically via the web? In this section, we explain the various techniques that you can use via Perl to produce graphical displays dynamically on the web.

5.5.1 Using R graphics in Perl

In the previous chapter, we saw how visualizations, such as plots, bar charts, and heatmaps can be created using R's powerful graphics capabilities. So, can we harness this feature of R from within Perl and use Perl to generate the web pages? Well, the good news is that we can, the bad news is that it is not the most elegant of solutions.

What do we mean by this? Basically, the perfect solution would be an easy to set up and use API for Perl to talk to and control R, so that you can set up your web pages and forms, and just use R to do the complex data manipulation or graphics as and when required. Unfortunately, there is not an easy to set-up and use API to marry Perl with R. There is the beginning of one available in the form of RSPerl (www.omegahat.org/RSPerl), but at the time of writing it is not yet easy to set-up and use, and therefore not suitable for our purposes.

The alternative solution relies on the fact that Perl has the generic capability to execute any process that can be run from the command line, and that R has the functionality to accept pre-written R programs for automated batch processing (this is done by using the command R CMD BATCH, followed by the program name). So we simply use our Perl programs to dynamically produce an R program, which we then run (with R) to perform any analysis and produce graphics plots required. We can then use these in our CGI driven web pages. This process is explained more clearly in the flow chart in Fig. 5.2.

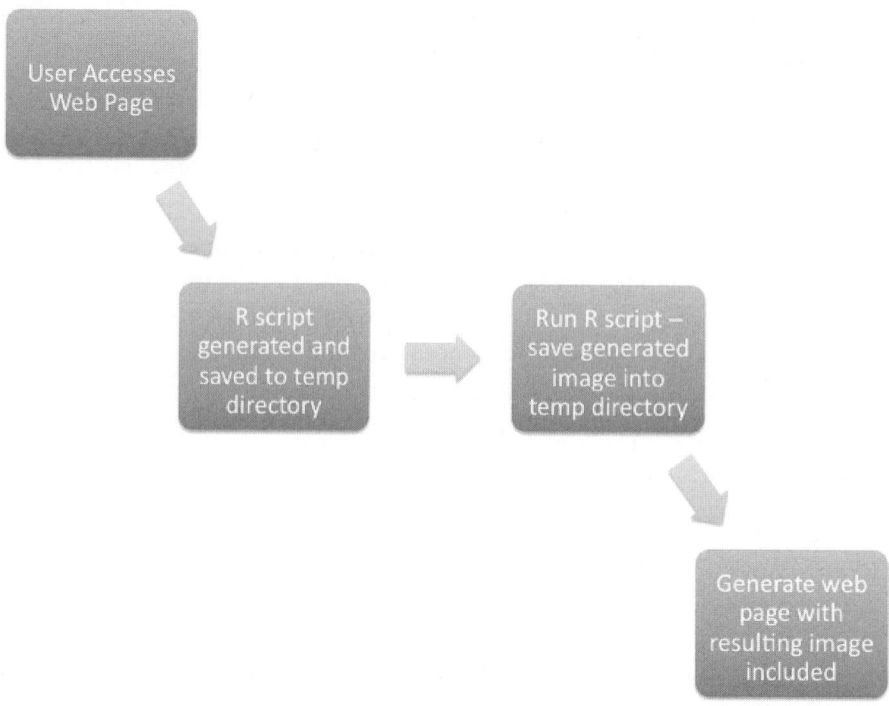

Fig. 5.2 A flow chart depicting the process followed by our CGI program that interacts with R to produce a graphical output on a web page.

Now that we have established how we are going to make this process happen. We need to do one setting up step before moving on to the code. This setting up step is creating a temporary directory for our R programs, their generated images and output files to be written to—this is going to be within our *htdocs* directory.

◆ If you are a Windows user (and your Apache server is running on Windows), simply create the directory `tempfiles` in your *htdocs* directory.

◆ If you are a Unix (Linux, Unix, Mac OS) user you will need to create the directory `tempfiles` (again in *htdocs*) as the root user, and then perform the following command on the directory to set the needed permissions: `chmod 777 tempfiles`. This `chmod` operation will then make the directory completely open so it is readable, writable, and executable by all users—this will ensure no problems when Apache needs to write its temporary files.

Now let's have a look at the code needed to interact with R and produce our dynamic web page:

```perl
#! /usr/bin/perl

use strict;
use warnings;
```

```perl
use CGI qw(:standard);
use CGI::Carp qw(fatalsToBrowser);
use DateTime;

# Set up our system parameters (Change these to suit your
  set-up)
my $htdocs = '/var/www';
my $tempdir = '/tempfiles'; # This is within the htdocs
  directory

# First we need to move to our temp directory, then create
  our R program
chdir($htdocs . $tempdir);
my $timestamp = DateTime->now();
open(RSCRIPT,">r-script-" . $timestamp . ".R");

# Print the contents of the program
print RSCRIPT '
  rangescale <- function(X) {
    Xmax <- apply(X, 2, max)
    Xscaled = scale(X, scale=Xmax, center=FALSE)
    return(Xscaled)
  }
';
print RSCRIPT 'X <- read.table("http://www.bixsolutions.net/
profiles.csv", sep=",", header=TRUE)'."\n";
print RSCRIPT 'Xscaled = rangescale(X)'."\n";
print RSCRIPT 'd <- dist(t(Xscaled), method = "euclidean")'.
"\n";
print RSCRIPT 'bitmap(file = "r-image-' . $timestamp . '.png",
type = "png256", width = 6, height = 6, res = 96)'."\n";
print RSCRIPT 'dendrogram <- hclust(t(d), method = "complete",
members = NULL)'."\n";
print RSCRIPT 'plot(dendrogram)'."\n";
print RSCRIPT 'dev.off()'."\n";

# Close the file
close RSCRIPT;

# Now run the R program
system('R CMD BATCH '.$htdocs.$tempdir.'/r-script-'
  .$timestamp.'.R');

# Finally create our HTML page using the image we generated
my $cgi = new CGI;
print
  $cgi->header,
  $cgi->start_html('Using R In Perl CGI'),
  $cgi->h1('Using R In Perl CGI'),
```

```
$cgi->p('Here is the resulting image from calling R within
Perl.'),
$cgi->img({
    -src => $tempdir . '/r-image-' . $timestamp . '.png',
    -border => 0,
    -alt => 'Combining the power of R and Perl'
    }),
$cgi->end_html;
```

In the above example we split the code into distinct sections:

* First we define the locations of our `htdocs` directory and the name of the temporary file storage directory that we have just created.

* We then create our R program within that directory. You will notice that we are recycling one of the R programs from Chapter 4 (clustering performed on the protein profiles dataset). The dataset in this instance is hard coded into the program (well, a link to the `.csv` file on the internet is); we only did this for brevity, so that the program is easier to read—this data could have just as easily came from a database query, or from user input via forms.

* At this point it is worth noting that in this section we use time stamped file names (through the use of `DateTime`)—this is because we are programming for a web page that could potentially be accessed multiple times by many different people, if we only had a single file name to use, we could be half way through writing one file when the next person comes along and starts overwriting it. This way, we try to ensure that these sorts of file complications are avoided.

* Next we execute our R program by using the `system()` function—this built-in Perl function allows us to call any command line driven application from within a Perl program.

* Finally, we create the HTML through the use of the CGI object and use our newly created image file as part of the web page.

In the above code we have only covered one relatively new thing, running other applications from the command line in Perl using the `system()` function, the rest we have seen in action before (writing data to files and producing HTML). Although it is a pretty clunky way of integrating Perl and R, it does work and is a good example of the generic approach used to harness the power of existing tools within Perl.

In many applications, we do not need the sophistication of processing and visualization provided by R. For these simpler applications, there are faster and simpler alternatives, which we introduce below.

5.5.2 Plotting graphs with GD::Graph

One of the most popular ways of producing graphics with Perl is to use the GD graphics programming library (www.libgd.org), and in particular, the Perl modules that use GD to produce graphs, `GD::Graph`. Before we get on to looking at using `GD::Graph`, we must first install it, as it is not a standard part of the Perl distribution.

Installing GD::Graph

As we said above, `GD::Graph` uses the GD graphics library to produce its plots. So, this must also be installed on your machine in order to use `GD::Graph` successfully.

- Windows. Unfortunately, at the time of writing, GD and GD-Graph are not currently located in the main ActiveState PPM repositories (the package manager that comes with the ActiveState Perl distribution for Windows). To install `GD::Graph` you will need to add the University of Winnipeg repository to your PPM setup (http://theoryx5.uwinnipeg.ca/ppms/), if you haven't already (you may have done this to install DBI in Chapter 3). You will find the option to add extra repositories in PPM's Preferences menu. Having done this, simply search for and install 'GD' and 'GD::Graph' within PPM.

- Linux. Installing the GD libraries and the `GD::Graph` Perl modules a straightforward process on Linux as it is included in the vast majority of distributions' package management tools. Simply search for `GD::Graph` in the package management tool that came with your operating system, then tell it to install `GD::Graph` and all of its dependencies.

- Mac OS X. Installing GD and `GD::Graph` on Mac OS X is also a trivial process thanks to the MacPorts and Fink projects mentioned in Chapter 3:

  - *Fink*: search for and install the relevant `GD::Graph` package for the version of Perl you have installed.

  - *MacPorts*: if you choose to install the Perl packages via MacPorts, it may require you to install a new version of Perl on your system (which, of course, it will do for you), but this will change the set up of Perl on your Mac, so that things are not installed on your system in the default locations. This is fine if you choose to let MacPorts upgrade your install of Perl, but can lead to problems if you use editors or programs that expect the default Perl installation. Our advice is that if you choose to use MacPorts, install the GD libraries themselves (search for 'gd') then use CPAN (via the terminal command: `sudo cpan GD::Graph`) to install the Perl modules—this way you will keep the default Perl setup on your system, but still have the Perl extensions you want installed.

Using GD::Graph

With GD and `GD::Graph` installed, we can write programs that produce graphics, such as the example below (`barchart.pl` at www.bixsolutions.net):

```
#! /usr/bin/perl

use strict;
use warnings;
```

```perl
use GD::Graph::bars; # we wish to draw a bar chart

# First load our data into an array - this is an array
# of array references
my @data = (
["1st", "2nd", "3rd", "4th", "5th", "6th", "7th", "8th", "9th"], # fields
[1,     2,     5,     6,     3,     1.5,   1,     3,     4],     # dataset 1
[1,     1,     4,     7,     2,     3,     7,     4,     6]      # dataset 2
);

# Declare our new GD::Graph image and its size (width/height in pixels)
my $graph = GD::Graph::bars->new(400, 300);

# Outline some paramaters for our graph (in a hash reference)
$graph->set(
  x_label           => 'X Label',
  y_label           => 'Y label',
  title             => 'A simple graph',
  y_max_value       => 8,
  y_tick_number     => 8,
  y_label_skip      => 2
) or die $graph->error;

# Calculate the graph and image
my $gd = $graph->plot(\@data) or die $graph->error;

# Print the image to a file
open(IMG, '>barchart.png') or die $!;
binmode IMG; # This sets printing to 'binary' mode - needed for images
print IMG $gd->png;
close IMG;

exit;
```

This code produces the graph shown in Fig. 5.3 in a PNG image file called
barchart.png.

The use of GD::Graph can be defined as six steps:

• Add in the use command relevant to the type of chart you wish to use. In our case we wanted to produce a bar chart, so we had use GD::Graph::bars. Other available chart types include lines, area, and pie.

• Define our dataset(s) within an array reference. Simply, you build up a two-dimensional array (or matrix) of data. The first array needs to contain the classification groups then all following arrays are treated as individual datasets.

• Create the graph object via the use of GD::Graph::bars->new(). It is also here that we define the dimensions of the finished plot in pixels.

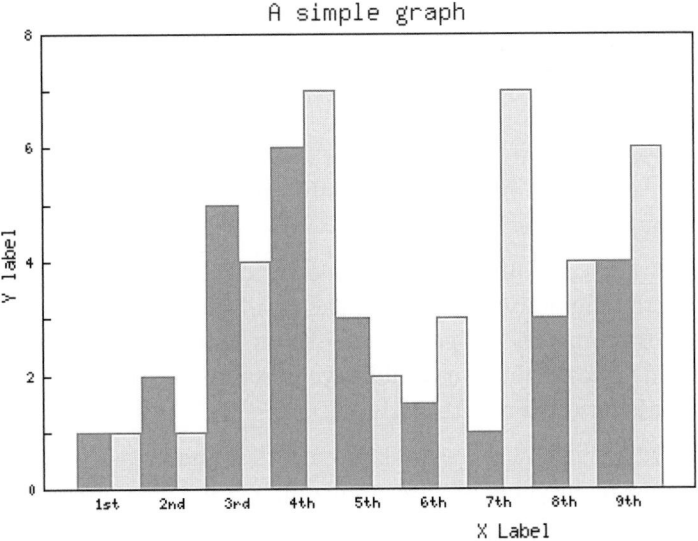

Fig. 5.3 A bar chart produced through the use of GD::Graph.

- Set any additional parameters that we want for our graph using the set() function. With this we can define the title for the graph, any axis labels, and a variety of other attributes.

- Calculate the plot using the plot() function—the plot() function takes our @data array reference as its argument.

- Print the plot out to a file using the standard Perl printing functions—the only extra thing that must be remembered here is to set the printing to binary (as opposed to text) through the use of the command binmode as this is required for the printing of images.

Before we move on, let's demonstrate how simple it is to change the type of graph that we are producing with GD::Graph. Simply edit your previous program and substitute the two occurrences of the word 'bars' for 'lines'. Your code will then neatly produce a line graph.

Using GD in CGI programs

You are probably already thinking that bitmaps produced by GD::Graph could quite easily be incorporated in dynamically generated web pages. We would like to tell you that it is as simple as cutting and pasting your GD::Graph code into a CGI program. Unfortunately, this is not the case, because the output of CGI programs can only be in one mode—images or text, but not both at the same time. So, if we were to put our GD::Graph code into one of our existing CGI programs we would just see a string representation of our image—not very pleasant!

This leaves us with two options to approach this task:

• We could adopt the same approach as we did with R, by first saving generated images into a temporary file storage area, then using these images in our web pages:

  ▪ The benefit of this method is that we have done this before (with R) and it works. It would also mean that we only have one program (file) to write to create our finished web page.

  ▪ The downside (and this is a very big downside) is that we are filling up our server with temporary files on each page load. If this is a busy site, the sheer volume of temporary images created could be enough to slow our server down and it means that we would have to set up measures to clear our temporary directory on a regular basis.

• We could resist generating any temporary files and create our images completely on the fly by generating separate graphics drawing programs:

  ▪ The benefit of this approach is that there is no need for any temporary file creation—everything is done on the fly.

  ▪ The downside is that we have to produce a few more files—one (HTML file) for the web page and one (CGI program) for each type of graph we wish to produce.

As we have already demonstrated, the first of these approaches with our R generated graphs, we would like to take this opportunity to show how you would use the second approach. As such, to get a dynamically generated image into our web pages, we must use a slightly different approach—we create a program to produce a graph and then just call this from elsewhere (a HTML page or another CGI program) whenever we need an image. This then returns the image into a separate text-based stream (the HTML page or program that called our image generating code).

So first, let's look at converting our graph drawing programs to work with CGI. Create a file `gd_example1.pl`, in your `cgi-bin` directory (make it executable if necessary) and enter the following code into it:

```perl
#! /usr/bin/perl

use strict;
use warnings;

use CGI qw(:standard);
use CGI::Carp qw(fatalsToBrowser);
use GD::Graph::bars;

# First load our data into an array - this is an array
# of array references
my @data = (
```

```
    ["1st",  "2nd",  "3rd",  "4th",  "5th",  "6th",   "7th","8th","9th"],
    [1,      2,      5,      6,      3,      1.5,     1,    3,    4],
    [1,      1,      4,      7,      2,      3,       7,    4,    6]
);

# Declare our new GD::Graph image and its size
my $graph = GD::Graph::bars->new(400, 300);

# Outline some paramaters for our graph
$graph->set(
  x_label          => 'X Label',
  y_label          => 'Y label',
  title            => 'A Simple Bar Chart',
  y_max_value      => 8,
  y_tick_number    => 8,
  y_label_skip     => 2
) or die $graph->error;

# Calculate the graph and image
my $img = $graph->plot(\@data) or die $graph->error;

# Print it to the page - this next line is important!
print "Content-type: image/png\n\n";
print $img->png;

exit;
```

As you can see, the code above is almost identical to our original graph drawing program, the only differences are that we include the CGI and CGI::Carp modules, and the way in which we print the image. That is all there is to it. Now do the same for the line graph drawing program and save that as a file called gd_example2.pl in the cgi-bin directory (making it executable again).

Finally, we can then create a HTML file in your *htdocs* directory—call this file gd_example.html:

```
<!DOCTYPE html PUBLIC "-//W3C//DTD XHTML 1.0 Transitional//EN"
  "http://www.w3.org/TR/xhtml1/DTD/xhtml1-transitional.dtd">
<html xmlns="http://www.w3.org/1999/xhtml">
  <head>
    <title>Basic GD Example</title>
  </head>
  <body>
    <h1>Basic GD Example</h1>
    <p>Here are some images generated by GD::Graph in CGI
    programs:</p>
```

```
   <p>
     <img src="/cgi-bin/gd_example1.pl" alt="my graph" />
     <img src="/cgi-bin/gd_example2.pl" alt="my graph" />
   </p>
  </body>
</html>
```

Now point your web browser at http://localhost/gd_example.html (substitute `localhost` for the name of your web server if you are not running it locally) and have a look at the results. You should now have a correctly rendered web page with two images (our dynamically created graphs) displayed. This is how you can use `GD::Graph` within a web page. You would not normally hard code all of your variables within your CGI programs. More typically, you would take data from the user, from a data analysis process, from a database query, or maybe a mixture of the three.

5.5.3   Plotting graphs with `SVG::TT::Graph`

The graphs generated by `GD::Graph` are perfectly functional, but they are not the nicest things to look at in an age of anti-aliased text and huge resolution monitors. A more modern alternative is `SVG::TT::Graph`.

Functionally `SVG::TT::Graph` is very similar to `GD::Graph`, the main difference is the final output format of the images. With `GD::Graph` you can produce a variety of bitmapped image files (JPEG, GIF, and PNG). `SVG::TT::Graph` produces SVG (Scalable Vector Graphics) images. SVG is a relatively recent graphics standard that allows the production of infinitely scalable high-quality graphics. SVG is an XML-based format, and is recognized and rendered well by the majority of modern web browsers, although at the time of writing it is not possible to view SVG images in Internet Explorer without first installing the Adobe SVG plugin (www.adobe.com/svg).

Installing SVG::TT::Graph

As with `GD:Graph`, before we can get started with `SVG::TT::Graph`, we must first get it installed onto our server. See below for the relevant instructions for your operating system.

* Windows. To install `SVG::TT::Graph` on Windows you will need to add the Trouchelle PPM repository to your PPM setup (http://trouchelle.com/ppm/). Then simply search for `SVG-TT-Graph` and install the package and its dependencies.

* Linux. To install `SVG::TT::Graph` on Linux, first look to see if the package is available in your distribution's package manager; if it is not, simply use the CPAN installation program to install it (enter the following command: `cpan SVG::TT::Graph` as the root user).

* Mac OS X. To install `SVG::TT::Graph` on Mac OS X, simply use the CPAN installation program via the following terminal command: `sudo cpan SVG::TT::Graph`. This will install the module and all of its dependencies.

Using SVG::TT::Graph

Using `SVG::TT::Graph` is very much like using `GD::Graph`. Let's start with our first example program:

```perl
#! /usr/bin/perl

use strict;
use warnings;

use SVG::TT::Graph::Bar;

# Field names for the x-axis
my $fields = ["1st", "2nd", "3rd", "4th", "5th", "6th", "7th", "8th", "9th" ];

# Our data sets
my $data1 = [1,      2,     5,     6,     3,     1.5,   1,     3,     4 ];

# Create our new graph object
my $graph = SVG::TT::Graph::Bar->new(
   {
   height               => '300',
   width                => '400',
   fields               => $fields,
   x_title              => 'X Label',
   show_x_title         => 1,
   y_label              => 'Y Label',
   show_y_title         => 1,
   scale_integers       => 1,
   stagger_y_labels     => 2,
   show_graph_title     => 1,
   graph_title          => 'A simple graph'
   }
);

# Add data to our graph
$graph->add_data(
   {
   'data'      => $data1,
   'title'     => 'Dataset 1',
   }
);

# Print our image to file
open(IMG, '>barchart.svg') or die $!;
print IMG $graph->burn();
close IMG;
exit;
```

The above code generates an output file called `barchart.svg`, which can be viewed in any web browser that can handle SVG graphics. When you run the program you may notice a few warning messages scrolling through your terminal window similar to `Argument "" isn't numeric in numeric lt (<) `—don't worry about these too much, they will not affect the end result of the program. The output looks like the graph found in Fig. 5.4.

As you can see this image is slightly more pleasing on the eye than the `GD::Graph` equivalent, so now let's go through the steps in the above example code to generate our image:

- As with `GD::Graph`, we have a `use` statement that declares what type of graph we are going to produce: `use SVG::TT::Graph::`*graph_type;*. The options are `Bar`, `BarHorizontal`, `Line`, `Pie`, and `TimeSeries`. Once again, we are going to show you the `Bar` and `Line` options—the others are just as straightforward.

- We establish the fields for our data to fit into and then we establish a data set. Note that these are both array references.

- We create a new `SVG::TT::Graph` object, passing it various attributes that dictate how the resulting image will look. Note the differences here between `SVG::TT::Graph` and `GD::Graph`—all of the attributes are set in the `new()` method with `SVG::TT::Graph`; and the fields are one of the arguments that we must pass within the new method (in `GD::Graph` they were loaded with the data sets).

- We load the data set into our graph with the use of the method `add_data`, also passing a title for the data set. If we're adding more than one data set (see below), you simply repeat this section of code with the new data set.

- Finally, we print out our image using the `burn` function. In the above example, we simply just print this to a file. Note that we do not need to set our print mode to binary—because SVG is XML-based the file consists only of text.

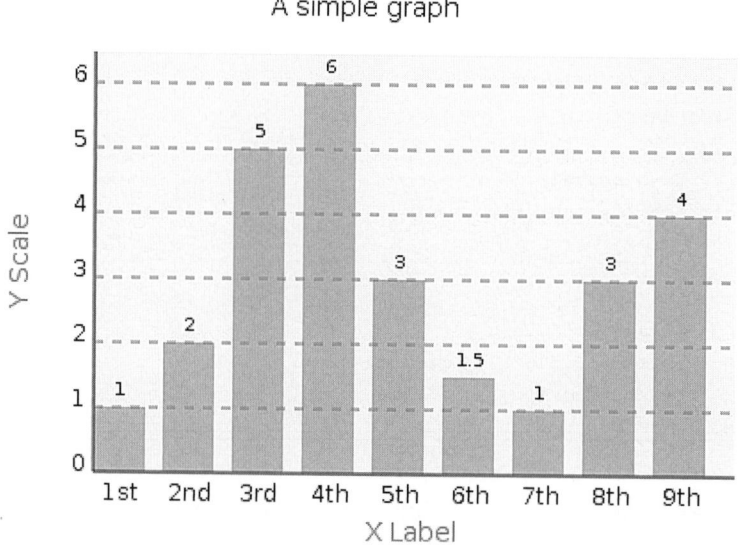

Fig. 5.4 A simple bar chart produced using `SVG::TT::Graph`.

Now that we have explained the basics of using `SVG::TT::Graph`, we can show you one of its major differences from `GD::Graph`, how bar charts handle multiple data sets. Here is some code to try to replicate the bar chart that we made earlier with `GD::Graph`:

```perl
#! /usr/bin/perl

use strict;
use warnings;

use SVG::TT::Graph::Bar;

# Field names for the x-axis
my $fields = [ "1st", "2nd", "3rd", "4th", "5th", "6th", "7th", "8th", "9th" ];

# Our data sets
my $data1 = [ 1,    2,    5,    6,    3,    1.5,    1,    3,    4 ];
my $data2 = [ 1,    1,    4,    7,    2,    3,      7,    4,    6 ];

# Create our new graph object
my $graph = SVG::TT::Graph::Bar->new(
   {
   height              => '300',
   width               => '400',
   fields              => $fields,
   x_title             => 'X Label',
   show_x_title        => 1,
   y_label             => 'Y Label',
   show_y_title        => 1,
   scale_integers      => 1,
   stagger_y_labels    => 2,
   show_graph_title    => 1,
   graph_title         => 'A simple graph'
   }
);

# Add data to our graph
$graph->add_data(
   {
   'data'      => $data1,
   'title'     => 'Dataset 1',
   }
);

$graph->add_data(
   {
     'data'      => $data2,
     'title'     => 'Dataset 2',
   }
);
```

```
# Print our image to file
open(IMG, '>barchart2.svg') or die $!;
print IMG $graph->burn();
close IMG;

exit;
```

If you run this program and look at the output, you will see that the way
SVG::TT::Graph handles multiple datasets in bar graphs is to produce compound bar graphs, where each dataset is overlaid in front of the other. This
contrasts with GD::Graph, which produces charts in which the datasets are
represented in separate bars. These types of compound bar graphs can often be
useful, but can easily become cluttered and hard to understand if many datasets are in use. One workaround for this is to use the line graph function of
SVG::TT::Graph. To do this, just replace the two instances of the word Bar in
the above program with the word Line and run the program again.

Using SVG in CGI programs

If all we wanted to do with our graphs was to view them locally, as we have done
so far, we would be better off using R. The benefit of doing it with Perl is that it is
an easier way to dynamically generate graphs for web pages, using CGI. In order
to use the SVG::TT::Graph generated graphs within CGI programs, we must
follow the same approach used with GD::Graph generated images—producing
separate programs for image production, and call these from another web page
or program. This is due to limitations found in web browsers—there are ways of
allowing in-line SVG generated images, but they do not work reliably across all
web browsers; hence, the need for this alternative method. Here is a program to
generate an image for use in a web page (save this file in your cgi-bin directory as
svg_example1.pl and make it executable):

```
#! /usr/bin/perl

use strict;
use warnings;

use CGI qw(:standard);
use CGI::Carp qw(fatalsToBrowser);
use SVG::TT::Graph::Bar;

# Field names for the x-axis
my $fields = [ "1st", "2nd", "3rd","4th", "5th","6th","7th","8th", "9th" ];

# Our data sets
my $data1 = [ 1,    2,    5,    6,    3,    1.5, 1,    3,    4 ];
my $data2 = [ 1,    1,    4,    7,    2,    3,   7,    4,    6 ];

# Create our new graph object
my $graph = SVG::TT::Graph::Bar->new(
  {
    height              => '300',
```

```
   width                  => '400',
   fields                 => $fields,
   x_title                => 'X Label',
   show_x_title           => 1,
   y_label                => 'Y Label',
   show_y_title           => 1,
   scale_integers         => 1,
   stagger_y_labels       => 2,
   show_graph_title       => 1,
   graph_title            => 'A simple graph'
   }
);

# Add data to our graph
$graph->add_data({ 'data' => $data1, 'title' => 'Dataset 1' });
$graph->add_data({ 'data' => $data2, 'title' => 'Dataset 2' });

# Insert our new graph we prepared above
print "Content-type: image/svg+xml\r\n\r\n";
print $graph->burn();
exit(0);
```

This program, like the GD::Graph ones earlier, required very little modification in order for it to be used via the web. Once again, we add in the CGI and CGI::Carp modules, then we change the way in which we draw our final image—instead of printing it to a file, we just simply print it (as Apache will direct our output to the web browser). Perform the same conversion on the code that was adapted for line drawing so that we can have a second chart on our web page, and save this file in your cgi-bin directory as svg_example2.pl and make it executable.

Finally, we come to the HTML file that will call the above two CGI programs. This is essentially the same as the example given in the GD::Graph section, except for one small difference. As we are now working with SVG output, the <img> tag no longer works when calling our CGI programs. Instead, we have to introduce a new HTML/XHTML tag: <embed>. The <embed> tag as the name might suggest, allows us to dynamically embed another file within a web page—in this case an SVG file. To use the <embed> tag, we simply have to pass it attributes for the source of the data (src), the type of the data (type), and then the dimensions on the page that we are to dedicate to its contents. See the example below for the actual code used in our example (copy this code and save it in a file in your htdocs directory as svg_example.html and make sure you give it the appropriate read permissions if necessary).

```
<!DOCTYPE html PUBLIC "-//W3C//DTD XHTML 1.0 Transitional//EN"
  "http://www.w3.org/TR/xhtml1/DTD/xhtml1-transitional.dtd">
<html xmlns="http://www.w3.org/1999/xhtml">
  <head>
    <title>Basic SVG Example</title>
  </head>
```

```
<body>
  <h>Basic SVG Example</h1>
  <p>Here are some images generated by SVG::TT::Graph in CGI
  programs:</p>
  <p>
    <embed src="/cgi-bin/svg_example1.pl" type="image/
    svg+xml" height="300" width="400" />
    <embed src="/cgi-bin/svg_example2.pl" type="image/
    svg+xml" height="300" width="400" />
  </p>
</body>
</html>
```

Now point your web browser to this file and have a look at the results. You should have a correctly rendered web page with two images (our dynamically created graphs) displayed, as shown in Fig. 5.5. As with GD::Graph, this is the easiest way to use SVG::TT::Graph to dynamically produce images for use in a web page. Again, just like we explained with the GD::Graph examples it is not normal to hard code data within your CGI.

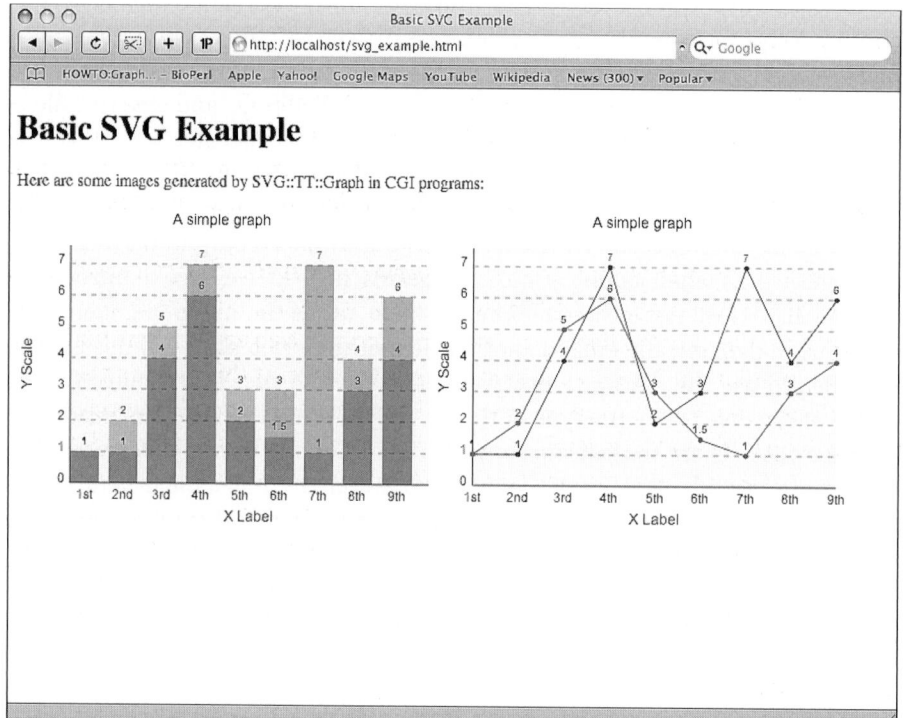

Fig. 5.5 Two dynamically generated SVG graphs, shown together on a single web page in the Safari web browser.

As one final word on SVG-based images and graphs, we should point out that, like all web-based standards, the quality of the implementation of SVG can vary greatly across different browsers and platforms—you need to take this into consideration if you decide to use SVG in any of your projects. Check that your images are rendered correctly in all browsers that your users are likely to use—as such our final example points out a flaw in the SVG rendering engine built into the version of Mozilla Firefox (v2.0.0.12) that we used for testing. Unfortunately, when the line graphs are embedded within a web page (and not a stand alone SVG image file), it cannot render the lines on the line graph correctly, thus making the line graphing function useless if our users use Firefox. Unfortunately, we can only hope that this fault gets fixed on future iterations of the browser.

5.5.4 Low level graphics in Perl

As in R there are low-level drawing functions available in both the GD and SVG graphics libraries. Although using these low level functions can be hard work, they do allow you to create very advanced bespoke graphics that can be extremely valuable in bioinformatics. For example, they can be used to display gene structure, mass spectra, and interaction networks. Much of the data visualization on bioinformatics web sites therefore employs these techniques. For more information about this topic, we refer you to the documentation for the `GD::Graph` and `SVG::TT::Graph` modules.

5.6 Summary

So that brings us to the end of this chapter and the end of the book. The main message from this chapter is that we can relatively easily add web interfaces to databases and data processing software produced in Perl, R, and MySQL. This completes the implementation of the conceptual bioinformatics solution depicted back in Chapter 1.

Something else that is clear from this chapter is that technology continues to evolve. Perl CGI is still the core of many web applications, but improvements on this, such as Ajax, are facilitating a new generation of web applications that have greater functionality. This is an important consideration at this point in the book, as we think about where to go next. We believe that the technical material in this book will be relevant for several years, but it is inevitable that details will change over time, and particular tool sets will come in and of fashion. However, the core principles of data storage, programming, and data analysis covered in this book have been established for several decades, and are likely to remain at the core of bioinformatics for decades to come. If you have grasped the concepts in this book, you should be well prepared for the future. We wish you every success.

References

Meyer, E. (2006). *CSS: The Definitive Guide*. O'Reilly: Sebastapol, California, USA.
Powers, S. (2006). *Learning JavaScript*. O'Reilly: Sebastapol, California, USA.

Appendix A: using command line interfaces

This appendix provides a brief tutorial in the use of command line interfaces, for the benefit of those readers who do not have experience of working with these. In this book, we use command lines to interact with three distinct programs: MySQL, R and the operating system (which may be Windows, Linux or Mac OS). Although specific commands vary between programs, all command line interfaces work in a similar way. In what follows we concentrate on the operating system as an example. Specific information about the command lines of MySQL and R can be found throughout Chapters 2 and 4.

A.1   Getting to the operating system command line

Depending on your computer's operating system the command line can have several names. On Windows PCs it is known as the *command prompt*, on Mac OS X and most recent Linux systems it is known as the *terminal* (older Unix variants, and people experienced with such systems may refer to it as the *shell*). The way the command line is accessed varies according to the operating system.

Opening the Windows command prompt

There are two ways of opening a command prompt window in Windows XP. You can either:

* Open the Windows Start menu.
* Click on Run....
* Type cmd in the box and hit the Enter key.

Or:

* Open the Start menu.
* Click on Programs.
* Click on Accessories.
* Click on the Command Prompt icon.

Using either of these methods should open a new window that by default has a black background with white text on it. In that window you will see the command prompt, which will look something like:

```
C:\Documents and Settings\Conrad>
```

The prompt tells you that the operating system is ready for you to type a command. It also shows you (in the section before then > symbol) which *directory* you are currently in. A directory is exactly the same as a Windows folder, but the term directory is more typically used in programming languages and at the command line. For example, you can list the contents of a directory by typing dir (short for directory) and hitting return. In the list of items that is returned, subdirectories are flagged with the label <DIR>.

You can move to another directory using cd (short for change directory). For example, to move into a subdirectory called Desktop, we would use the command:

```
cd Desktop
```

Most folders contain a special folder denoted by two dots (..). This is actually a short cut to the parent folder. So, issuing the command below will move you up one folder:

```
cd ..
```

The above examples move you to directories relative to the directory you are currently in. If you want to move directly to a directory regardless of your current location, you need to specify the new location from the disk drive downwards, for example:

```
cd c:\Progam Files\R
```

This will take you to the R directory, within the Program Files directory on your C: drive. In cases like this, where a file or folder name contains a space it is good practice to enclose the name in quotation marks to avoid confusion.

```
cd "c:\Progam Files\R"
```

To change to another drive, just type the letter of that drive followed by a colon. So, to change to the E: drive just type e: and hit the Enter key.

Opening a Linux terminal

Depending on how you have Linux configured, you may not have a graphical interface and will therefore already be at the command line. If not, you first need to open up a *terminal* (or *shell*) window. To do this, look for an icon that looks either like a picture of small computer monitor in black with white writing on it, or, in some instances, an icon that looks like a sea shell! If you can't find any such icon, go to Applications and choose Terminal.

Any of these methods should open up a window that will have a solid background with contrasting text, often white on black. Within this window you should see the Linux command prompt, which will look similar to the following:

```
$ /home/User>
```

This shows you your current directory—in this case your own home directory. You can see the contents of the current directory by typing `ls` followed by hitting the Enter key. As in Windows, you can change directory using `cd`. For example:

```
cd BBS
```

takes you to a folder called BBS.

```
cd ..
```

takes you up one directory.

```
cd /usr/local/
```

will take you to the directory `local` within the `usr` directory. Note that the slashes delineating the different directory levels are forward slashes, whereas Windows uses backslashes.

Opening a terminal in Mac OS X

Mac OS X has a terminal application very similar to the ones found in Linux. You can find this in the Applications > Utilities directory. Once you have opened up the Mac OS X terminal (also sometimes referred to as 'Terminal.app'), the situation is very much the same as Linux, and the instructions described above apply.

A.2   General command line concepts

Working directory and path

In operating systems and in R the concept of the *working directory* is important when using the command line. The working directory is the directory you are in at any given time. If you try to execute a file by typing its name, this is the first place the operating system will look for the file. If the file is not in the working directory it will not be found, unless its location is included in the *path*. The path is a list of directories that you want the operating system to search every time you try to access a file. Depending on the command line you are using, there are various ways of viewing or modifying the current path. For example, in Windows, the directories in the path can be seen by typing `path` at the command line, and in Linux and Mac OS you can achieve the same by typing `echo $PATH`.

Parameters, arguments, options, and switches

Some commands, such as `ls` and `dir` are very simple and can just be typed by themselves. Many other commands require one or more parameters to be specified. This is known as *passing* parameters (or *passing arguments*) and is done by typing these parameters after the command, on the same line. One example is the cd command shown above, which required the name of the target directory to be specified after the command.

On a similar theme, some commands have options or *switches*, which are used to modify their behaviour. A good example of this is the Perl version switch (-v) demonstrated at the start of Chapter 3. If this switch is included as part of the Perl command, as shown below, Perl will just print its version number to the screen, instead of actually doing anything.

```
perl -v
```

Through a combination of command line arguments and switches, we are able to control the behaviour even very complex programs. A good example is the blastall program (available from www.ncbi.nlm.nih.gov/blast/download.shtml) used to search for a sequence in a database. An example of this in use is shown below.

```
blastall -p blastn -d nr -i seq1.txt
```

Here, the combination of switches and parameters defines precisely how the search is conducted. Specifically, the nucleotide version of BLAST (blastn) is chosen with the -p switch. The nr sequence database is selected with the -d switch and the query sequence (the sequence we want to look for) is specified by the -i switch. Looking at the documentation for blastall at NCBI we can see that it supports many other possible options, but where we are happy with an option being set to a default setting we can simply omit these options.

Although this might seem arcane and typing such long commands may be prone to error, it actually becomes much more efficient than using a graphic interface if the same—or similar—operations need to be completed repeatedly. In particular, it is easy to automatically generate and execute these commands in Perl using its system() function, as described in Chapter 5.

A.3   Command line tips

There are various shortcuts that make life in the command line a little easier. The details of these will vary according to which particular program or operating system you are using, but something that is common to most is the ability to recall previous commands using the up and down arrow keys. This is particularly useful if you want to repeat a command or type a command very similar to one that you entered earlier (for example, if you made a typing error the first time or if you just want to change one of the switches).

On later versions of Windows and most Linux systems, the Tab key may also be used to attempt to automatically complete directory, file, and command names before you have finished typing them. This can speed up typing considerably as you only need to enter the first few letters of a directory or file then press Tab; however, the letters you enter should uniquely point to a single instance, or you may either be given a list of possibilities or, on some systems, one of the options will be selected for you. It is therefore wise to check any automatically completed text. Automatic Tab completion for table and field names is also enabled on some versions of MySQL.

Another handy feature is the path, described earlier. Having key tools, such as Perl and MySQL, in your path makes life a lot easier because you don't have to spend so much time switching between directories. Similarly, file *associations* can be useful. A file association is a link – known to the operating system – between a specified file type extension, and a program that deals with such files. An example of such an association would be to associate `.pl` files with the Perl interpreter program, `perl.exe` (on a Windows system-it's just called `perl` on Linux and Mac). If this has been done, then a Perl program can be executed simply by typing its name at the command prompt, so typing `hello_world.pl` on a Windows system, or `./hello_world.pl` on Linux/Mac would run the program with that name directly, without you having to specify that Perl is needed to run it.

Finally, we should note that, throughout this book, when we show examples of commands to be entered at the command line we do not show the command prompt. The only exception to this is where we illustrate a sample command line session, and in those cases the command prompt is used to differentiate between text that is typed in by the user and text returned to the screen by the computer. This is most frequently used to demonstrate interactions with R in Chapter 4, and occasionally with MySQL in Chapter 2.

Index